Class in Modern Britain

Also by Ken Roberts

Class in Modern Britain

Ken Roberts

palgrave

First published 2001 by
PALGRAVE
Houndmills, Basingstoke, Hampshire RG21 6XS and
175 Fifth Avenue, New York, N.Y. 10010
Companies and representatives throughout the world

PALGRAVE is the new global academic imprint of
St. Martin's Press LLC Scholarly and Reference Division and
Palgrave Publishers Ltd (formerly Macmillan Press Ltd).

ISBN 0–333–79311–0 hardback
ISBN 0–333–79312–9 paperback

This book is printed on paper suitable for recycling and
made from fully managed and sustained forest sources.

A catalogue record for this book is available
from the British Library.

Library of Congress Cataloging-in-Publication Data

Roberts, Kenneth, 1940–
    Class in modern Britain / Ken Roberts.
        p. cm.
    Includes bibliographical references and index.
    ISBN 0-333-79311-0 (cloth)
        1. Social classes–Great Britain. 2. Great Britain–Social conditions–20th century.
I. Title.

HN400.S6 R63 2001
305.5'0941–dc21   2001027365

Printed in Great Britain by
Biddles Ltd, King's Lynn, Norfolk

Contents

List of Tables, Figures and Boxes

Acknowledgements

The author and publishers are grateful to the following for permission to use copyright material: Palgrave for Tables 3.1 and 3.3 (pp. 49 and 54–5) in P. Dunleavy *et al.*, *Developments in British Politics*, 1997; Figure 10.1 (p. 216) in I. Holliday *et al.*, *Fundamentals in British Politics,* 1999; Tables 5.1 and 5.2 (pp. 85 and 91) in A. Felstead and N.H. Jewson (eds), *Global Trends in Flexible Labour*, 1999; Polity Press for Figure 3.11 (p. 58) in N. Abercrombie and A. Warde, *Contemporary British Society*, 2000; Oxford University Press for Figures 2.3 and 3.1 (pp. 38 and 61) in D. Gallie *et al.*, *Restructuring the Employment Relationship,* 1998. Every effort has been made to contact all the copyright holders, but if any have been inadvertently overlooked, the publishers will be pleased to make the necessary arrangements at the earliest opportunity.

1

Introduction

We live in a most unequal world. The wealth of the world's top 358 billionaires is equal to the combined annual incomes of nearly a half (45 per cent) of all the world's people, roughly one-and-a-half billion of them. In 1993 a single individual, George Soros, the financier, 'earned' £724 million. His income in that year exceeded the gross national products of 42 countries (Rojek, 2000).

Within Britain inequalities are relatively modest. We have none of the world's top 20 billionaires, and the poor in Britain have much higher incomes than their African counterparts. But even in Britain there are vast inequalities in wealth, income and virtually everything else. The most wealthy 1 per cent of the population holds approximately a sixth, and the bottom 50 per cent holds hardly any of all personally-held wealth. Compared with children of top professionals and managers, the children of unskilled workers are 50 per cent more likely to die in infancy. As adults, the unskilled group are roughly twice as likely to die before reaching retirement age, and 10 times more likely to have no natural teeth. Children from the top group are six times more likely to go to university, and they are also six times more likely to stay in the top group than are those born at the bottom to rise to the top (Reid, 1998). Class is related to many other things – the ages at which people marry, how they vote, church attendance and risks of criminal conviction. These inequalities may not, in themselves, prove that society is divided into separate classes. The challenge is: can anyone explain these inequalities without a theory of class?

In this opening chapter we first consider the meaning of the word class. We then explain why sociologists have, and still do, pay so much attention to class. We also review the case against class: that its importance has been exaggerated in sociology and that, in any case, class divisions are no longer as strong as earlier-on in history. As you would expect in a book on class, rejoinders (hopefully persuasive) to the 'decline of class' thesis are presented. The chapter then concludes with a book plan – an explanation of the ground to be covered in each of the subsequent chapters.

What is Class?

Anyone who is not entirely new to sociology knows that, although class is one of the most-used terms in the entire discipline, there is no agreed definition. All books on the subject must necessarily point out that Marx and Weber, and functionalist sociologists, have defined class in different ways. Actually there are no longer any sociologists who stick faithfully to the original ideas of Marx or Weber, or full-strength functionalism, so the prefix 'neo' is often attached to present-day Marxists, Weberians and functionalists.

Karl Marx (1818–83)

Marx was a German, a travelling scholar and would-be revolutionary, who settled in England from 1849 where he collaborated with Friedrich Engels who was also from Germany, from a family engaged in the textile industry. Engels became a socialist while a student, became Manchester-based while representing his family business, wrote a book about the industrial working class in that city, then began his association with Marx.

Everyone has heard of Marx because he developed a theory that was to become the world's main change ideology of the twentieth century. He is the source of the most powerful critique of capitalism that has ever been produced. Marx argued that there were just two main classes in capitalist societies. First, the owners of the means of production, the bourgeoisie or capitalist class. Second, the proletariat or working class. Phrases such as 'means of production' will be properly defined in due course. For present purposes Marx's meaning will be clear. Marx forecast that over time other classes would tend to disappear, that capitalist societies would be progressively polarised into their two main classes, and that conflict between these classes would lead eventually to the downfall of capitalism.

Present-day Marxists do not necessarily believe any of this. In sociology they are most likely to believe only that Marx's ideas are a good starting point. They recognise that capitalist societies have not become polarised, and that, in addition to the two main classes, there are additional classes in so-called ambiguous or contradictory locations. Again, these terms will be explained properly later on. Present-day Marxists acknowledge that the working class has not become a revolutionary force and seek to explain why. They are also most likely to accept that, while classes have an economic base, other factors – politics, ideology, race and gender divisions – can play important roles in class formation. Indeed, so many modifications to the original theory have been introduced that it is sometimes difficult nowadays to distinguish the ideas of Marxists from those of other sociologists, except that the former always start by identifying classes in terms of their 'relationships to the means of production'.

Max Weber (1864–1920)

Weber was another German, but, unlike Marx, Max Weber spent his entire working life in his own country. Weber came a generation after Marx, and it is often said, with justification, that Weber's work is best understood as a debate with Marx or, probably more accurately, a debate with the ghost of Marx since it was the Marxist thinking of Weber's own lifetime with which he was engaged.

Whereas Marx said that classes were defined by their relationships to the means of production, Weber claimed that classes arose in marketplaces, the labour market being the crucial marketplace in this context. So there was a class of people who hired, and another who sold their labour power. These seem very much like Marx's two main classes. True, but whereas for Marx it was experiences at work (relationships to the means of production), for Weber it was the processes of gaining work (or hiring labour) and the rewards (life-chances) that arose from all this, that were crucial. Also, Weber's conceptualisation allows classes with different types of property, and selling different types of labour power, to be identified, and there is no assumption that over time other divisions will weaken and that we will be left with just two main classes. Any sociology that places people into classes according to the types of labour that they offer or the jobs that they do (manual or white-collar, for example) is liable to be categorised as neo-Weberian.

All told, Weber took the view that matters were much more complicated than Marx had suggested. Apart from offering a different definition of class, Weber also distinguished class from status. Scholars still argue over exactly what Weber meant by class and status, but for present purposes it is sufficient to understand how and why Weber is seen as having advocated a multidimensional view of stratification. He argued, as explained above, that classes were formed in marketplaces, whereas, in Weber's view, status groups could be identified by the honour or prestige attached to their styles of life. Whereas Marx believed that other inequalities arose from an economic base of class divisions, Weber argued that different inequalities had different sources, and that although in the real world the different types of stratification (into classes and status groups) interacted, neither was reducible to the other. Weber believed that political parties could be based on either class or status groups, or factions of either, but that political success or failure was not governed entirely by the strength of parties' bases because much depended on the political skills of the movements' leaders.

Nowadays sociologists can qualify for the Neo-Weberian tag in many different ways. It may be their interest in market processes and outcomes; it may be their identification of class divisions among workers; it may be because they do not prioritise any, but recognise many factors (jobs, education and housing, for example) as helping to fix individuals' positions in the system of stratification (see Box 1.1). Or it may be because they focus on status, probably, in practice, the prestige attached to occupations (though this is not what Weber himself meant by status), when measuring class. Indeed, any non-Marxist, non-functionalist (see below) sociology is liable to be labelled as neo-Weberian.

Functionalism

This theory was popular and influential in mid-twentieth century North American sociology. It explains social practices in terms of the functions that they perform for their wider societies. So functionalists have argued

---

Box 1.1

Social stratification and social divisions

Social stratification is the most all-embracing term used in sociology when analysing inequalities. There is a deliberate geological analogy (which should not be taken too literally) – strata of rock (people) lying on top of one another.

All known societies have been stratified, and sociologists have identified different types of stratification systems – slavery, estates, castes and the class systems of modern societies. Weber introduced a further distinction between class and status. Class systems are different from the types of stratification that existed in earlier societies. First, classes are relatively open, meaning that mobility is possible (and quite common). Second, classes have an economic base (how we earn our livings) rather than being based on law or religion. So mobility does not require legal verification, or a religious ceremony, or the permission of one's owner: people simply change their jobs.

Social divisions is an even more all-embracing term. Here the groups may exist in parallel rather than above and beneath each other. Stratification is just one possibility: one of many types of social division. Sociologists usually speak of gender and ethnicity as bases for social divisions. The extent to which one group (a sex or ethnic group) is above others, and how class, gender and ethnic divisions interact, then become matters for research and debate.

that social stratification is functional. They claim that inequalities motivate people with the required talent to compete to enter, then to perform as effectively as possible in, important positions. They also argue that inequalities help to integrate societies by affirming the importance of well-rewarded positions, and expressing the wider society's approval and gratitude to the incumbents.

Nowadays full-strength functionalism has few, if any, supporters in sociology, and the criticisms have been devastating. Functionalism confuses effects with causes. As regards stratification, it has been counter-argued that, rather than integrating society, inequalities are at least just as likely to provoke conflict. Also, inequalities can obstruct the ascent of talent to important positions. However, functionalism still reigns in everyday commonsense and economic theory. It is said that the higher earners must remain so, or become even better paid, in order to keep them in their jobs, and that the rewards that they receive are necessary compensation for the effort, training or responsibility, and no more than commensurate with the value of their work to society.

There is a softer version of functionalism in sociology which maintains simply that there are functional prerequisites or imperatives for the survival of any society: that there must be procedures for rearing children and resolving disputes, for example. It is argued that all practices can be analysed to establish the ways and extent to which they are functional (and dysfunctional). Sociologists who have examined stratification in this way have claimed that some inequality is inevitable, for the reasons given by full-strength functionalism, but they admit that this does not explain the particular types and degrees of inequality that are found in different societies.

Nowadays most sociologists concur that 'conflict theories' offer the more plausible and powerful explanations. Both Marx and Weber are regarded as conflict theorists for these purposes. They explained inequalities in terms of the relative power that different groups were able to mobilise; in Marx's case in the relationships of production, and for Weber in marketplaces (in the case of classes).

Functionalism lives on in sociological class analysis only in so far as some sociologists conceptualise class 'gradationally'. Positions or individuals are portrayed as positioned along a continuous scale on which there are no clear divisions. This is the view of class that functionalism fosters – a ladder up which the talented can climb, with people at every level admiring and emulating those above. The theory (functionalism) that accounts for the sliding-scale outcome is usually pushed well into the background nowadays, but some sociologists still believe that its model of inequalities is the one that approximates most closely to social reality.

Making a Living

Sociologists are not in total agreement, but neither are we hopelessly at loggerheads over how to define class. When we debate class we tend to focus on points of disagreement, but this happens in all subjects. What can be missed is that all the definitions of class have common denominators. Sociologists (whether Marxist, Weberian or functionalist) are agreed that classes have an economic foundation: they are composed of people with common experiences of making their livings. So people are invariably 'classed' on the basis of their occupations.

We are also agreed that modern societies' class systems of stratification are very different from the estates, castes and master–slave relationships that have been present elsewhere (see also Box 1.1). Feudal estates were legally-defined entities; the different estates of the realm (lords, church and commoners) all had their own legally defined rights and responsibilities. Under a caste system people are born into and must remain in a particular caste. The system is legitimised by religion, and all the castes have prescribed total ways of life from which the members cannot escape. Under slavery one group actually owns another rather than just purchases their labour power. None of the sociological theories of class confuse this system of stratification with estates, castes or slavery.

It is impossible to conduct a systematic examination of Britain's (or any other society's) class structure without opting for one or another of the theories of class. Neutrality is not an option. One or other of the main theories will be implicit in any way of organising all the material. However, this is not the right point at which to opt for Marx, Weber or functionalism. On what basis would a choice be made? It would be guesswork or ideology. It is better to wait until the theories are confronted by some evidence, then to judge their success in handling it. This is done in Chapter 2 where we consider the class schemes that have been developed on the basis, or which correspond with the assumptions, of either Marxist, Weberian or functionalist views of class. The outcome of this assessment is signalled in the rest of this book's chapter headings. If you cannot read the signals at this point, don't worry: everything will become clear as we proceed.

Class Matters

Another point of agreement among all class theorists is that class matters. Class theorists would say that, wouldn't they, but the evidence really is overwhelming. We have already seen that class is related to people's wealth, health and education, but this is just the beginning of the list.

Compared with unskilled workers, managers and professionals are twice as likely to have made a will, to regard religion as very important, to do voluntary work, to go to the cinema, to visit wine bars and to take holidays away from home. The unskilled are twice as likely to 'worry all the time about being a victim of crime'. The managers and professionals spend four times as much on leisure goods and services, and the mothers with children aged under five are 30 times more likely than unskilled working-class mothers to have full-time jobs (Reid, 1998). Why are all these things class-related? The relationships are strong. Class differences are huge. There is usually no need to apply statistical tests to see if they are significant. Class theory seeks explanations.

Arguing that class matters is not implying that other social divisions like race/ethnicity (see Box 1.2) and gender are unimportant or even less important. The situation here is not zero-sum. It is possible for huge class, huge gender and huge racial/ethnic inequalities to co-exist. Class is not a completely separate type of social division. Sociologists could hardly suggest that this was the case given our insistence on the inter-connectedness of things. Who enters particular types of employment can be, and in practice

---

Box 1.2

'Race' and ethnicity

Nowadays 'race' is often written (and sometimes spoken) with inverted commas. This is to dissociate the user from racist views. It is no longer believed that humanity is divided into races whose genetic make-up leads inexorably to significant psychological or social differences. However, people may still treat each other differently depending on their physical characteristics, including the races to which they appear to belong. People may subscribe to beliefs which justify this treatment. Science has discredited racial theories, but racist beliefs and behaviour are still everyday realities in most parts of the world. These beliefs, attitudes and related behaviour are described as 'racial' or 'racist'.

The word ethnicity is never put in inverted commas. Ethnic groups consider themselves, and are likely to be regarded by others, as sharing characteristics (knowledge of their history, language, religion, dress-codes and so on) that set them apart from other groups. They may seek, and, sometimes irrespective of this, they may be accorded different treatment on the basis of their ethnic characteristics.

Clearly, although they are conceptually separable, race and ethnicity are often thoroughly interwoven in real-life situations.

often is, influenced by both race and sex. In turn, these characteristics of the entrants can infuse the occupations themselves. Occupations can be gendered and racialised – given masculine or feminine qualities or characteristics (wrongly or correctly) attributed to particular ethnic or racial groups. There are many examples in the following chapters. At present, one will suffice. The task mix in office jobs would almost certainly be different if most of the employees were men. Most of these jobs are considered particularly suitable for women. So women tend to be drawn into the occupations and excluded from 'masculine' jobs, not by law which insists on equal opportunities nowadays, but by the self-concepts of men and women, their likelihood of applying, assumptions that are built into hiring processes, and workplace cultures which can make the 'wrong person' feel uncomfortable.

This book is primarily about class, but other divisions, especially gender and ethnic divisions are discussed throughout. Race and gender are not dealt with in separate chapters, they are treated within all of them. There are class differences among both men and women, and within all ethnic groups, and what it means to belong to any class differs by gender and ethnic group. Other divisions have to be drawn into class analysis which, in turn, can contribute to an understanding of the other divisions.

Class in the Head

Sociologists who study class have other things in common; we share what we all feel to be well-grounded assumptions. Marxists, Weberians and functionalists all agree that their class locations are liable to get into people's heads and make impressions on their minds, their consciousness and unconsciousness. It is impossible to explain all the things that are related to class unless there is such imprinting. Income and wealth are likely to be the mediating variables in some things that class predicts, like going to the cinema and wine bars, and on holidays. But class is also related to people's attitudes: the importance that they attach to religion, whether they believe that it is government's job to provide citizens with jobs if they want them, to provide decent housing if people cannot otherwise afford it, and to reduce income inequalities (Reid, 1998). Why should any of this be so if class did not somehow get into people's heads?

It would be remarkable if class had no such effects given that we spend so much time at work, women as well as men nowadays, all those hours per week, and all those years throughout our adult lives. People do not necessarily stick in the same jobs, but, as we shall see in later chapters, they tend to stick in the same classes of jobs. If not, they tend to follow characteristic trajectories, like from skilled worker to supervisor, or junior to senior manager. Class is related to income which affects, well, most things in a society which is so commercialised. People tend to associate with others in the same classes – at work, in their neighbourhoods – and so they also tend to marry one another.

Among class researchers there has been a rough division of labour between, on the one hand, those who study the shape of the class structure, mobility flows and rates, and who typically conduct large-scale surveys with representative samples, then, on the other hand, those who study class consciousness and related behaviour, typically using case-study methods (Crompton, 1996a). Yes, there is a difference, but these are not competing groups of class researchers. Neither set of investigators has tried to stake monopoly claims for its own speciality within class analysis. Everyone wants to 'put it all together'. It is simply difficult to handle everything simultaneously.

Valerie Walkerdine and her colleagues (2001) argue that, 'Class is not something that is simply produced economically. It is performed, marked, written on minds and bodies. We can "spot it a mile off" even in the midst of our wish for it no longer to be there'. Their own study, of 33 girls growing-up in London, provides vivid illustrations of class getting into pretty well every aspect of the girls' lives. However, the book is less revealing on the reality 'out there' that was doing the marking and writing on the girls' bodies and minds. This is not a criticism. It is impossible for any single project to do the lot. The observation that class is not simply 'out there' is not new. Marx distinguished a 'class in itself' from a 'class for itself'. Classes may be defined initially by their relationships to the means of production, but they become more than simple aggregates of people only when the actors begin to develop common types of consciousness.

We need to be cautious here. Present-day class analysts do not assume that the members of any class will develop a particular, easily predictable, type of consciousness, and certainly not necessarily the kind of solidaristic and revolutionary consciousness that Marx believed would develop in the working class. People may not identify themselves with any class. In practice, most people do place themselves in a class (usually the middle class or the working class) when invited to do so by researchers, but it does not follow that these same people will think in class terms at any other time. In their everyday lives people are more likely to think of themselves as women, husbands, parents, neighbours and so forth.

Class analysts certainly do not assume that it is only class that gets into people's heads. Age, gender and ethnicity have the same capacity, and it is only in the course of all these things getting into people's minds and bodies that they become mixed together. So we should expect men and women, for example, and members of different ethnic groups, to experience being working-class or middle-class in rather different ways.

Class analysts do not assume that people will regard other classes as enemies of their own. As a matter of fact, in response to survey questions, most people, roughly the same proportion nowadays as in the 1960s, say that there is a class struggle (Abercrombie and Warde, 2000). They also say, again in surveys, that the government represents a particular class (the upper class and the middle class rather than the working class in the case of the New Labour government in the late-1990s). However, an extreme form of individualism, an outright refusal to think in class terms, an insistence that there is no such thing as society, only individuals (a phrase made famous by Margaret Thatcher), and a belief that all classes share common interests, can all qualify as characteristic forms of class consciousness. Class analysts do not assume, because they know full well that it is not the case, that most people are dedicated class warriors.

Class and Politics

Another point of agreement which transcends Marxist, Weberian and functionalist theorists is that class and politics are most likely to be thoroughly interconnected. This is another mediated link. How people make their livings cannot directly cause them to take part in any political action. The mediator will be class's imprint on their minds and social networks. It is presumed throughout class analysis, or at least envisaged, that (class) structure will lead to (class) consciousness which in turn will lead to (political) action. Thus class analysis seeks to unravel the relationships between economy, society and politics. Causation can be multidirectional; the organisation of economic life determines class divisions from which particular kinds of consciousness and political action arise, which may then feed back, via government policies, into the economy and society.

'Politics', as the term is being used here, is not confined to party politics. Voting for a political party, becoming a member and involved in its campaigns, are political, but so too is any other collective action that is intended to change or preserve the macro-structure of society. So trade unions, professional associations, tenants' organisations, women's groups, racial equality movements and all other pressure groups are equally political.

When people identify with a class, and vote for a party because it is seen as representing the class in question, the link between class and politics is clear-cut, but this is not the only possible way, and it is probably not the usual way, in which political action is class-related. There seems to be a general tendency for people to attribute stronger class solidarity and motivation to others than they do to themselves. Conservative and Labour politicians alike, especially when in government, have always claimed that their own parties represent all classes of people, and have accused the other side of being in hock to sectional interests. Labour used to claim that the Conservatives were dominated by out-of-touch aristocrats. In more recent times the accusation has been of sleazy links with business. For their part, the Conservatives have accused Labour of being dependent on (working-class) trade unions. When in office the leaders of both parties have claimed to be creating a classless Britain. Harold Macmillan, a Conservative prime minister in the late-1950s and early-1960s, thought that he was destroying the proletariat by enabling its members to enjoy rising standards of living. John Major claimed to be creating a classless society in the 1990s. His successor as prime minister, Tony Blair, claimed to be creating ladders of opportunity which would open middle-class positions (middle Britain) to all. Political leaders have realised that they stand any hope of office only if they can attract votes from more than one class.

For their part, members of all classes know from first-hand experience just how divided their people are. Those who live on council estates know that not everyone votes Labour. Trade union activists know how difficult it is to maintain appearances of solidarity during negotiations, and especially during industrial action. Viewed from a distance, all classes appear more united than from within. So workers have resented how the upper and middle classes keep them down. The upwardly mobile sometimes feel frustrated at being unable to penetrate 'old boy networks'. Meanwhile, the higher classes have felt threatened by an organised working class. All these are characteristic forms of class consciousness and they are all political, that is, likely to persuade those concerned to support a particular party and specific policies.

All macro-social patterns are clearer when viewed from a distance, including historical distance. Looking back in time, it is fairly easy to see that class schisms and struggles have been major determinants of the direction of historical change. It would be difficult to begin to explain the rise of industrial capitalism without referring to how an ascendant class, the bourgeoisie, pioneered new forms of enterprise, and, with the wealth thereby generated, contested the position of the older, ruling, landed classes, and thereby reshaped society. Equally, it is impossible to explain the twentieth century without mentioning that, by its beginning, a working class had already been formed and was organising itself into trade unions and creating the Labour Party. The politics of the twentieth century was largely about the achievements and failures of working class power.

Is Class in Decline?

Of course, all that was in the past. Many people are convinced that the present is very different. No change here. Talk of class being in decline is not novel, it is one of the constants. Some of the arguments recently in vogue have been reborn, others are completely new, there has always been such a mixture. As in previous decades, the role of class in our present time will become clearer only when the turn-of-the-millennium can be viewed from a distance, sometime in the future. Old class formations are in decline which is easily mistaken for a decline of class itself. So every generation has suspected that class has been in decline, only for its persistence to be rediscovered later on, thereby triggering another round of debate.

Class would decline if one or more of three things happened. First, there would be a decline of class if occupations ceased to be arranged in 'clumps'. The 'fences and ditches' analogy is inappropriate in class analysis: there is too much mobility and class boundaries are too indefinite. 'Mountains and hillocks' is a better metaphor. It is meaningful to speak of classes only if clusters of occupations have sufficient in common to make a characteristic impression on the minds of those involved. If there was no clustering we would have a situation of classless inequality. However, we shall see that there are still 'mountains and hillocks'. Second, class would decline if occupations eased to make an impression on the minds of the practitioners, in which case people's views and feelings about the wider society, and their own positions in it, would most likely be governed entirely by other divisions. Why this is unlikely will become clear in the chapters that follow. Third, we could speak of a decline of class if the clustering of occupations, and the associated forms of consciousness (and unconsciousness), were insulated from politics. Again, as will become apparent, highly improbable.

All claims that class is dying rest on the view that one or more of the above developments has occurred. There are a number of separate arguments, some old, others relatively new. The arguments are interrogated in detail in appropriate places throughout the following chapters, but it may be useful to introduce the entire bunch at this point. The arguments are all mistaken. A common mistake is to confuse change with decline. Some former mountains are becoming mere hillocks, while former hillocks are becoming mountains. There are always 'underground' changes in the character of the mountains and hillocks. Some do decline in significance, but up to now at any rate, not class in general.

Embourgeoisement

This is the oldest of all the arguments, and the argument itself never changes. It is claimed that as their incomes rise, members of the working class are able to buy and do things that formerly signalled middle-class status. As this happens, manual workers are supposed to jettison their working-class identities, and adopt forms of consciousness associated with the middle class. Hence the old class division is supposed to crumble.

These arguments were first heard towards the end of the nineteenth century when workers were experiencing year-on-year rises in their real earnings and living standards. Many were moving into, and, with the assistance of the recently-created building societies, some were actually buying the new terraced housing built to conform with local authority bye-laws. Some workers were adopting 'respectable' bourgeois lifestyle habits, like saving and spending annual holidays at the seaside.

Basically, the same claim has undergone several rounds of recycling. The working class has emerged intact from one cycle of changes only for the old claims to be reasserted. The embourgeoisement thesis was revived in the 1950s, another period of rising living standards, full employment, and three successive Conservative election victories. The thesis was considered laid to rest by the Luton-based Affluent Worker study by John Goldthorpe and his colleagues (1969) (see Chapter 4), only to be revived again in the 1980s – a period of four successive Conservative election victories, and when home ownership was spreading among manual families, assisted by the government policy of selling council houses to sitting tenants.

The detailed evidence in respect of all the alleged slayers of class is in subsequent chapters, but the principal objections can be stated succinctly. There are three basic weaknesses in the embourgeoisement thesis. First, whenever the working class has improved its income levels and living standards, the middle class has advanced in line, so there has been no catching up. Over the long term, class-related income inequalities have remained remarkably stable. Second, it is necessary only for something to become common within the working-class for it to lose its middle-class associations. This has happened to seaside holidays, television sets, washing machines, motor cars and owner-occupied dwellings. In the 1950s manual families who were rehoused from the inner cities to suburban council estates were regarded as upwardly mobile. Nowadays being a tenant on most of the outlying estates has entirely different social connotations. Third, even if manual workers caught up with middle-class income and spending levels, they would simply be affluent workers rather than middle-class. Their jobs – their day-on-day and lifelong experiences of earning their livings – would remain very different from those of senior managers.

Please note that the argument here is not that rising living standards have changed nothing. Living standards, and other changes that are considered below, may well have altered the character of specific classes and their relationships to others. The current argument is simply that the changes in themselves have been insufficient to cause even the decline, let alone the death of class.

The Property-owning Democracy

This is a variant of the embourgeoisement thesis. The claim here is that wealth has ceased to be confined to a small class of owners of industry, thereby obliterating the owner–worker class division. This claim became particularly strident in the 1980s and 1990s when a series of privatisations, and the conversion of building societies into banks, were said to be transforming working-class 'Sids' into share-owners. However, very similar claims had been made earlier on as more and more workers built up savings in bank accounts, insurance policies and pension funds, and as ownership of assets such as houses and motor cars became widespread.

There are three reasons why claims about a classless property-owning democracy are patently false. First, even after all the privatisations and building-society conversions, less than a fifth of all households own any shares, and in most cases their holdings are so small that the individuals' life-chances continue to depend on how they earn their livings. Second, there is a difference between investments from which a never-ending stream of income can be drawn, and assets such as houses and motor cars which are for personal use. Third, there is a similar difference between wealth that can be held intact and passed on down the generations, and savings which are simply deferred spending until the annual holiday, or from one's working life into retirement.

Managerialism

This is another old argument. It dates from the time when the creation of joint-stock, limited liability companies enabled ownership to be scattered among dozens, or hundreds, and sometimes thousands of investors. During the first half of the twentieth century analysts counted the number of companies where there had ceased to be a single majority owner. Investors were often scattered geographically, and in many cases the size of their investments would not justify the time and trouble of acquainting themselves with, and endeavouring to play any active part in, the management of the companies. The result, it was claimed, was control by managers, a 'managerial revolution' according to James Burnham (1941). A related argument was that sensible investors would not object to the management of their funds being left in the hands of people with the detailed knowledge and expertise necessary to run steel mills, railways and so on.

The alleged disempowerment of owners has been complemented by claims that managers, unlike bosses who own and run their own companies, are 'accountable', legally to boards of directors and via the boards to the shareholders, but also to other 'stakeholders' because managers need to take account of the demands of organised and unorganised labour, plus whatever economic policies are being pursued by the government of the day. Managers, it is claimed, are appointed on the basis of their qualifications, experience and expertise to coordinate the interests of all the relevant parties and to run enterprises efficiently. A likely outcome may well be a very unequal society but, this argument runs, not class divisions.

These arguments are considered fully in Chapter 7 where we shall see that they encounter two fundamental objections. First, the owners of firms have not been disempowered; their power has been depersonalised rather than removed. Second, in so far as salaried managers have gained a share of power, the evidence shows that this is used not equally for the benefit of all 'stakeholders' but primarily in their own and the share-owners' interests. In so far as the class division between owners and all workers has been displaced, it has reappeared beneath the upper echelons of the new middle class of salaried managers and professionals.

Social Mobility

Throughout the twentieth century every generation appeared to believe that it was witnessing an increase in the rate of social mobility and that people's life-chances were ceasing to depend on their social origins. Educational reform, and employment on the basis of qualifications rather than connections were supposed to be accomplishing this. Every generation of working-class children must have been told repeatedly that they had far better opportunities to get on than their parents. Educational reform was certainly successful in creating this impression: first when scholarship places in secondary schools were introduced following the 1902 Education Act, then when secondary education for all of a type suited to each child's ability, aptitude and interests was decreed by the 1944 Education Act, then following the waves of expansion in higher education after the Robbins Report (1963) and again in the 1990s. High rates of social mobility are supposed to erode class divisions. As cross-class family links increase, class barriers are supposedly broken down.

The problem with these arguments is straightforward: the objective evidence refutes them. As far as we can tell, the rate of social fluidity, meaning the social mobility that is not structurally inevitable on account of class differentials in birth rates and changes in the proportions of positions at different levels, is roughly the same at the beginning of the twenty-first century as it was at the beginning of the twentieth. Modern social classes have never been closed groups. In this respect class societies are unlike caste societies. But most people have always ended up, and continue to end up, in either the same class, or in a class close to where they were born. In any case, social mobility transfers people between classes without necessarily weakening the roots of class divisions, meaning differences in characteristic lifetime experiences in employment.

Citizenship

This argument arose in the years following the Second World War amid the expansion of the welfare state that was then taking place (Marshall, 1950). It was claimed that citizenship was developing, and expanding, through successive stages. The original citizenship guaranteed no more than protection under the law. Then a political dimension was added – citizens became able to elect their rulers. Subsequently, people were able to use their political power to elect governments which conferred new social rights. Thus citizenship acquired a social dimension. This included the right to a minimum income, educational opportunities, health care and adequate housing. In the immediate postwar years it was widely believed that the welfare state, and the social rights which it conferred, would expand remorselessly, and, in the process, remove many of the inequalities in which class grievances had been rooted.

   We now know that citizenship rights can be rolled back as well as extended, but the basic objections to the idea of citizenship superseding class are twofold. First, even in the heyday of the welfare state, there were class inequalities in people's ability to benefit from their social rights – educational opportunities for example. Second, many of the new rights – levels of social security benefits, for instance – were always minimal, and there remained plenty of class-related inequality above the citizenship floor. This, of course, has applied also in housing and health care.

Post-Industrialism

This is among a set of late-modern trends and is therefore a relatively recent addition to the arguments about the death of class (see Pakulski and Waters, 1996). Post-industrialism, as the term is used here, refers to the shift of labour from manufacturing to services, and from manual into white-collar occupations. These trends would not, in themselves, challenge class divisions, but an effect is said to be that brain power supersedes both money capital and brute labour as the key factor of production. The latest technological revolution, based on micro-chips, computers and information processing, is said to be accelerating this trend. Hence, it is claimed, the heightened importance of education in economic competitiveness, and, within countries, in determining individuals' achievements. The resultant hierarchy is said to be unlike the earlier class society in inequalities being gradational and reflecting merit.

In reality all this is plain bunk. It completely neglects, first, the extent to which access to information, qualifications and knowledge remain class-based, and, second, the ways in which credentialism either reinforces older, or creates new class divisions.

Post-Fordism

Fordism is explained fully in Chapter 3. For present purposes it is sufficient to say that in the Fordist era large firms were among the most reliable and could offer relatively secure jobs – jobs for life in some cases. The post-Fordist era is said to be characterised by the flexibility that is required to cope with the pace and dramatic implications of current technological changes, and the competitive processes unleashed by globalisation. Successful businesses need to be flexible and this, it is claimed, requires them to make their workforces flexible. Hence the much-reported demise of jobs for life and high rates of labour mobility. Class divisions are said to dissolve in the flux.

However, later chapters will show that flexibility has rather different meanings in different social classes, and moreover, the increased mobility is horizontal rather than vertical. Individuals tend to move between basically similar occupations. Class divisions thereby remain intact, but as with the other changes being considered here, there are likely to be significant implications for the character of the various classes. Specifically, they are in fact becoming less communal and solidaristic. The basic mistake in this argument is to imagine that classes must have communal, solidaristic roots.

Other Divisions

It is sometimes argued that certain long-standing divisions – by age, gender and ethnicity – have ceased to be subordinate to or overshadowed by class, and now play stronger roles in identity and social consciousness formation, and in political action. The only mistake here is to imagine that we are witnessing something entirely new, and that any role played by other divisions must be at the expense of class. In fostering particular kinds of consciousness, which may lead to political action, class has always interacted with other social divisions. The change is that in former decades, in most of the UK, other divisions could simply be taken for granted. Until the 1970s, except in Northern Ireland, national identity was simply not a major political issue, but rather than Ulster being anglicised, the national question has spread into the politics of Scotland and Wales, and into England with the immigration of non-white minorities since the Second World War. For members of the minorities, if not the majority population, 'race' has become the big political issue. Gender was once taken for granted in both social science and politics, but second-wave feminism has changed this. Women are now more prominent in the labour market and in other areas of public life including party politics.

Just like class positions often are, gender and ethnicity are (nearly always) life-long statuses, and must be expected to make a major impression on everyone's consciousness. Age is different: everyone is young once and only once. However, in times of major change, whether in fashion or politics, young people are always likely to respond most strongly to the trends. People who have become working-class or middle-class since the 1970s have faced rather different, though still class-specific, experiences compared with their counterparts in the 1950s and before. Many things, including class locations, now have different meanings than formerly. The sole point of crucial relevance here is that all age groups, ethnic/national groups, and each sex remain as class divided as ever.

Book Plan

Before beginning to explore the details of class in modern Britain an appropriate class scheme, a map of the territory is needed. Lay people subscribe to class schemes. When they identify themselves as working-class or middle-class they usually have some ideas about which, if any, classes are above and beneath their own. Lay schemes are often vague and incomplete, and sociology's class schemes are not based squarely on lay conceptions. One should expect sociology's class schemes not to mirror, but, at the end of the day, to explain lay people's conceptions of class.

All sociological schemes are based on theories about the genesis of classes, and as we have seen, there has never been a theoretical unanimity in sociology. So it should be no surprise that there is no unanimously agreed class scheme. Even so, sociologists are not hopelessly divided over which class scheme to use. When, in the 1990s, British sociologists were invited to recommend a replacement for the Registrar General's older social classes, there was broad agreement on a slightly modified version of a class scheme originally developed by John Goldthorpe in the course of conducting a large-scale study of social mobility in Britain in 1972. Chapter 2 presents this class scheme, together with the alternatives. This chapter also tackles the vexed question of who should be classified – individuals or households/families. This turns out to be one of the questions to which it is currently impossible to propose an answer that is right for all cases.

The main classes identified in the Goldthorpe scheme are a service class, which is referred to as the new middle class or simply as the middle class, throughout this book, and a working class. There are also intermediate classes – lower-level white-collar workers and a petit bourgeoisie comprising self-employed non-professionals and proprietors of small businesses. To these, the new (1998) official classification adds a bottom stratum, in effect an underclass, and most sociologists will concur that although it is fruitless to try to capture its members in survey research, the scheme should really be topped by an upper or over-class.

Equipped with this class scheme, Chapter 3 traces the class effects of recent economic changes. These have led to a numerical decline of the working class and an expansion of the new middle class. This is well-known, but we shall see that there have been at least equally important changes in the occupations within all social classes, and in their social composition. There are likely to be implications here for typical forms of social consciousness and political proclivities within all the main classes.

Chapters 4 through 7 consider successively all the main and intermediate classes. Chapter 4 deals with the working class. It is shrinking but remains the largest single class. Since the 1960s the main change in the working class has been its disorganisation, and, despite its still considerable size, the working class has declined drastically as a cultural and political force. This has been due to the steep contraction in manufacturing employment, the shift of employment from large to small establishments, the destruction of working-class communities by a combination of rehousing, television and the motor car, higher absolute rates of upward mobility, the spread of unemployment and precarious jobs, and manual workers becoming more mixed in gender and ethnicity. In the course of all these changes the working class has lost its former organisations – trade unions and the Labour Party. Chapter 4 also considers the likelihood, actually the probability, of the persistence of high unemployment, and the intensification and spread of poverty, creating an underclass or excluded groups beneath the employed working class.

The intermediate classes – lower-level white-collar workers and the petit bourgeoisie – are the subjects of Chapter 5. These are smaller than both the working class and the new middle class and lack the demographic base for full class formation. Membership of these classes is unstable, but this does not make the classes inconsequential either socially or politically. If office workers were assimilated into the working class, this would again be the majority of the population. The self-employed and proprietors of small businesses can play a major ideological role in (apparently) demonstrating that anyone with sufficient enterprise can make it, and they were among the most enthusiastic Thatcherites in the 1980s.

Business people and self-employed professionals were the core of the old middle class. Nowadays they are vastly outnumbered by salaried professionals and managers, the core members of the new middle class, the subjects of Chapter 6. Their numbers grew steadily throughout the twentieth century, and sometime in the twenty-first century they could become the largest class. As a demographic entity, the new middle class is still in formation. Its recent growth rate means that its current members could not but include many who have been upwardly mobile. There are numerous divisions within the new middle class – by levels, between managers and professionals, according to whether they work in the public or the private sector, and by lifestyle. They are certainly not a solidaristic class. Nor are they particularly conservative any longer. The middle class is no longer a small minority, needing to defend itself in the face of working-class power. The new middle class has various discontents – sometimes about the macroeconomic and political orders, but mainly about its own career situations. The new middle class is politically important if only because it now provides a clear majority of the activists in all the main political parties.

The old upper class comprised the monarchy, aristocracy and related families. The new upper class, or over-class, examined in Chapter 7, has money at its core. The central members are capitalists – very wealthy individuals. They fulfil the demographic criteria for being treated as a class due to their ability to transmit their private property down the generations. The upper class is in fact contemporary Britain's best example of a well-knit class, aware of its vital interests and able to act in a concerted way when necessary to protect these interests. The very wealthy have access to political elites, and are able to associate with titled folk and other celebrities. This network constitutes the modern upper class. The individuals concerned amount to less than 1 per cent of the population but they are currently the most powerful of all the classes.

Chapter 8 deals with social mobility. Most interest in this topic is about the extent to which people have equal opportunities, but in class analysis an at least equally important issue is the extent to which classes are demographic entities with critical masses of life-long members and/or distinctive life chances. The presumption is that unless a class is demographically distinct it is unlikely to develop a characteristic consciousness and all that follows. We shall see that the working class has met this test for many, many decades. The new middle class is on the way to becoming a stable demographic entity but will become properly formed only several decades into this twenty-first century. Class formation is a long-term process and it is still much too early to give a final answer as regards the consciousness and politics of the new middle class.

The long-term and ongoing trends are towards people born into the working class enjoying improved chances of social ascent, and the new middle class becoming self-recruiting. There have been major changes over time in absolute rates of social mobility. Relative rates, in contrast – the relative chances of people who start at different levels reaching a specific class destination – have remained remarkably stable. And these rates are similar in all modern societies. There are several explanations for this stability but none are totally convincing; this is one of the turn of the century's unresolved sociological puzzles.

Chapter 9 is on contemporary politics. In a sense, this is the crunch chapter. A promise of class analysis has always been to unravel the links between the economy, society and politics. If there were no such links, class analysis would be a feeble exercise. It will be argued that politics has in fact been de-aligned from older class divisions, but that only a class explanation can account for how politics has changed. Contemporary politics reflects the new balance of class forces: a disorganised and disarmed working class, an ascendant upper class, and a new middle class that is more likely to address its discontents through career strategies and lifestyle choices than through politics.

The new middle class supplies nearly all our current members of parliament, but these are better treated as one among many middle-class career groups rather than as class representatives. Except in places where nationalism has filled the void, politics is now substantially divorced from the people. This is the result of a particular balance of class forces. What will the outcome be? What can be said with confidence is that, just like previous balances, the current state of the class struggle is unlikely to last for long.

Summary

This chapter has explained how class is defined by Marxist, Weberian and functionalist sociologists, and noted common features. All regard class as having an economic base. All concepts of class group together people with similar ways of making their livings, that is, people in similar occupations. All sociologists who study class have additional common interests. They are all interested in how the class divisions that arise in economic life are liable to spill over into people's minds and wider social relationships, and the implications for their political activities and preferences through which there may be feedback loops with politics impacting back on economic life, the class structure and the rest of society.

This chapter has also considered briefly the reasons given for an alleged decline of class: embourgeoisement, a property-owning democracy, managerialism, social mobility, citizenship, post-industrialism, post-Fordism, and the increased prominence of other social divisions. We have seen that while the shape of the class structure and the composition of specific classes may well have changed in important ways, there are good grounds for rejecting the view that class itself has become a thing of the past.

The next chapter will introduce the main sociological class schemes that correspond broadly with Weberian, Marxist and functionalist views of class. It will discuss which scheme gives the best results, and thereby lay out a framework for the later chapters' detailed examination of the main classes in present-day Britain, how these are changing in some ways, and remaining much as ever in others.

2

Class Schemes

Introduction

The previous chapter has established that class remains very much alive and still plays a major part in virtually everyone's life. In order to explore the contemporary class structure in detail we need an outline map. In other words, we need a class scheme. This chapter describes the Registrar General's social class scheme that was first used to analyse the 1911 census. It then considers the main alternative class schemes developed by sociologists:

* The Goldthorpe (Nuffield or Oxford) scheme;

* The schemes developed by the American sociologist, Eric Ohlin Wright; and

* The Cambridge scheme.

The strengths and limitations of each scheme are discussed, and it becomes clear why a modified version of the Goldthorpe scheme has been adopted (since 1998) as the new official UK class scheme. The chapter then considers who should be classified – individuals or households – and, if the latter, whose occupations should be taken into account. Related issues of how to incorporate gender and race into class analysis are also considered.

The (Pre-1998) Registrar General's Social Classes

Even today, the best-known British social class scheme is probably the Registrar General's that was first used in the 1911 census, and remained the UK's official (government) class scheme up to 1998. The scheme had a long life, and its replacement is not so very different. This is despite the new scheme having an entirely different theoretical rationale. Whatever their theoretical bases, class schemes usually identify much the same main divisions, which is hardly surprising because none of the schemes are works of pure theory – the constructors have always had at least one eye on the same surrounding inequalities.

The old Registrar General's scheme had six classes. Classes I and II consisted of higher and lower-level professionals, managers and administrative employees. Class IIIa comprised lower-level white-collar workers, while classes IIIb, IV and V were the skilled, semi-skilled and unskilled manual grades. It was claimed (until 1981) that the classes grouped together occupations of similar social standing. Then in 1981 it was decided (by the government and the Registrar General's office) that the classes in fact represented skill levels. There was no wholesale reassignment of occupations despite this major change in the alleged theoretical base.

Skill is rather difficult to measure. The length of time required to learn a job, and the level of qualification needed to enter, may not be technically necessary. There is always a huge judgemental factor in assessments of skill. How do we compare objectively two entirely different jobs? Is it to be in terms of the intrinsic difficulty or the severity of the consequences when mistakes are made? Is the surgeon's job technically more difficult than the butcher's?

Sociologists were never really satisfied with the Registrar General's original classes, firstly because of the absence of a plausible theoretical justification. Few sociologists believe that either social standing or skill are the principal bases on which classes are formed. Second, there had never been thorough large-scale research to justify the placement of occupations. From time to time, occupations were reclassified on the basis of new evidence and expert opinion. For example, air pilots (who were originally classed with other drivers) were promoted into the professional grades, and postal delivery workers (who were originally placed with other public officials) were demoted into the semi-skilled manual class. New occupations such as computer programmer had to be newly classified in the same way – on the basis of any hard evidence that was available plus expert opinion. It was all rather messy and unsatisfactory. Despite this, sociologists were normally happy to use the scheme. Its longevity made it widely understood, and its widespread use, especially in analysing government information, meant that new data that was classified in the same way was comparable with many existing sources.

The ONS 1998 Class Scheme

Nevertheless, when the research community was invited in the 1990s to propose a replacement class scheme it responded willingly, and its

Table 2.1 The 1998 official class scheme

ONS classes	Goldthorpe names	Book's names
1.1 Employers (large organisations) and senior managers		
1.2 Higher professionals	Service class	Middle class
2 Lower managerial and professional		
3 Intermediate (e.g. clerks, secretaries, computer operators)	Intermediate classes	Intermediate classes
4 Small employers and own-account non-professional		
5 Supervisors, craft and related		
6 Semi-routine (e.g. cooks, bus drivers, hairdressers, shop assistants)	Working class	Working class
7 Routine (e.g. waiters, cleaners, couriers)		
8 Never worked, long-term unemployed	—	Underclass

proposal (Rose and O'Reilly, 1997), adopted in 1998 by the Office of National Statistics (by then the responsible government department), is a slightly modified version of a class scheme originally developed in the early 1970s by John Goldthorpe. The new official classification is presented in Table 2.1 along with the original Goldthorpe class labels, and the labels used throughout this book.

Market and Work Situations

Now that this has become the UK official classification, the scheme may be generally regarded as a linear scale (which in fact it is not), and as representing social standing or skill (whereas in fact neither is a principal consideration in placing occupations). The scheme purports to group together occupations which have common market situations (see Box 2.1) and work situations.

The strength of an occupation's market position is reflected in the rewards from work that practitioners can expect. These rewards include, of course, the level of pay, and any fringe benefits such as health insurance and the use of a company vehicle, but future expectations (career prospects) can be at least as important as current earnings, and job security also needs to be taken into account.

An occupation's work situation is its typical position in the system of authority and control, and the degree of autonomy that incumbents

---

Box 2.1

Markets

- Markets exist when large numbers of buyers and sellers interact, and when prices are fixed by the interplay between supply and demand. There can be markets for anything – capital, goods, services and labour.

- Markets have existed since ancient times, but played a relatively minor role when much production was by families and local communities for their own use, and/or when people were required to make their labour or goods available to a specific land-owner or governor.

- Markets are never completely free. What we regard as free markets are in fact regulated by law, which allows buyers and sellers to interact 'freely', safeguards everyone from coercion, and enables bargains (contracts) to be enforced.

- Markets can be regulated in additional ways – by governments, cartels of firms, professional associations and trade unions. The object may be to set a floor or ceiling for prices, or to drive prices (for labour or goods) above what would otherwise be the market level.

- Under communism, state and party regulation largely replaced market mechanisms. The outcome was a distinctive kind of modern society, and a rather different class structure to those that have arisen in countries with market economies.

- Max Weber (see Chapter 1, p. 3) was the founding father of modern sociology who highlighted the role of markets in the formation of classes.

- Nowadays, markets have been globalised, and market forces (regulated in different ways and to varying extents) play a pivotal role in class formation throughout the entire world.

---

possess when performing their jobs. How closely are they supervised? How much discretion do they exercise? Are they responsible for, and do they have control over, the work of others? There are in fact just four basic work situations. One can be an employer, self-employed, a manager (performing ownership functions – see Box 2.2), or a worker.

The Goldthorpe/ONS class scheme is widely regarded (within sociology) as neo-Weberian because it classifies occupations according to their market situations as well as their work situations (relationships to the means of production in Marxist terminology). As explained in Chapter 1 (see pp. 3–4), Max Weber himself believed that classes were formed in markets, in labour markets in the cases of people who needed to sell their

---

Box 2.2

Ownership functions or functions of capital

One way of identifying these is to ask what the owner would do in a small enterprise where he or she was in sole command of the entire workforce. Among other things, he or she would hire staff, fix rates of pay, allocate tasks, make investment decisions, fix prices, maybe personally sell the products, and keep the books. As enterprises grow in size it becomes necessary to employ managers and professionals to perform many of these tasks.

Marxists (see Chapter 1, p. 2) have sometimes argued that in a society where the means of production are collectively owned, all such 'unproductive' or 'socially unnecessary' functions of capital will be eliminated and the associated jobs will disappear. Others argue that it will always be necessary to have managers to coordinate workforces, accountants to keep the books, and so forth, though the managers and professionals might work differently, according to different priorities. In other words, the occupations and their functions are not necessarily unique to capitalist societies, though in such societies the relevant staff must necessarily be capitalism's functionaries.

---

labour. Weber recognised employers and workers as two major classes, but he also identified other class divisions depending on the assets (skills and qualifications) that individuals could offer in the labour market. Goldthorpe is entitled to insist that his scheme is really just as Marxist as Weberian because it pays equal regard to work situations. However, Marxist sociologists prefer to classify occupations or jobs solely on the basis of their relationships to the means of production (see below).

As we shall see later (p. 28), Goldthorpe's scheme (like Marxist schemes) is relational (not gradational) in that it regards classes as being formed largely through their relationships with one another – employing one another, and controlling or being controlled by one another at work, for example. Now it is claimed (by the Goldthorpe scheme's supporters) that when occupations are grouped simultaneously according to their market and work situations, we find that they cluster into a limited number of classes. When the Goldthorpe scheme was first used (in Goldthorpe's 1972 social mobility survey, see Chapter 8), it was not entirely clear how all the occupations had been placed, but the clustering has subsequently been confirmed in the analysis of large data sets which contain all the necessary information about work and market situations (see Evans and Mills, 1998).

The Goldthorpe/1998 ONS Classes

There are just two main classes in the Goldthorpe scheme. One is composed of managers and professionals (classes 1 and 2 in the ONS scheme). These occupations are characterised by their high and secure incomes that rise progressively as individuals' careers develop, by the authority that incumbents exercise in their work organisations, and by the discretion that they enjoy. Goldthorpe has placed great emphasis on the 'trust' or 'service' relationship with their employers. Managers and professionals do not normally have fixed hours of work, and their work is not monitored closely. They are trusted to act responsibly and to use their skills in their employers' interests. In exchange they are given relatively secure jobs, high incomes and progressive careers. Goldthorpe labels this class the 'service class' to stress its distinctive 'service' terms and conditions of employment, but this label is always liable to be misunderstood as referring to people who work in services as opposed to manufacturing, or servant-like occupations. It is doubtful whether anyone outside sociology identifies with the service class. New middle class, or just plain middle class, is just as good a label: it is the self-description used by most of the people in the class, and throughout the remainder of this book.

The second main Goldthorpe class is the working class, subdivided by skill levels (classes 5, 6 and 7 in the ONS scheme). These occupations are the polar opposites of the middle class. People are paid by the number of hours that they work, or according to how much they produce, and they are usually paid far less than people in management or professional jobs. On average, male white-collar workers earn half as much again as male manual employees, and female white-collar staff have a similar earnings advantage *vis-à-vis* their female manual counterparts. There is little trust in the working-class employment relationship. Terms and conditions of work are strictly contractual, and the jobs are generally less secure than those of managers and professionals so risks of unemployment are greater. Career prospects and fringe benefits are usually distinctly inferior, or non-existent, and most manual employees are not responsible for the work of any other staff. They do not exercise, but are expected to submit to authority. Table 2.2 presents some of the findings from a nationally representative sample that was questioned about their jobs and labour market experiences in the early 1990s. The table illustrates the stark contrasts between middle-class and working-class jobs. The chances are that a middle-class employee will initiate and decide his or her own daily tasks, and supervise someone. The chances are that a working-class employee will do none of these things.

It is sometimes claimed that the staff–works distinction is a thing of the past, but this would be untrue even if everyone used the same canteens

Table 2.2 Automomy, responsibility and social class

	Prof./Man. (%)	Skilled (%)	Non-skilled (%)
Decides daily tasks	75	33	37
Initiates new tasks	75	45	38
Has supervisory responsibilities	68	35	21

Source: Gallie *et al.* (1998).

and addressed each other using forenames (which in practice is still the exception rather than the rule). Occupations at all levels have changed over time, and these changes are discussed at length in the next chapter. In certain technical aspects, the old blue–white-collar divide has crumbled. For example, mechanisation has taken much of the brute labour out of manual jobs; and, meanwhile, offices have become stocked with technology. Nowadays manual workers and managers may both be required to work with computers. However, in terms of career prospects and other basic features of the market and work situations, there has been no collapse, or even a weakening, of this long-standing class division (Gallie, 1996).

The Goldthorpe/1998 ONS classification identifies two intermediate classes. One consists of lower-level office and some sales staff. These jobs usually possess some middle-class features, for example there are often short career ladders. The jobs are thereby set above manual occupations but remain very inferior in all respects to occupations that are in the middle class proper. The intermediate position of these occupations is reflected in the occupants' collective uncertainty about their class locations. The majority of manual workers describe themselves as working class, while the majority of managers and professionals identify with the middle-class. People in lower-level office jobs divide roughly 50:50 into middle-class and working-class identifiers.

The second intermediate class is the petit bourgeoisie – people who work for themselves or who own and run small businesses, except professionals who are placed, alongside other members of their occupations, in the service/middle class. Members of the petit bourgeoisie differ enormously in market success but they have such a distinctive work situation – working for themselves and being the boss – that they are grouped together on this basis.

The 1998 ONS classification also has an 'underclass' (class 8) which was not in the original Goldthorpe scheme. This class is for people who have never worked, the long-term unemployed, and others who depend long-term on state social security. The case for recognising such a class has strengthened since the 1970s due to the level of unemployment, and the extent to which social security benefits have dropped further and further behind average earnings. However, whether the people concerned really are a class apart is considered carefully in Chapter 4.

An objection to the Goldthorpe/ONS scheme is that it does not recognise an upper or capitalist class. One reason why there is no such class in the ONS version is simply that the scheme classifies people by their occupations rather than by their wealth, and company directors are placed in the top class. The original Goldthorpe scheme was intended to be used in survey research where, as we shall see later (in Chapter 7), it is probably pointless to try to identify an upper class (most people who are so classified in large-scale surveys turn out to be neither very wealthy nor very powerful). However, if anyone wishes, for whatever reasons, to distinguish an upper class (as this book certainly does for reasons that will become clear in later chapters), this class can simply be placed on top of the ONS scheme.

A point to note is that the Goldthorpe scheme is not consistently hier-archical. The middle class is certainly above the working class, class 1 is above class 2, and classes 5, 6, 7 and 8 are in rank order, but lower-level office workers are not believed to be above the petit bourgeoisie, and it is not implied that all of the latter are beneath all members of the middle class, or above all members of the working class. The intermediate classes are simply distinct classes most of whose members occupy the intermedi-ate space between the two main classes – the middle class and the work-ing class. Goldthorpe has always insisted that we can speak unequivocally of someone having been socially mobile only if the person has moved from the middle class into the working class, or vice-versa. Movements into and out of the intermediate classes do not necessarily indicate that those concerned have risen or fallen. It is most likely that, in its ONS guise, the scheme will often be treated as a fully linear scale, but sociologists will (or should) know better.

Strengths of the Scheme

The original Goldthorpe scheme was received sometimes critically, but generally enthusiastically, in British sociology, as being superior to both its predecessors and contemporary rivals. The Goldthorpe scheme has sev-eral distinctive advantages. First, there is an explicit theoretical rationale; one can see why each occupation has been placed in its particular class, and if anyone suspects that an occupation has been misplaced there are ground rules for resolving the dispute. This also applies whenever new occupations are created. Second, the scheme sidesteps arguments about whether occupations should be classified according to their work or market situations by employing both criteria simultaneously. One no longer has to be either a Marx or a Weber supporter. Third, in separating lower-level white-collar occupations from the middle class proper, the Goldthorpe scheme disarms critics of class analysis who query whether there really is a major division between the middle and working classes, meaning all white-collar and all blue-collar workers respectively. The crucial contrast in the Goldthorpe scheme is between a middle class proper of managers and professionals on the one hand, and the working class on the other. The fact that some occupations are intermediate need not mean that there are no clear class divisions.

The ONS/Goldthorpe scheme predicts things that one would expect a class scheme to predict (self-assigned class identities and political partisanship, for example, and much else besides), but, of course, virtually any class scheme will do this. It must be said that after all the careful conceptualisation and dedicated research, the new class scheme is not all that different from the Registrar General's older social classes with a petit bourgeoisie and an underclass added. However, the ONS 1998 scheme has a stronger theoretical justification. The old scheme's original construction and survival owed much to its reliance on everyday common-sense. This is not foolproof; If it were, then sociology would be redundant. So it is always necessary to have common-sense confirmed. But, as we shall see, for sociology deliberately to ignore the potential value of everyday common-sense (what we 'know' as ordinary members of our societies) can be foolhardy.

Marxist Schemes

Objections to other Schemes

The Goldthorpe/ONS scheme has faced criticism from two flanks. First, from Marxists. Their class schemes are rarely used in present-day Western or post-communist Eastern sociology, but the arguments never die. As in politics so in sociology: Marxism is a perpetual opposition.

Marxists object, of course, that the Goldthorpe scheme does not identify a separate capitalist class, but, as we have seen, this absence is easily corrected, if desired. More fundamentally, Marxists object to people being classed according to technical features of their jobs (whether they work mainly with their hands or with their heads, for example), and according to how well they are rewarded. Marxists insist that people should be classed solely by their social relationships to the means of production (see Box 2.3). They object to people being separated from the working class for what, to Marxists, are inadequate reasons, like being highly-paid.

Box 2.3

Forces, means, relationships and modes of production

These terms are associated with Marxism, but they can be detached from this body of theory.

The forces or means of production are the raw materials upon which people work, and the equipment that they use.

Relationships of production refers to the social (rather than the technical) division of labour, and, therefore, the social relationships into which people enter in order to use the forces/means of production. Marx, of course, regarded the employer–worker relationship as the principal, definitive relationship of production in capitalist societies.

A mode of production encompasses the forces/means, and the corresponding relationships of production. Hence Marx identified the feudal mode, the capitalist mode, and so on. It was Marx's view that throughout history, under successive modes of production, the forces of production had been developed progressively as far as the existing relationships of production would allow. However, he believed that points were reached when 'contradictions' arose between what the prevailing relationships of production would permit, and the potential of the forces of production. Thus under capitalism there was said to be an unfolding contradiction between the possibility of new technology releasing everyone from want, and capitalist relationships of production which condemned the working class to a subsistence existence, the persistent threat of unemployment and the severe deprivations involved. The inevitable (in the long term) outcome of such a glaring contradiction was said to be revolutionary change (the advent of a new mode of production), with the momentum supplied by a formerly exploited class, or a faction of it. The working class was expected to develop a revolutionary consciousness as it became aware of the contradiction between its treatment under capitalism, and what the forces of production with which they worked were capable of delivering.

Contradictory Class Situations

For a long time Marxists have acknowledged that capitalist societies are not being progressively polarised into just two main classes. All their class schemes distinguish employers from workers, but for over a century Marxists have recognised additional class divisions and situations, as did Marx himself. Since the 1960s, Marxists have responded to the need to solve the middle-class problem – how to classify them – and their solutions have involved the identification of various so-called contradictory or ambiguous class situations. Even if employers and workers are not the only classes, Marxists have continued to insist that class situations are defined essentially by workers' relationships to either or both of these two main classes.

Marxists have always expected that, once classes are correctly identified, we will see exploitation, domination, struggle and consciousness-formation more clearly than through schemes that mis-locate the proper class boundaries. By their fruits we shall know them! We shall see that in practice the results achieved with Marxist class schemes have been inferior to the performance of the Goldthorpe/ONS scheme. Hence the latter's premier position in contemporary British sociology.

The Wright Schemes

The best-known, and most widely used, Marxist class schemes have been constructed by Eric Ohlin Wright (1979, 1985, 1994, 1996), an American sociologist. His ideas have not been dismissed out of hand, they have been treated very seriously. Indeed, his class schemes have been used in an international comparative research project to which the British contribution was *Social Class in Modern Britain*, a study conducted by Gordon Marshall and his colleagues (1988), all then at Essex University.

Wright himself has always been open-minded and willing to revise his ideas in response to criticism; in fact he undertook a major overhaul of his class scheme in the 1980s. His earlier scheme (see Table 2.3a) had recognised a (grand) bourgeoisie, small employers, a petit bourgeoisie, managers (in the contradictory position of being employees yet performing functions of capital – see Box 2.2), semi-autonomous employees, a category that was meant to capture professionals but in practice became something of a rag-bag since cooks and caretakers, for instance, were sometimes placed there, and a working class.

Wright decided that his first attempt at a class scheme was too simple and that in practice there were more contradictory locations than he had identified. So he attempted to rectify these faults by making his scheme more consistently Marxist (so he said). His revised scheme (see Table 2.3b) removes people from the working class depending on whether they own the businesses in which they work, or whether they control organisational assets (perform management functions), or whether they hold any credentialled skill assets (useful qualifications). One might wonder what place credentials have in a Marxist scheme. Other Marxists (for example, Gubbay, 1997) have queried the revised Wright scheme's Marxist pedigree. Wright appears to be trying to keep people such as university professors, who may have no management responsibilities, out of the

Table 2.3   Wright's original and revised class schemes

(a) Wright's original class scheme

1. Bourgeoisie
2. Small employers
3. Petit bourgeoisie (self-employed, no employees)
4. Managers and supervisors
5. Semi-autonomous employees
6. Workers

(b) Wright's revised class scheme

	Assets in the means of production			Organisation assets
Owners	*Non-owners skill/credential assets*			
	Experts	*Skilled employees*	*Non-skilled*	
1 Bourgeoisie	4 Expert managers	7 Semi-credentialled managers	10 Uncreden-tialled managers	*Managers*
2 Small employers	5 Expert supervisors	8 Semi-credentialled supervisors	11 Uncreden-tialled supervisors	*Supervisors*
3 Petit bourgeoisie	6 Expert non-managers	9 Semi-credentialled workers	12 Proletarians	*Non-management*

---

working class. In his original scheme the semi-autonomous employee category was designed for this purpose but in practice the category had a wider embrace. The Marxist reasoning behind classifying people partly on the basis of their credentials, or lack of any, provided that the qualifications are relevant to and used in their jobs, is that those concerned have acquired special skills that are useful to their employers in exchange for which they receive a share of the surplus value (see Box 2.4) that other workers produce. If you find this reasoning unconvincing, you are not alone.

A noteworthy feature of Wright's scheme, or more strictly its use, is that individuals are classified not according to their occupations but by their jobs. Wright criticises procedures (see Box 2.5) that assume that everyone with a common occupational title will be doing broadly similar jobs. Classifying people according to the character of their particular jobs is

---

Box 2.4

Surplus value

Most present-day economists (and sociologists) have no use for this concept. However, the concept occupied a central place in Marx's theory about the operation and development of capitalist societies, and some (though not all) present-day Marxist sociologists continue to use the term.

We need to begin with the labour theory of value which asserts that the basic value of any commodity depends on the amount of labour required for its production. So the relative value of commodities depends primarily on how long it takes a worker, or workers, to produce them.

Labour itself has a basic value depending on its costs of production and reproduction. Workers need to be fed, clothed, housed, and so on, and they also need to be born, reared, educated and trained. So there can be variations in the basic value of different kinds of labour power. In market situations, commodities (including labour power) may be bought and sold at prices in excess of their basic value. The difference between the two is said to be surplus value which may be appropriated by an employer. It is also possible for workers themselves to acquire surplus value from the sale of their labour power on the basis of the particular skills and experience that they can offer, but this always depends on the employer being able to recoup the costs in the surplus value (profit) gained from the sale of the workers' output. It is only when the forces of production (the tools and machinery with which people work) have been developed to a level that enables workers to produce in excess of their own subsistence needs, that some people can engage in 'unproductive labour' or work that is not 'socially necessary' (to reproduce the worker). Examples include artists of various kinds and religious functionaries, plus a separate class of owners and the people who they employ (managers, for example) whose principal function (so Marxists claim) is not to create value but to extract surplus value from the real producers (see Box 2.2).

---

expected to lead to the discovery of stronger relationships between social class and most other things than occupation-based classifications. Wright has always suspected that many jobs with middle-class occupational titles are really proletarian. When constructing his original scheme he was influenced by the ideas of Harry Braverman (1974) who had claimed that the development of capitalism led to a progressive degradation of labour as, in the search for profit under competitive conditions, employers subjected labour to forever tighter control. As this happened, both manual and white-collar jobs were said to be vulnerable to deskilling. Wright argues that classifying according to job characteristics enables everyone, whatever their job titles, to be classified correctly.

Box 2.5

Classifying people

Wright's scheme is the exception here; with virtually all other class schemes this is a multi-stage process. First, individuals' jobs must be assigned to 'occupational unit groups'. Around 25,000 different occupations are currently recognised in official (government) registers: too many for all but the most common to be present in useful numbers even in large samples. So occupations are allocated to one or another of the 370 or so groups in the government's standard occupational classification (SOC) (which has been used since 1990). Each group of occupations is supposed to perform similar work, which requires similar experience, skills and qualifications. Neither the list of separate occupations, nor the standard groups (SOCs) are stable; new occupations are being created constantly. Likewise, entire new categories of occupations can be brought into existence – para-medical occupations, public relations experts, call-centre occupations more recently, and, even more recently still, occupations connected with electronic commerce. The standard occupational classification is being revised constantly. It is only at the next stage in classifying people that most sociological class schemes begin to do their original work.

The schemes classify SOCs, not separate occupations. So SOCs can be allocated (using computer programmes nowadays) to the Registrar General's (pre-1998) social classes, or alternatively to the 17 socio-economic groups (SEGs) that are also recognised. Goldthorpe (and Hope) originally ranked occupational unit groups into 36 groups of occupations, each with reputedly similar social standing. These 36 groups were then collapsed into the seven original Goldthorpe classes, which have been modified and extended to eight in the new official classification. The Cambridge class scheme (see below) is also based on occupational unit groups (the SOCs nowadays). So once occupations have been allocated to SOCs, it is fairly straightforward for sociologists to experiment, and to compare the results obtained with different class schemes. This is how Gordon Marshall and his colleagues (1988) were able to compare Goldthorpe's with other class schemes. There are never-ending debates about the classes into which particular SOCs should be placed, especially when the occupations are completely new or when the character of the work has changed radically. It has been argued (successfully) that supermarket check-out staff should be placed in the working class rather than in the intermediate class, where they would accompany people who sell motor cars and insurance policies, and who work in more traditional department stores. There is still a debate about where to place call-centre staff (intermediate at present in the official classification). Technical and supervisory jobs are another group of occupations whose location is currently controversial. Should they are be grouped together in an intermediate class (as in the original Goldthorpe class scheme)? Or, as in the new official classification, should most of them be either downgraded into the working class or upgraded into the middle class?

However, Wright's insistence on ignoring occupational titles leads to some peculiar-looking placements (see Marshall *et al.*, 1988). For example, investment brokers, purchasing officers and others can appear in the working-class because, according to the answers that they give to interviewers, they are non-owners, do not have management responsibilities, and possess no job-relevant credentials. Maybe the jobs really are working - class and all the other class schemes, are wrong! With the exception of the owner and worker categories, Wright's entire revised scheme flouts common-sense. None of the contradictory class positions are recognisable in everyday life, although this does not necessarily mean that the scheme must be wrong. However, neither Wright himself nor anyone else has ever found any of the non-owner classes, except the workers, displaying a distinctive type of consciousness or political proclivities. No matter how the Wright scheme is collapsed, it fails to yield as strong predictions (correlations) as other class schemes with measurements that are expected to be class-related (see Marshall *et al.*, 1988). Small wonder, then, that most investigators prefer Goldthorpe.

Wright's problem could be his application of Marxism, and other Marxists have distanced themselves from him. For example, Jonathan Gubbay (1997) has criticised the Weberian elements (like credentials) in Wright's revised scheme and has called for a more rigorous application of Marxist thinking. Gubbay would like classes to be recognised by examining flows of surplus value (see Box 2.4) – who generates it and who receives it. Surplus value, according to Gubbay, is everything that is produced in excess of what is needed to reproduce labour power in the prevailing social and cultural contexts. So everyone who is paid above the minimum on which individuals are able to continue to work is declared to be receiving surplus value. It is possible to establish who receives more than this minimum income (nearly everyone nowadays, though to very different extents), but identifying where surplus value is created is far more difficult. Within any firm it is always difficult to measure how much of the collective output is due to each particular worker.

The fundamental problems in the Wright scheme, and other Marxist attempts, are not the applications, but Marxism itself. The theory discourages scheme constructors from classifying workers according to how much they are paid, their job security, career prospects and other rewards from work – the market-situation part of the Goldthorpe rationale. Even John Westergaard (1994), whose sociology has always been basically Marxist, has protested against the futility of trying to exclude 'who gets what' from class analysis.

Marx believed that the owner–worker division would become the main class schism in capitalist societies, and that other divisions would diminish in significance. He was wrong, and his basic approach is simply unable to cope with history having shown that employer–worker is one major division, but that there are additional class schisms among employees whose basic work situations (wage or salary earning) are very similar. Addressing these plain facts requires committed Marxists either to betray their own theory (by admitting Weberian elements into their work) or produce class schemes whose resemblance to social reality is tenuous, or a mixture of the two.

The Cambridge Scheme

Over the last 20 years the challenge of Marxism has faded. Nowadays the main challenge to neo-Weberian class schemes is from sociologists who prefer to conceptualize class gradationally. The Weberians and gradationalists have always been the main class camps in North American sociology and Europe has now fallen into line.

Marxist and Weberian concepts of class have an important feature in common: they are both relational. Each class is defined by its relationships with others – employing or being employed by them, or controlling or being controlled by them, for example. Classes are conceived as being formed by these relationships. Gradational concepts, in contrast, identify classes in terms of how much they have of whatever is considered crucial – power, income, status or whatever. These schemes identify class differences rather than clear divisions. The class hierarchy is conceived as a series of steps rather than antagonistic groups. American sociologists have normally been comfortable with gradational class concepts. Functionalism (see Chapter 1, pp. 4–5), the best-known theoretical underpinning of this view of class, was always most influential on the west of the Atlantic. European sociology has always been more hospitable to conflict theories and their relational class concepts.

Criticisms of 'Box' Schemes

In Britain the main gradational class scheme currently in use has been developed by a Cambridge group of sociologists (Robert Blackburn, Ken Prandy and Sandy Stewart). Their ideas are not hot-off-the-press; they began to develop their class scheme at the same time as the Goldthorpe (Oxford) scheme was being conceived for the 1972 social mobility survey. At that time the Cambridge group believed that Goldthorpe was leading the sociological study of class down a false trail.

They have four basic objections to Goldthorpe's and other box schemes, and an alternative. The first objection, of course, is that class is in fact gradational, not relational. The Cambridge group point out that all the alleged determinants of class position are distributed gradationally: that in reality the situation is not that some people's jobs are totally secure and others the exact opposite, and likewise with job autonomy, career prospects, pay and everything else. 'Putting people into boxes' is said to be a misleading, and unnecessary, sociological habit. The Cambridge group argue that sociology was on the right lines with the old Registrar General's social classes – six groups of occupations, each believed to be of broadly similar social standing. They believe that sociology took a false turn by trying to define the boundaries between classes more accurately instead of working towards positioning everyone more precisely along a continuum.

The second objection to the Goldthorpe methodology is that it is pointless to try to define class precisely, in terms of market situation, work situation or anything else, and, in particular, to try to follow Weber in separating class from status. In practice, the Cambridge group argue, everything is merged into general stratification arrangements with actors located at various levels.

Third, the Cambridge group take exception to identifying classes objectively, in terms of market or work situations which are said to create class positions which actors then fill. The Cambridge view is that social classes, if they deserve the label, can only be formed in the course of actors evaluating their own and other's positions.

Fourth, the Cambridge group believe that, ideally at any rate, class analysis should always incorporate a longitudinal, biographical dimension. They argue that how people respond in given positions will always depend, at least in part, on where they are coming from, and where they believe they are heading. They have argued, for example, that if the positions are occupied only temporarily, lower-level office jobs may have proletarian characteristics without the actors themselves being proletarianised. As we shall see in Chapter 8, there is in fact a great deal of social mobility, which, according to the Cambridge group, makes it unrealistic to portray the population as occupying fixed 'boxes'.

The Cambridge Alternative

The Cambridge group have not been armchair critics of the Goldthorpe classification. They have been out 'in the field', gathered their own data, and built an alternative Cambridge class scheme. This is constructed by asking people to think of four friends and their occupations, as well as naming their own. The same information, about the subjects' and their partners' occupations, has also been collected about pairs at the time of their marriages. These questions have been asked of roughly 10,000 individuals, yielding approximately 70,000 pairs of occupations (chosen by each other). Occupations (SOCs in practice, see Box 2.5) that are paired frequently are said to be socially close (near equals). Frequency of pairing is used as a measure of social proximity and distance, and the more frequently occupations choose each other, the closer they are said to be.

When this information is analysed it is found that people in different occupations give symmetrical answers. Things do not simply have to turn out this way; plumbers could name accountants as friends more frequently than accountants named plumbers, or vice-versa, but in practice there are no major inconsistencies of this type. It is also found that when all occupations are placed in relation to each other, as described above, they spread out along a single axis. Again, this does not simply have to be the case. In theory there could be several circles or networks of occupations that tended to choose one another, but in practice this is not what happens – occupations are spread out along a more-or-less straight line. Common-sense is used to tilt the line: the end with the accountants and doctors is set at the top, and the end with the road sweepers and labourers is set at the base. The axis is then calibrated at equal intervals and each occupation can be given a numerical score depending on its typical position. The scale is said to be measuring social class by grouping together occupations whose members associate with one another as equals, and, it is suggested, share similar lifestyles and occupy the same levels of advantage and disadvantage in society's general stratification arrangements.

The first version of the Cambridge scheme was developed on the basis of surveys of manual workers in Peterborough and white-collar workers in East Anglia in the 1960s and 1970s, and was presented in the 1980 book, *Social Stratification and Occupations* (Stewart et al., 1980). Instead of being gratefully adopted, the Cambridge scheme was virtually ignored by British sociology whereas at that time the Goldthorpe scheme was receiving a generally favourable reception. So the Cambridge group persisted. They revised and consolidated their scheme on the basis of additional research (Prandy, 1990), and have proceeded to show that it gives superior results to any of its rivals. The results are said to be superior in that the correlations are stronger with everything that social class is supposed to predict – children's education and the subjects' own voting intentions, for example. If the Cambridge scheme is divided arbitrarily into the same number of classes, the relationships with dependent variables are shown to remain stronger than those obtained with the old Registrar General's and the new official (Goldthorpe) classification (Blackburn, 1998; Prandy, 1998 a,b; Prandy and Blackburn, 1997). So why has the Cambridge scheme not been adopted more widely?

Objections

One objection to the Cambridge scheme is that it is not based on research with a nationally representative sample, but the Cambridge group have an adequate reply here. Since people at all levels appear to rank occupations in basically the same order, and since there appear to be no major differences by region or anything else, there are no reasons to suspect that the scale would be any different if derived from a random sample of the entire UK population.

A second objection is that the predictive power of the Cambridge scale is simply irrelevant. OK, the scale yields stronger correlations with, for example, children's educational achievements, than the Goldthorpe scheme. Does this mean that the Cambridge group have a superior measurement of class? Critics say that this is not necessarily so: that the true relationships between social class and the dependent variables may be weaker than the Cambridge scheme suggests, and that the strength of its relationships with dependent variables cannot be accepted as a test of whether an independent variable is being measured accurately (Evans, 1998; Rose, 1998). This argument would carry more weight had not the Goldthorpe scheme's supporters been willing to cite its own superior predictive power as a reason for preferring their scheme to Wright's (Marshall *et al.*, 1988). Maybe this kind of evidence is less than decisive, but the ability to predict what any theory of class would lead one to expect cannot be dismissed as neither here nor there.

Third, and getting closer to the heart of this matter, it can be objected that, contrary to the Cambridge group's view, classes are not aggregates of people (in specified occupations) who associate as equals: that these social relationships may be consequences of class but they are not what class actually 'is'.

Fourth, and related to this, the Cambridge group accept, alongside nearly all other class theorists, that actors should be classified according to their occupations, but the Cambridge scheme is not based on a theory which offers possible explanations, which can then be tested, of why occupations are ranked as they are. The Cambridge scheme may measure occupational rank accurately, but the scheme has no variables comparable to the market and work situation that might explain each occupation's class position.

Fifth, the Cambridge scale's critics argue that occupations are in fact grouped in clusters: they are not spread evenly in social space (Evans and Mills, 1998). It may be true that all the separate indicators of market situation – pay, job security and career prospects for example – are distributed gradationally, and likewise the pertinent features of work situations. But when occupations are grouped taking into account all these variables simultaneously, we see that some occupations consistently achieve positive scores, others negative, and other groups, like the petit bourgeoisie have distinctive packages – employing oneself, and maybe other people, in combination with either a strong or weak market position. The justification for 'putting people into boxes' is not that there are clear boundaries (akin to ditches or fences) between classes which might act as barriers to mobility or friendships, but that the members of each class are scattered around concentrations or 'clumps' of occupations, each clump having a qualitatively distinctive class profile.

Sixth, the Cambridge scheme does not lead to any theoretically based predictions about the kinds of consciousness and related political action that are most likely to develop at a given social level. The scheme has no underlying theory to explain, for example, the rise of the working class as a political force earlier in history, or to predict equivalent future developments. In short, the Cambridge scheme does not offer enough. It gives precise measurements which lead to strong predictions of some of the short-term consequences of class, but it is weak on explanations, especially explanations of class formation and the likely longer-term political consequences.

Readers who are new to these debates, who have no history of partisanship in the arguments, may wonder why supporters of the Goldthorpe/ Oxford and Cambridge schemes cannot reconcile their differences. Why not treat the Cambridge scale as a ruler which gives precise measurements of the hierarchical positions of occupations within classes, and the distances between classes, while the Oxford scheme is allowed to identify the main divisions? The answer is that this type of harmonisation would require both sides to compromise their positions, which neither is willing to do. The Cambridge group wish to define class gradationally and argue that introducing any divisions or 'boxes' misrepresents reality. The Goldthorpe scheme is not consistently hierarchical and its supporters have no wish to make it so, since, in their view, this would misrepresent class realities.

Who to Classify?

Whatever the class scheme, we have to decide who to classify. In practice the choice is between individuals and household/families, and, if the latter, whether to take account of everyone's occupations or just one member's.

The Conventional Approach

The conventional practice in sociology has been to classify households according to the (usually male) head of household's occupation. There are persuasive reasons for treating the household as the unit that is stratified. Until the 1980s the persuasiveness of this practice was usually considered overwhelming and was rarely challenged. Members of a household were regarded as sharing common standards and styles of living. Children were, and usually still are, regarded as having single family class backgrounds. The idea that members of a family might have different, even antagonistic class interests used to be considered ludicrous. It was argued that class conflict had to be kept out of the home otherwise the family would be unable to perform its own vital functions.

A related conventional practice is to classify each household according to the occupation of the (usually male) head. Women living singly have been classified according to their own occupations. In the case of couples, it used to be nearly always, and it is still usually, the male who has the most continuous employment, who works the longest hours, who earns the most and thereby, it is said, governs the entire household's standard of living and general social standing. Hence the justification of conventional practice.

John Goldthorpe has been a consistent defender of conventional practice subject to the qualification that the occupation of the household member with the dominant attachment to the labour market (not necessarily, but in practice still usually, a male) should be used to classify the family group (see Goldthorpe, 1983; Erikson and Goldthorpe, 1988). An assumption or implication in conventional practice is that male employment is normally more important than female employment as a determinant of not only households' class positions but the shape of the entire class structure. Hence the justification for studying social mobility and class structure with male-only samples. All 10,000 respondents in Goldthorpe's 1972 social mobility survey were men (Goldthorpe *et al.*, 1980).

During the last 20 years this conventional practice has come under fierce, broadly-based attack. Indeed, virtually the only British defenders (in print) have been John Goldthorpe himself and his Oxford-based colleagues. Second-wave feminism in sociology has chosen the conventional way of doing class analysis as one of the bastions of patriarchal assumptions that must be overturned. The criticisms of the conventional approach now look just as persuasive as the latter once did.

First, the view that the members of a household share the same standard of living, style of life and class position has been challenged. Marriages are not always equal partnerships; there is not necessarily financial equality. The status and public recognition attached to the male's occupation are not necessarily passed on to his marital partner.

Second, nowadays women comprise nearly a half of the workforce (see Chapter 3). It was more realistic in the past to treat the male as the family's main link with the macro-social structure, mainly via the labour market, and the woman's main role as domestic. Nowadays single women are just as likely to have paid employment as men, and roughly two-thirds of married women hold paid jobs. Career breaks following childbirth have become shorter, and more-and-more women have been taking maternity leave rather than terminating their employment. Given these trends, it has become difficult to justify ignoring women's employment in class analysis. There are more households where deciding which member's labour market attachment is dominant is anything but straightforward. Moreover, it is impossible to explain the distribution of men between the different occupation-based class groups, and their mobility chances, without referring to the fact that some types of jobs are done mainly by women (see Hayes and Miller, 1993).

Third, more women (and men) are living singly or cohabiting outside marriage as a result of the rise in the typical age of first marriages, and the rise in rates of divorce and separation. People are living longer into old age and, as men tend to die younger, there are far more widows than widowers, and the former do not usually inherit their partners' full occupational pensions. Given these trends, one would expect more and more women to regard their own life-chances as depending more upon their own education, skills and occupations rather than who they first marry, or with whom they are currently cohabiting. The foundations in the real world on which conventional practice once rested have certainly weakened.

Individual Classification

An alternative to conventional practice is to classify individuals, not households, so that everyone, males and females, can be classed according to their own occupations. Individual classification now has a wide body of support, and those who advocate this alternative in writing are mostly, but not exclusively, women. They have been able to show that women's own occupations make a difference (after controlling for the influence of their partners' occupations) to women's subjective class identities and political partisanship (Abbott, 1987). They have even been able to show that women's occupations have some influence on their husbands' politics (Hayes and Jones, 1992a,b). In Britain young women have been shown to base their perceptions of their class positions on their own education and occupations, and to view their life-chances, including the resources that will be available to them following marriage, as being determined mainly by their own backgrounds and education (Stanworth, 1984; Charles 1990). Female sociologists expect their own achievements to govern their own career prospects; they feel entitled to be placed in their discipline's social classes according to their own occupations, and demand commensurate treatment for other women.

However, there are two big problems with individual classification. First, women in similar occupations are all placed in exactly the same class, and the most common employment for women is low-level white-collar (see Chapter 5). So all these women, if classified individually, are placed in intermediate class positions on the Goldthorpe/ONS scheme. This is despite some of the married women having partners who are either company directors, doctors and so on, while others have partners who are manual workers, with all that this entails for the women's standards and styles of living.

Second, all the investigations that have conducted multivariate analysis with large data sets have discovered that the husband's occupation is still, even today, a better predictor of the wife's politics and class identity than her own job (Mills, 1994; Roberts and Marshall, 1995; Zipp and Plutzer, 1996). Her husband's employment is the best predictor of a woman's lifestyle and her chances of avoiding poverty (Breen and Whelan, 1995). The Goldthorpe scheme's supporters, who dismiss the Cambridge scheme's stronger correlations with class identities and so on as irrelevant to its validity, do not hesitate to use the same kind of evidence to defend 'conventional practice'.

Why should their own occupations make a greater impression on men's own standards of living, class identities and politics, than women's own occupations make on their's? Why should women be more responsive to their husbands' occupations than men are to their wives'? The only plausible answer is that, despite the protests of feminist thought, many women still see the domestic role as their primary role, and place themselves in society, and judge their interests, according to their male partners' occupations. And it is still usually the male who has the highest and least interrupted earnings (even though the number of exceptions has increased), and whose occupation therefore, has the most influence on the household's standard of living and the lifestyles that all its members can afford.

There are powerful arguments both for and against conventional practice, and at present neither side can win because society is changing, the pace of change is uneven between social groups and among households within social groups, and no single method of classification is going to be right for everyone. In the USA, Davis and Robinson (1988) have documented a trend over time towards women basing their class identities on both their own and their husbands' occupations rather than the latter's alone. They have also shown that in the USA males have not changed: they have always assessed, and continue to assess, their own class positions entirely on the basis of their own achievements. The chances are that the trends over time, and the sex difference, are basically the same in Britain. In so far as sociology's class schemes need to take popular conceptions into account, the change and dissensus currently found in society are bound to be reflected, some way or another, within sociology.

A Different Class Scheme for Women?

If men and women are to be classified individually, each according to their own occupations, the question arises as to whether the same class scheme is going to be equally appropriate for both sexes. The Goldthorpe scheme was initially developed from information about men's occupations. All well and good, if only men's occupations are to be taken into account when classifying the entire population. Can the scheme cope with women's jobs?

This question arises because even a quarter of a century and more following Britain's equal pay and equal opportunities legislation, men and women still tend to do different jobs. Labour markets remain segmented by gender, and there are still many occupations that are done mainly by women. The inclusion of women's occupations in class analysis certainly alters the apparent shape of the class structure. Women are more likely to be in the middle, intermediate grades, than anywhere else, whereas men are more likely to be in the middle class proper and the working class. The social class profile of men exhibits the hour-glass shape, while women's profile bulges in the middle. Amalgamate the two, and the class structure looks more like a pillar. But this is not the only difference that women's inclusion in class analysis could make; their inclusion in the research from which class schemes emerge could change the outcomes, the main clusters.

Advocates of the Goldthorpe scheme argue that it is gender-neutral: that women's manual jobs, professional jobs and lower-level office jobs possess much the same market and work-situation features as men's (Evans, 1996). Others are sceptical. Within broad categories such as professional, management, office and manual occupations, men and women still tend to choose, or to be channelled into, different kinds of jobs. For example, routine non-manual women are more likely than men to do typing/word processing. The men are more likely to do administrative tasks that place them on career ladders. So would we be trying to place women (and men) in the same social class categories if women's occupations had been included when constructing the schemes? Or would we have identified rather different social class groups?

Angela Dale and her colleagues (1985) have shown that cluster analysis using features of just women's occupations produces groups that resemble, but are not exactly the same as, the Goldthorpe classes. They found that women's occupations formed the five main clusters in Table 2.4. It can be argued additionally that, among women, class analysis really ought to take into account the inequalities between full-time and part-time jobs. Part-time jobs, that are filled mainly by women, tend to be interior to their full-time equivalents in most respects – pay per hour, job security, fringe benefits and promotion prospects. This applies at all levels, in retailing, and from junior office jobs to university lecturing. All the class schemes developed by studying, and in order to study, mainly men, ignore the full-time/part-time dichtomy. It can also be argued that housewives would be recognised (given a class of their own) in a truly woman-friendly scheme. Critics argue that ignoring the domestic division of labour is masculinist: that it marginalises women and conceals much of their work, their contributions to society (Crompton, 1996b).

Class analysis is threatened with grotesque complications, like using two entirely different class schemes and dispensing with the view that there is just one national class structure, and crediting children with dual social origins according to their mothers' and fathers' occupations. Maybe this latter complication will not be a distortion for the many children who nowadays have two sets of parents/step-parents.

Joint Classification

A way of avoiding some of the above complications without returning to the conventional approach is to classify households using all the adult members' (usually the husbands' and wives') occupations. One argument for doing this is basically the same as the case for the Cambridge scheme – it gives the best predictions, the strongest correlations, with everything that class analysis is expected to predict like standards of living, political partisanship and children's educational attainments (see Britten and Heath, 1983; Lampard, 1995; Leiulfsrud and Woodward, 1987). But as with all the other answers to 'Who to classify and how?' there are serious problems.

Table 2.4   Women's occupational classes

i.	Professional and administrative
ii.	Technical and supervisory
iii.	Clerical, cooks, postwomen and bus conductors
iv.	Service and production workers
v.	Other manual employees in manufacturing

Source: Dale *et al.* (1985).

One is that joint classification records more instability in people's class positions than any of the alternative procedures. This is because households' class positions (appear to) change if and when women move out of and back into the labour market, and therefore do or do not have occupations to be taken into account in determining the households' class positions. A household where the husband was a doctor would appear to have experienced downward mobility if his wife began to work as the medical practice's secretary. Maybe the appearances cast by joint classification are correct and there really is more instability in class positions than other methods of classifying the population record. Or maybe the error is in the joint classification method.

A more basic problem with joint classification is that households can gain identical scores from various combinations of husbands' and wives' occupations. So the classes that are identified are not composed of people with common experiences. In other words, the measurement does not distinguish classes in the ordinary meaning (within and outside sociology) of the term. As with the Cambridge scheme, joint classification is fine if the objective is to develop the best possible predictors of children's educational attainments, standards of living and so on, but this is not exactly the same as identifying actual class groups.

Social Change, Gender and the Class Structure

As already indicated, at present there can be no single, unambiguously correct choice of method. The best choice will depend on the purpose. Individual classification has the edge when seeking the shape of the occupational class structure – the proportions of positions in different classes. On balance, at present, joint classification or the conventional practice are better when seeking class predictions – of the types of consciousness and political action that are most likely to be produced.

Changes in gender roles – both in the home and in the labour market – make it more difficult than formerly to classify the population whatever class scheme is used, and the changes in gender roles themselves are altering the shape of the class structure in ways that are discussed in greater detail in later chapters, but deserve an introduction here. Class and gender are entwined in one another; they are different social divisions, and neither can be reduced to the other. But they interact, as when gender influences people's jobs opportunities. More subtly, each division becomes implicated in the other. So occupations can be gendered – considered most suitable for, and in practice entered by, mainly men or women. In some way or another, gender infiltrates all classes and class processes. This is why it is impossible to treat gender adequately in a separate chapter in a book on social class: gender must be treated throughout. For the time being, we can note just two (there are many other) ways in which changes in gender roles are affecting the shape of the class structure.

First, increased labour-market participation by women has increased the proportion of cross-class households with adults in occupations in different classes. This is despite there being a strong tendency for like to marry like. Middle-class men are more likely than working-class males to marry middle-class females, but there are many males in both classes who marry women whose own occupations are intermediate (office work mainly). This tends to blur class divisions. The blurring occurs in standards of living: gross income and spending levels are less clearly class-divided than would be the case if only males were employed. Dual-earning working-class households may have higher gross incomes than single-earner middle-class households.

Second, and simultaneously, women's increased labour-market participation is tending to push the ends of the social class structure further apart. Like does tend to marry like. So there are now more households than in the past with two adults in well-paid middle-class jobs. At the other extreme, there are more households containing adults of working age in which no-one is employed.

Class and Ethnic Divisions

Following the above section, readers might be expecting a corresponding treatment of ethnic divisions. Gender and ethnicity pose some similar problems for class analysis. One is whether ethnic divisions (like gender) have independent effects on processes that are class related, like children's educational and occupational attainments, and how people vote. The alternative possibility (in the case of ethnic divisions) is that gross differences between ethnic groups could be due to their different social class distributions. In practice, as we shall see throughout the following chapters, we find that ethnicity usually has independent effects, but these differ from minority to minority, and sometimes between males and females within the same ethnic groups. In other words, the ethnic picture is extremely complicated.

All ethnic minorities, like men and women, have distinctive occupational distributions. Just as occupations can be gendered, so can they be racialised – considered most suitable for, and in practice filled disproportionately by, members of particular ethnic groups. Ethnic restaurants are the clearest example, but there are many others. Despite racial discrimination having been outlawed, many occupational cultures remain racialized. Office or shopfloor small-talk may make members of minority groups feel uncomfortable, even unwanted, and there is still covert racial discrimination in recruitment and promotion in many organisations. Ethnic-minority employees sometimes complain that even when they are admitted to certain professions, like teaching and social work, they tend to be channelled into what are regarded (by their colleagues and bosses) as appropriate niches, like work in multiracial neighbourhoods.

Which occupations are generally regarded as suitable for, and most accessible to, ethnic minorities may change over time. In the 1950s and 1960s – the postwar years of full employment – immigrants were welcomed into low-level jobs. In the tougher labour markets of the 1970s and subsequently, there have been recurrent cases of sections of the white working class acting informally to hold on to 'their' jobs – in car plants, and as hospital ancillaries, for example.

The class opportunity structures confronting ethnic minorities are different from those experienced by the white population, which raises many of the same issues for class analysis which arise with gender. Do we need different or modified versions of the normal class schemes in order to portray ethnic minorities' positions? If so, how should we treat ethnically-mixed households?

These issues will be revisited throughout the following chapters. At present we can note simply that the constructors and users of class schemes have usually preferred to side-step ethnic issues. There are sound reasons for this. One is the sheer complexity of the relevant situations: there are numerous ethnic minorities, and the implications of belonging to any of the groups can vary by gender. In total the minorities amount to no more than 6 per cent of the current UK population, though this figure will rise over the next generation – 11 per cent of current schoolchildren in England and Wales are from ethnic-minority groups. Second, Britain's class and race researchers alike are nearly all committed integrationists. Rather than construct alternative class schemes, which might reinforce the minorities' separation, they have preferred to investigate the obstacles to their assimilation into the dominant white class structure.

Summary

This chapter has appraised the main class schemes developed and used by British sociologists: the Registrar General's original class scheme, the Goldthorpe scheme, the Wright schemes, and the Cambridge scheme. We have seen that the Goldthorpe scheme has special strengths, which is why it has become the scheme most widely used by present-day British sociologists, and increasingly in other countries also, and why, in a slightly modified form, it has been adopted as the new official UK classification. Over time the Goldthorpe scheme is bound to become more widely known and, perhaps, better understood.

This chapter has also considered whether individuals or households should be the units that are classified, and, if the latter, whose occupations are to be taken into account. The related issue of whether the same class scheme can be equally suitable for males and females, and all ethnic groups, has also been considered. We have seen that there are problems with all the solutions to these issues that have been proposed (when any have been sought – in practice when handling gender). This means that the issues cannot be considered settled and set aside: we must remain sensitive to the problems throughout all the following chapters.

3
Economic Change

Introduction

If a person's class depends on his or her occupation (see Chapter 1), then economic changes that alter the kinds of jobs that people are able to enter are bound to reshape the class structure. Here the Goldthorpe scheme (the 'best buy' from all the available class schemes – see Chapter 2) is used as a background 'map' for revealing some broad class effects (details are added in later chapters) of recent economic and occupational changes, and developments in the UK's labour markets.

The first section examines the new (economic) times in which we are now said to live: how globalisation and new technologies have undermined Fordism, increased labour market flexibility, expanded precarious, non-standard forms of employment (part-time, temporary and self-employment), led to more frequent job-changing for men, broken-up linear careers, contributed to the spread of unemployment and greater insecurity for people still in jobs who are generally expected to do more than in the past in some way or another, all amid wider income inequalities.

The second section focuses on changes in the occupational structure: the shift from manufacturing to service-sector jobs, and from manual to non-manual occupations, and the implications for class demographics and social mobility. The third section discusses the spatial scattering of the workforce that has occurred as a result of large firms introducing labour-saving technology and work practices, and doing more sub-contracting, the rise in self-employment and in the proportion of jobs in small businesses, the decline of public sector employment, and the separation of places of work and residence. The final section deals with ongoing changes in the age, gender and ethnic composition of the workforce, and the interaction between these trends and the above developments in the economy and labour markets. The implications for the shape of the class structure (the proportions of the workforce in different classes), and the character of the main classes, are considered throughout.

New Times

It is doubtful whether we really do live in an era where either the pace or the immensity of economic change is more dramatic than ever before. After all, there was an industrial revolution; and during the twentieth century there were two world wars. All generations seem to believe that they are experiencing especially momentous changes. After the Second World War the survivors were impressed by the contrast between the prewar depression on the one side, and the full employment and steady economic growth of the new era. Since the 1970s commentators have contrasted their own new era with the '30 glorious (postwar) years'. Change is endemic in modern industrial societies; they are inherently dynamic. A stable state is not an option. So there is nothing really new about our present age having novel features. Every generation has been able to comment on something new, and two phrases that occur again and again in accounts of recent and current changes are globalisation and information technology. Both changes have profound direct and indirect implications for employment and the class structures in Britain and all other countries.

Globalisation and New Technology

In some respects globalisation (see Box 3.1) is ironing-out inter-country differences. It has become impossible to escape McDonalds; wherever we go we encounter the same news (probably from CNN), music, international cuisine and consumer goods. Yet in other respects globalisation sharpens inter-country differences. Tourists travel in order to see something different, and local populations may accentuate local customs as a way of resisting global forces. So everywhere globalisation results in a unique mixture of the global and the local. A new word, glocalisation, has been coined to describe this process.

Here we are concerned primarily with the economic aspects of globalisation, which is certainly not ironing-out inequalities in standards of living. Indeed, the gap between rich and poor countries widened in the closing decades of the twentieth century. Every country has to establish, or finds itself driven into, a particular niche in the global economy. The key globalising developments in the world economy have been the creation of transnational companies, hauling-down trade barriers (tariffs), and the growth in the proportion of all output that is traded internationally. One result of all this is fiercer competition. A related consequence is that national governments are less able to manage their national economies according to their own priorities, oblivious to global trends. They can be

Box 3.1

Globalisation

This is not completely new, for example there have been world religions for several centuries. Nevertheless, it is only during the last 30 years that the term 'globalisation' has been used extensively. It refers to a large number of interacting trends, some completely new, and others that have intensified.

- The growth of transnational companies that plan their activities on a global scale.

- The growth of international trade.

- Satellite communications and the internet.

- The creation of worldwide (television) audiences for world sports events such as the Olympics and football's World Cup.

- The same music, fashions and consumer goods now being available in all parts of the world.

- The growth of international tourism.

- Sensitivity to the global scale of, and the need for global solutions to, problems such as environmental sustainability and AIDS.

- The global scope of new social movements such as Marxism (at one time), and, more recently, the peace and green movements.

- The development of world political and judicial institutions such as the United Nations and the various international courts.

helpless in the face of international flows of capital; if they try to control the export of capital they can be sure that little will flow in. Virtually all kinds of businesses – banking, motor cars, clothing and so on – have lost their former holds over their domestic markets. This is despite the fact that most of the goods and services that we buy are still produced locally. The proportion of exports in the UK's GNP rose from 11 per cent in 1950 to 25 per cent in 1996. Exports as a proportion of world output grew from 7 per cent to 16 per cent over the same period (Genov, 1999). Globalisation is a trend, certainly not an absolute state, even though the trend itself is unmistakable. Maybe at some point the trend will be arrested. The street protests, and the failure to reach agreement at the 1999 Seattle meeting of the World Trade Organisation (whose remit is to promote trade) perhaps indicate the beginning of a grassroots reaction against the global environment, and the economies of developed and less-developed countries alike, becoming matters that elected (or any other) governments are unable to control.

Technological change is not new, but the latest generation (which satellite communication, computers and the Internet have helped to promote globalisation) has several novel features. First, micro-computing affects virtually all products, industries and occupations in some way or another. Its applications are neither industry nor occupation specific, and there can be few people whose working lives have been completely unaffected by the microchip. Second, the new technology is micro, and cheap. It can be installed virtually anywhere – inside washing machines and even wrist watches, and in study bedrooms. It is unnecessary nowadays to be a giant firm in order to take advantage of state-of-the art technology.

Globalisation and technological change are the forces behind a variety of recent and ongoing shifts in the workforce which are examined in greater detail below: between business sectors, especially from manufacturing to services, and from larger to smaller establishments. There have been equally important implications in the world's labour markets. In Europe, levels of unemployment have been higher since the 1970s than during the preceding 30 years. Related to this, more jobs are precarious. More jobs are part-time, officially temporary, and permanent jobs are felt to be less secure than formerly. People in employment are having to work harder, and income inequalities have widened. New technologies and globalisation have played a part in all these changes. They have not been the cause of, but the above trends have interacted with the UK workforce becoming more compressed in terms of age, more balanced in terms of gender, and more mixed in terms of ethnicity. We shall see that the effects of all these interacting changes have not been exactly the same – in fact they have often been completely different – in different sections of the workforce.

Flexible Labour Markets and Workers

The hard data do not always suggest that there have been major changes. The shift from full-time to part-time jobs is the exception here: from around 17 per cent to around 25 per cent of all jobs in Britain between 1979 and 1997 (see Table 3.1). A problem when measuring the shift from permanent to temporary posts is that until the 1980s, government statistics did not make the distinction; previously this had not been an issue. Clearly, therefore, something has changed. However, in 1997 over 90 per cent of all jobs were still permanent, that is, with open-ended contracts (see Table 3.1). The change here has not been a wholesale switch of permanent staff onto temporary contracts, but an increase in the proportion

Class in Modern Britain

of new starters, following unemployment for example, who enter temporary posts. In 1994 approximately a quarter of all exits from unemployment were into temporary jobs or government schemes: only 35 per cent
were into permanent full-time jobs (see Table 3.2). Thus the unemployed
can find themselves trapped. Their rungs on their ladder of opportunity
are likely to snap soon after the individuals begin to climb; people find
themselves on a 'black magic roundabout', experiencing successive cycles

Table 3.1   Full-time and part-time jobs, and self-
employment (percentages of all in employment)

	1979	1984	1990	1997
Full-time	76.7	69.7	67.1	65.2
Permanent	–	67.4	64.8	61.7
Temporary	–	2.3	2.3	3.5
Part-time	16.1	18.8	19.4	22.2
Permanent	–	16.5	17.2	19.2
Temporary	–	2.3	2.2	3.0
Self-employed	7.2	11.3	13.4	12.5
Full-time	6.5	9.4	11.3	9.9
Part-time	0.7	1.9	2.1	2.6

Source: Robinson (1999).

Table 3.2   Positions entered by formerly unemployed
people

	1979	1985	1994
Full-time employment	53.5	49.2	47.0
Permanent	–	38.4	35.1
Temporary	–	7.9	9.1
Government schemes	–	1.8	2.4
Part-time employment	41.2	40.7	40.9
Permanent	–	26.5	26.7
Temporary	–	10.6	8.7
Government schemes	–	3.6	5.0
Self-employment	3.7	9.8	12.1
Full-time	2.5	6.2	7.9
Part-time	1.2	3.6	4.2

Source: Robinson (1999).

of government schemes, short-lived jobs, and periods of unemployment. The term 'sub-employment' is sometimes used to describe these career histories.

One view is that the much proclaimed end of 'jobs for life', and the advent of unprecedented workforce flexibility and worker insecurity, are largely the result of press scares and hype-books. Since 1977 the average lifespan of men's jobs has fallen only slightly, from 6 years 6 months to 5 years 9 months. Meanwhile, the average lifespan of women's jobs has risen from 3 years 7 months to 4 years 4 months (the result of more women exercising their statutory right to maternity leave rather than terminating their employment). In other words, the main trend has been towards gender equality, not all-round insecurity. Only a fifth of the workforce has ever been made redundant, and most job movements are still voluntary. Three-quarters of all employees say that they are not worried about losing their own jobs, and in this respect there has been little change since the 1970s (Denny, 1999).

However, labour turnover figures may be unsatisfactory as indicators of job security and insecurity. Employees may cling-on because they are uncertain of finding new jobs. Voluntary departures may be prompted because the alternative is demotion or geographical relocation; workers often jump before being pushed. Brendan Burchell and his colleagues (1999) interviewed 340 employees and managers in 20 work establishments in various parts of Britain. All the businesses had faced pressure to become more flexible as a result of tougher market competition, customers who wanted everything just in time, right first time every time, and at lower prices, and from shareholders who wanted higher dividends and share values. All the businesses were achieving the necessary flexibility by some combination of redundancies, contracting-out, and changed work practices which could include multi-skilling, teamwork, delayering, changing hours of work (upwards, downwards or towards greater flexibility), and the relocation of jobs. Only 23 per cent of the employees said that there was 'any chance' of them losing their own jobs during the next 12 months, but many still felt insecure. This was not because they regarded job loss as likely, but through fear of the consequences should this occur. Social security benefits have become less generous, and the chances of finding a new job without loss of status have diminished. Also, the workers felt that their managers could not be trusted. The workers knew that managements' guarantees would become worthless if customers so decided (by taking their business elsewhere) or if the shareholders decided to sell the company.

Under-30-year-olds experience far more changes of status today than in the 1950s and 1960s, sometimes in and out of government schemes or educational courses rather than straight from job to job. This is plain fact, not hype (Pollock, 1997). There has been talk of workers becoming 'wandering troubadours', constructing self-designed apprenticeships and treating jobs as projects in which they can expand their portfolios of skills, thus enhancing their employability (Arthur *et al.*, 1999; Bridges, 1995). This can sound splendid, but in their 1992 survey of a nationally representative sample of the British workforce, Gallie *et al.* (1998) found that 47 per cent said that they had little or no choice when looking for their present or most recent jobs.

Labelling the Era

A new vocabulary has been coined as an aid to understanding all these changes. We have already encountered globalisation, labour market flexibility, and portfolio careers. It is also said that we have become a *post-industrial society*, meaning that there are fewer jobs in manufacturing (well under a third of all jobs today – see below), and that most employment is now in services. We are said to have become an *information society*, recognising here the extent to which change is information technology-driven. We are said to have become a *learning society* in two senses: there are more high-level jobs that demand qualifications (see below), and the pace of change requires education and training to be recurrent, and life-long.

Post-Fordism (see Box 3.2) refers to how everything has become more flexible – enterprises, labour markets, occupations and workers. The name Ford is used because this firm led and typified the earlier era. Ford created a mass market for its cars through the mass production of standardised products, which enabled unit costs to be hauled down, thereby bringing private motoring within the average American family's means. Its success enabled Ford to employ thousands of workers in highly specialised and fairly secure jobs (for life if they could stand the pace). Firms like Ford, their products and their jobs, were among the most secure fixtures on the socioeconomic landscape. They were affected by recessions, inevitably, but could be relied on to survive. We are now in new, post-Fordist times.

Non-standard Employment

This term has been coined in recent years to acknowledge the spread of jobs with different terms and conditions to those that became standard, meaning full-time and permanent, earlier on under Fordism. The largest segment of Britain's non-standard sector consists of part-time jobs. Nearly a half of all Britain's female employees are on part-time schedules (defined in government statistics as under 30 hours a week), and the proportion of

Box 3.2

Fordism

This term was coined by Antonio Gramsci (1891–1937), an Italian Marxist, a theorist, but also a leader of Italy's communist party, and a prisoner in Mussolini's gaols from 1926 until 1937. As often happens, the word Fordism has become widely used only since the system began to decline.

The name Ford is used because the firm pioneered what, at the time (in the 1920s), was a novel way of organising industrial production. Ford introduced the mechanised assembly line, and pioneered the mass production of a standardised product which enabled costs and prices to be hauled down to a level that stimulated mass consumption. The key features of Fordist production are:

- Capital intensive
- Inflexible production processes
- Hierarchical and bureaucratic management
- Extensive use of semi-skilled labour performing routine tasks
- Strong trade unions

Prior to and following the Second World War, Fordist methods were adopted in the manufacture of a wide range of consumer goods.

males with part-time jobs (now over 10 per cent) has been rising. It has also become common for students aged 14–15 and upwards to take part-time jobs. Many nominally full-time university students have taken such jobs, largely from financial necessity as student grants have been replaced by loans and fees introduced. However, another crucial fact of this situation is that there are more opportunities to work part-time nowadays, mainly in consumer services.

It is only fair to point out that many women (and some men) prefer part-time to full-time schedules (see Hakim, 1996). Women often find part-time employment more easily reconciled with their domestic roles, and something very similar can be said of students. But it must also be said that the arrangement is equally convenient for employers. Nowadays part-time jobs are less likely to be created because the employers are unable to fill full-time posts than to fine-tune the numbers of staff at work to fluctuations in workflows, and to ensure that labour costs are no higher than absolutely necessary. So office staff may be hired for just 30, 25 or 20 hours a week if, in the employer's view, that is all that is required. Retail and other consumer services which need to be provided so as to coincide with consumers' life rhythms use part-time staff so that the workforces can be strengthened, often doubled or tripled in size, in the evenings and/or at weekends. The use of part-time staff is one way in which firms can achieve numerical flexibility. A rather controversial employer strategy is to guarantee no specific hours of work but to require staff to be on call whenever required. In the 1990s one fast-food outlet gained notoriety by requiring staff to sign-off and sign-on when customers left and entered the premises.

Another form of non-standard employment is temporary. We have seen that the proportion of employees on officially temporary contracts – with specified end-dates – is in fact quite small, around 5 per cent. But to this we need to add workers who are on government 'training' schemes. The use of temps (who may have indefinite contracts with their agencies) is another way in which employers can achieve numerical flexibility and avoid carrying excess labour. Rather than staffing-up so as to be able to accommodate staff holidays and illnesses, employers have increasingly opted for lean-and-mean profiles, and have brought in temporary staff as and when necessary. Another advantage of using such staff, from the employer's point of view, is that they are usually not eligible for any union-agreed terms and conditions applicable to directly employed staff. And any temps who prove less than satisfactory can be dispensed with very quickly.

A third type of non-standard employment is self-employment which has become more widespread since the 1970s, and is discussed in greater detail later in this chapter. Add together all the types of non-standard employment and they amount to around a quarter of all jobs. As explained above, the workers concerned would not all prefer standard, full-time permanent contacts. The point remains that all non-standard forms of employment are more precarious than the mainline jobs of the Fordist era.

The spread of non-standard employment is sometimes applauded as evidence of businesses making themselves flexible so as to cope with post-Fordist conditions – rapid technological change and shifts in consumer preferences. As always, however, this is just one side of the story. In conditions of high unemployment it is possible to recruit to low quality jobs because workers have no choice. Indeed, as we have seen, nowadays the route from unemployment to a full-time permanent job is often via part-time, temporary positions. Non-standard employment is often a way in which employers transfer risks away from themselves and onto their workforces, and the least-skilled, lowest-paid workers have been the most vulnerable (Purcell *et al.*, 1999).

Unemployment

Some would say that this has been the really big change in the labour market since the 1960s: the result of certain other trends like the collapse of manufacturing and manual employment, and the cause of others such as the spread of poor quality, non-standard jobs. As ever, levels of unemployment rise and fall alongside business cycles, but around a much higher centre-point than from 1945 up to the mid-1970s.

The official unemployment rate understates how many people are affected. This is not because anyone is deliberately fiddling the figures; although this accusation may have been justified in the 1980s when the method of calculating unemployment was changed on over 30 occasions, always with the effect of reducing the numbers. For example, it was decided that only unemployed claimants would be counted (so unemployed married women and other groups who were ineligible for benefit were excluded). In 1988 youth unemployment was abolished at a stroke by making virtually all 16 and 17-year-olds ineligible for benefits. Nowadays the government's preferred way of measuring unemployment is from the Labour Force Survey, using the International Labour Office's criteria. People are counted if they are not in work, actively seeking employment, and prepared to start more or less immediately if offered a suitable job. The people who are still excluded are 'discouraged workers' who have given up searching, but who would return to the labour market if they believed that they stood a chance of being offered suitable jobs.

Another way in which all 'snapshot' figures are misleading is that they understate the numbers who are unemployed at some time or another. In the five years up to 1984, a third of the workforce was unemployed on at least one occasion (Marsh, 1988). In their survey of a nationally representative sample in 1992, Gallie *et al.* (1998) found that 40 per cent of the men and 30 per cent of the women had experienced at least one spell of unemployment while in their twenties. Between 1990 and 1995 there were four million redundancies in Britain (Noon and Blyton, 1997). School-leavers and university graduates have come to accept it as simply normal to job-search for a while after completing their studies. It was different before the 1970s: beginning workers could expect to receive several job offers from which they could choose prior to completing their courses.

For most people unemployment is a temporary experience, and one which they detest. Unemployment is bad for people's physical and mental health, family relationships, standards of living and virtually everything else that they value. And the damage that unemployment inflicts seeps into sections of the workforce who realise that their own jobs are insecure; they know that they cannot rely on finding further jobs of equivalent status immediately (Gallie *et al.*, 1994). People often manage to escape from unemployment only having lowered their sights and accepted demotion to inferior jobs to those that they formerly occupied. Getting back into work has become tougher. We have seen that by 1994 only 35 per cent of people leaving unemployment were entering full-time permanent jobs. The rest were taking part-time work, temporary positions, places on government schemes, or trying to work on their own accounts (Robinson, 1999).

The official European Union view, and the UK government's, is that the answer to unemployment is faster economic growth which is expected to create more jobs, coupled with better education and training for young people and for the adult unemployed, so that they will be equipped for the jobs that come on-stream. The European Commission (1998) claims that new technology has created far more jobs in Europe than it has destroyed, and that the total number in employment at the end of the twentieth century was higher than ever before (European Commission, 1999). But one important, often overlooked, fact of this matter is that the growth of part-time employment accounts for more than all the additional employment over and above the level of the 1970s. There are fewer full-time jobs in the European Union today than there were in the 1970s (European Commission, 1999). It is doubtful whether there really is more paid work around, and, moreover, recorded unemployment figures take no account of the declining rate of economic activity among EU adults of working age (European Commission, 1999). Unemployment has been concealed by people taking early retirement, young people prolonging their education, and an amazing rise in the UK (given the general improvement in health) in the numbers who are recorded as unable to work due to incapacity. By the late-1990s a fifth of all UK households that contained adults of working age had no-one in employment, and two-thirds of all men aged 60–65 were out of work (Campbell, 1999).

Doing More

These are amazing times. In the last quarter of the twentieth century the UK had more people than formerly without any work, more who were in and out of jobs, and more who were working part-time. Meanwhile, full-time employees were working longer and harder than ever. The lengthening of working time has been most pronounced in the management and professional grades, and this is one way in which some sections of the workforce are now doing more. It is partly a consequence of all the delay-ering and cutting back of core payrolls to the lowest possible levels. Businesses have become reluctant to carry any slack which, in many cases, has meant the staff who are retained carry heavier workloads. The pre-sent-day worker is often a tired worker. Salaried staff are often expected to take any excess work home and complete it in the evening or at week-end. Warhurst and Thompson (1998) claim that work intensification is in fact the main recent change in people's experiences of work.

There are additional senses in which people in jobs are doing more. While seeking numerical flexibility in some grades (generally the lower-skilled grades for which suitable staff can be easily found and replaced), firms have been demanding functional flexibility from their permanent core staff. In some cases this has meant the multiskilled worker replacing older, specialised trades. Sometimes functional flexibility has been achieved through 'teamwork' which requires all members to be able to cover for each other's absences, and usually requires the team itself rather than managers or supervisors to accept responsibility for the quality and quantity of their work. Multi-skilling often means recurrent training and further education simply to keep abreast of changing technologies and work requirements.

In the 1970s Harry Braverman (1974) forecast a progressive degradation of work which was to result from an increasingly clear division between conception (the responsibility of management) and execution (the worker's role). Braverman anticipated jobs at all levels becoming less skilled and more routine. In practice, the trend has been in exactly the opposite direction. Most employees in all grades report that their jobs have become more demanding, and that doing the jobs requires more skills, training and qualifications than in the past. In this sense there has been a general process of job enrichment. In a 1992 survey of a nationally representative sample of the workforce, 63 per cent reported that the skill requirements in their jobs had increased during the previous five years. The majority of employees in every grade made this claim, but the majority also reported that their work had been intensified and had become more stressful (Gallie and White, 1993). An earlier national research programme in the 1980s, the Economic and Social Research Council's Social Change and Economic Life Initiative, also found that most employees reported that the skill requirements in their jobs were increasing (Penn *et al.*, 1993). This trend continued into the 1990s. Even so, many jobs still require little in the way of qualifications and skills. Thirty-four per cent of the respondents in the 1992 survey said that their jobs needed only low qualifications or none at all, and 22 per cent said that it took less than a month to learn to do their jobs well. Forty-two per cent said that they had received no training whatsoever in their present jobs

(Gallie *et al.*, 1998). The workforce is becoming more skilled and more highly trained, but these trends are obviously from rather modest starting points.

Income Inequalities

Another well-documented trend in recent times has been a widening of income inequalities. Since the 1970s the highest earners have been receiving the largest pay increases in both absolute and per centage terms. Company directors have fared best of all, followed by managers and professionals, followed by skilled and office workers, with the least skilled lagging behind everyone else. And behind all of these, the groups dependent on state benefits have seen their incomes falling further and further behind the earnings of those in employment.

The most popular explanation for all this is market forces. At any rate, this is the explanation favoured by politicians and newspaper editors, and probably by those who are doing best and who like to believe that they are gaining only the proper rewards for their hard work and scarce skills. Income inequalities are said to have widened because skill requirements have been rising, and workers with the necessary skills (presumably like the City of London financial professionals who earn six-figure salaries plus six-figure bonuses) have been able to benefit.

The problem with this explanation is simply that the facts don't fit. This has been known since the 1960s (see Routh, 1965), but the mass of contrary evidence does not seem to prevent the explanation being repeated time and again. The explanation fits classical economic theory which is often confused with how real economies work. All the evidence shows that pay relativities fluctuate only marginally in response to labour shortages and surpluses. In any case, over the last 30 years the workforce's qualifications have improved more rapidly than skill requirements have risen. The number of university graduates has risen steeply, from less than 15 per cent at the beginning of the 1980s to over 30 per cent of all young people today. If the market forces explanation was correct, this increase in supply should have depressed graduates' earnings. In practice the earnings differential between graduates and other employees has widened. How can this be explained? We shall see that class theory proves far more helpful than classical economics in resolving this paradox. Company directors and senior managers are able to fix their own remuneration; other grades have to negotiate, individually or collectively, or are simply told how much they will receive. The incomes of state-dependents are determined by politicians whose positions depend on the votes of the population in general.

The Changing Shape of the Occupational Structure

The preceding section has identified changes that have swept through the UK economy affecting all sections of the workforce, albeit, as we shall see in later chapters, to different extents and in rather different ways. Here we identify how, amid these tidal waves, the workforce has shifted between different types of jobs. There have been two main shifts: sector shifts – from manufacturing into service sectors, and occupation shifts – from manual into non-manual jobs.

Sector Shifts

It is misleading to speak of a collapse of British manufacturing since output is as high as ever. Even so, over the last generation the decline of employment in manufacturing (and extractive) industries has been steep. Over half of the manufacturing jobs that existed in the 1970s have gone, and in some industries the workforces really have collapsed. Huge steel plants, for example, have closed. Coal-mining used to employ three-quarters of a million: in 1981 the National Coal Board still had 211 collieries and employed 218,000 miners, but by 1994 British Coal had just 17 mines and 8500 miners (Fieldhouse and Hollywood, 1999). In the early 1980s few people believed that, before the end of the century, Britain's coal-mining industry would be all but closed-down. Arthur Scargill (the leader of the coal-miners union) was accused of scare tactics when he led the 1984–85 coal-miners strike against an alleged programme of pit closures. The scale and speed of pit closures following the strike actually exceeded Scargill's forecasts.

The downward trend in manufacturing employment is sometimes described as a second industrial revolution. In the first industrial revolution labour moved from the countryside to towns, and from agriculture into the mines and factories that were then opening. At the beginning of the nineteenth century, agriculture was far-and-away the country's main employer; today less than 2 per cent of the workforce is in agriculture, but output from the land is greater than in the nineteenth century. Much the same is now happening to manufacturing. Output is being maintained – increasing slightly in the long term – but with far fewer workers. The explanations are the same as applied in agriculture over a century ago – more efficient working practices (enforced in recent times by international competition) and technology boosting the productivity of each worker.

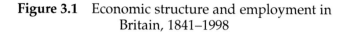

Figure 3.1   Economic structure and employment in
Britain, 1841–1998

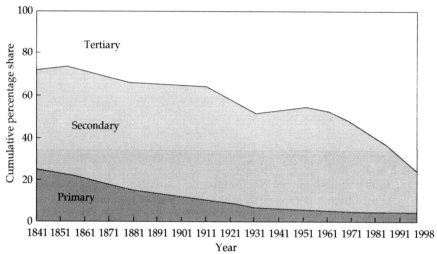

Primary = Agriculture, forestry, fishing; secondary = manufacturing, mining,
construction, utilities; tertiary = services.

Source: Abercrombie and Warde (2000).

Figure 3.1 describes the division of Britain's workforce between agriculture, manufacturing and other industries (including mining), and services, since the beginning of the nineteenth century. Note the steep decline in agricultural employment in the nineteenth century, and the slower fall subsequently. Employment in manufacturing expanded until the interwar years, at which time around a half of all jobs were in manufacturing and mining. Subsequently there was a slow decline, then note the steeper decline from the 1970s onwards: the effects of new technology and globalisation. By the end of the twentieth century well over 70 per cent of all jobs in Britain were in services.

The steep dip in manufacturing employment since the 1970s is sometimes described as de-industrialisation (see Box 3.3). Some old 'rust-bucket' and 'smoke-stack' industries have been all but wiped out; in addition to coal-mining, these include ship-building and steel production. The impact has varied from region to region. Regions that were heavily dependent on older manufacturing and extractive industries (the midlands, the north of England and Scotland) saw their levels of unemployment rocketing upwards in the 1970s and 1980s. South-east England, in contrast, has experienced the greatest benefits from the job creation that has occurred. Some workers in declining regions have stayed put; family commitments, the

---

Box 3.3

De-industrialisation

This can be a misleading phrase. It is true that manufacturing employment has declined steeply, but this does not apply to output. Some industries have all but disappeared from the economic landscape, but Britain is doing OK in many manufacturing sectors, and excellently in some. Food-processing and chemicals are OK; so is motor manufacturing thanks to all the foreign-based (but really transnational) firms that assemble here. We are the world's number one in producing Formula One. We are world class in other high-tech areas – weaponry, aircraft and pharmaceuticals are just three examples.

---

social and economic costs of relocation, and fears of being unable to afford housing in the south-east have tied them down. But many have moved. So by the end of the twentieth century in the UK, regional disparities in unemployment rates were narrower than at any time since the First World War. Nowadays there are growth spots and unemployment blackspots within all regions, though there are still more of the former and fewer of the latter in the south-east than anywhere else. Needless to say, regional imbalances and population movements are anything but novel. During the industrial revolution the north and the midlands attracted new labour to the mines and factories that were then opening. In the nineteenth century the countryside was largely depopulated, and levels of unemployment rose in many rural areas. Rural unemployment is still an apparently intractable problem in many parts of the UK, though in the late-twentieth century some out-of-city areas experienced an economic boom as businesses moved on to greenfield sites (see Box 3.3).

The expansion of employment in services (anything that you cannot drop on your foot) has more than compensated for the loss of manufacturing jobs, but we may now be on the verge of a third industrial revolution. From the 1940s up until the 1970s employment in public services expanded; there were more jobs in central and local government, teaching and health services. Subsequently this all-round public sector growth has ground to a halt. Financial and other business services were a major source of new jobs from the 1960s up to and through the 1980s, but this trend is now being reversed. Financial services, like agriculture and manufacturing previously, are introducing labour-saving technology and downsizing in terms of staff. Nowadays the main source of employment growth is consumer services – retailing, hotels and catering, and other leisure industries.

Manufacturing jobs have been lost because Britain, along with other advanced industrial countries, has been unable to increase sales and output sufficiently to maintain the earlier armies of workers. Part of the explanation is the switch of production to less-developed, lower-cost countries in the Far East, Latin America and Eastern Europe (an aspect of globalisation). New labour-saving technology is another part of the story; and another reason is that in countries like Britain demand for goods is growing more slowly than spending power. People still have a huge appetite for manufactured goods – cars, televisions, videos, computers, mobile telephones, gardening equipment and so on. But as standards of living rise, we all tend to spend higher proportions of our incomes on 'being served' – with holidays and meals out, for instance.

What are the class implications of this? These are explored fully in later chapters, but two implications can be noted immediately. First, there are fewer manual jobs because in service sectors white-collar employees are generally larger proportions of the total labour forces than in manufacturing. Local government, the civil service, banks, hospitals and universities have top-heavy occupational profiles. However, it is important to bear in mind that not all service-sector jobs are white-collar. Hospitals employ porters as well as doctors. The service sector includes cleaning and security businesses, restaurants and supermarkets, as well as banks and solicitors. Indeed, the consumer services in which employment growth is now concentrated have bottom-heavy occupational profiles.

A second class effect of the shift to services is to change the character of the manual jobs that remain. The old working class was employed in coal mines, shipyards, steel plants and engineering workshops; the new working class is employed in supermarkets, security firms, contract cleaners, fast food and other catering establishments, and suchlike. The full implications of this are discussed in Chapter 4.

Occupation Shifts: The Shrinking Working Class

There have been simultaneous changes in the distribution of employment between the various grades within some business sectors, and especially within manufacturing, and the main shift has been upwards. Manual employment has sometimes been decimated and sometimes trimmed, while white-collar employment has held steady or increased. Production workers have been replaced by technology. Meanwhile, new higher-level occupations have been created connected with the design and management of the new technical systems.

Occupation shifts have combined with sector shifts to reduce the number of manual workers. Table 3.3 presents information from two major

Table 3.3 Class distributions

Class	After Goldthorpe et al. (1980)		After Savage and Egerton (1997)
	Respondents' fathers (%)	Male respondents (%)	Male respondents (%)
Service	14	27	36
Intermediate	31	30	21
Working	55	44	43

surveys in which occupations were classified using the Goldthorpe class scheme. The first is the 1972 social mobility survey conducted by John Goldthorpe himself in 1972. The centre column in the table gives the class breakdown of the respondents, who were adult men at the time. The left-hand column gives the class breakdown of the respondents' fathers. So we have information about the class distribution in the early-1970s, and a generation earlier. The right-hand column gives the class breakdown of the male respondents in a survey in 1991 of a National Child Development sample who were all born in 1958, then followed-up into adulthood. In 1991 they were aged 33. One point to note is the expansion of the service (middle) class: from 14 per cent to 27 per cent to 36 per cent of all male jobs. Over time the proportions of males in the working class, and in the intermediate classes, are shown to have declined. This is the basis of the claim that we have become, or are becoming, a middle class society. This is true in that nowadays less than 40 per cent of all jobs (when women's jobs are included) are in the working class. This class is no longer the mass of the people as it was at the beginning of the twentieth century when, at the time of the 1911 census, three-quarters of all occupations were manual. However, the extent to which, and the speed with which, the working class has declined numerically should not be exaggerated. It is still the largest single class. If we discount the intermediate classes, we are still some distance from having a middle-class majority. We are certainly not on the verge of an age when we will all be stockbrokers, accountants, brain surgeons and so on. There is still plenty of 'donkey work', and around a quarter of all jobs require no formal qualifications and very little training.

However, we have already become a mainly middle-class society in terms of how people see themselves. The change has been slow but remorseless. In the 1950s just over a half of the population described themselves as working class and just less than two-fifths described themselves as middle class. By 1999 these proportions were almost exactly reversed (see Figure 3.2).

Figure 3.2   Subjective class identities

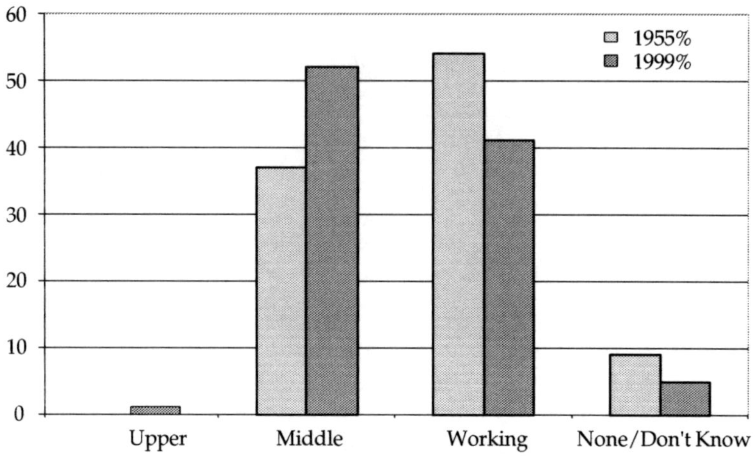

Source: Travis (1999).

Class Demographics

The numerical decline of the working class is not a new trend. It is a very long-term trend that began around the time of the First World War, and there have been profound implications not just for the size, but also for the character of all the main classes, not just the working class. A large class (like the working class) that is in long-term decline tends to become overwhelmingly self-recruiting. Most adults in the class today, and yesterday, were born into it. So for a long time Britain's working class has been composed mainly of life-long members. In this sense the working class is a mature demographic entity and will remain so well into the twenty-first century.

In contrast, the growth of the middle class has required many of these positions to be filled from beneath. The proportion of the workforce in professional and management occupations more than doubled in the second half of the twentieth century. There was no way in which all these positions could have been filled by the children of middle-class parents – there were simply not enough of them. So, unlike the working class, the middle class has been, and still is, composed of people with diverse origins. High proportions have been upwardly-mobile (drawn from the working and intermediate classes), as we shall see in Chapter 8. The middle class will stabilise demographically only as and when its growth rate slows, as it must because no group can double in size again-and-again-and-again because at some stage it comprises over half the population and its growth rate simply has to slacken. As the middle class grows ever larger, and as the rate of growth slows, it will become increasingly self-recruiting (see Noble, 2000). Well into the twenty-first century, the middle class is likely to become as well-formed demographically as the working class was in the twentieth century.

An effect of middle-class growth is to create more opportunities for working-class children to experience upward mobility. Again, we shall see in Chapter 8 that throughout the twentieth century the chances were growing of children who started in the working class moving into the middle class. More and more working-class parents, themselves usually life-long members of this class, have seen their own and their neighbours' children ascend. These changing class experiences become important when we consider the types of consciousness and political action that have characterised different classes, and how these have changed over time.

Spatial Scattering

This has been the result of several separate trends, the combined effect of which has been to break up large, communal concentrations of workers.

Downsizing

Large firms have downsized (another new term), often dramatically, simply because they have had the greatest scope to save labour by introducing new technology and new working practices. Just like the decline in manufacturing employment, large firms have not necessarily declined in terms of turnover and profits – just in terms of the numbers on the payrolls.

Downsizing has also been due to the spread of subcontracting (or outsourcing as it is called in North America). Businesses have been stripping-down to their core functions (enabling managers to concentrate on what they do best) and subcontracting their cleaning, catering and so forth. Oil refineries have become less likely to employ their own staff to repair buildings and transport their output. This development has occurred at all occupational levels. More work is now passed out to various types of consultants – engineers, solicitors, recruitment specialists and so on, which this is one way in which enterprises have been making themselves flexible. Specialists are hired only as and when needed. Also, the hirer is able to go to whoever has the most expertise or the lowest price. Subcontractors often pay their own staff less than the union-negotiated rates in large companies; and the firm which subcontracts ceases to be hampered by what may be the limited and out of date experience and expertise of its own staff. Private and public-sector organisations have been equally keen to strip down to essentials.

Self-employment

Meanwhile, small businesses have been growing in number. The number of self-employed persons (with or without employees) has doubled from around 1.5 million in the 1970s to over 3 million, around 13 per cent of the workforce today. Far from disappearing as Marx predicted, the petit bourgeoisie is flourishing. This is another side of the coin of subcontacting by large organisations – there are more opportunities for small businesses. So staff at all levels – with professional, office and craft skills – have often found that they can earn more, and enhance their career prospects, by moving out of employment and into self-employment.

There are other developments, apart from subcontracting, that have contributed to the growth of self-employment. In the 1980s there was much talk about the spread of an enterprise culture. It was a myth; there was no sea-change in attitudes. The population did not become more entrepreneurial than formerly, though it is true that, ideologically at any rate, the government at that time was sympathetic and supportive towards small businesses.

Unemployment-push was and remains one of the forces behind the growth of self-employment. There has been a great deal of survival self-employment – people setting-up on their own accounts due to their inability to obtain proper, secure and decently paid jobs. However, new technology has also played a part in the growth of small businesses. Small is not necessarily beautiful, but it can be, especially in the age of micro-computing. Small businesses can now afford, and are able to use, state-of-the-art technology. So small independent companies are able to produce recorded music of much the same quality (technical as well as artistic) as the giants of the industry. Small radio stations can be commercially viable, as can desktop publishing.

The Shrunken State

Another dispersal has been from jobs with the biggest of all employers – government. There has been no decline in the proportion of the national income that the government spends, but more of its spending is channelled through quasi-autonomous agencies – hospital trusts, for example. They spend public money, but the employees are not public servants. However, the major cut-backs in public-sector employment accompanied the privatisation of a series of nationalised industries in the 1980s and 1990s – steel, British Airways, oil, gas, electricity, coal, water, telecommunications and subsequently the railways. In all these industries there is no longer one large monopoly operator; competition has been introduced. There are now scores of telecommunications businesses. In 1980 the public sector accounted for 30 per cent of all jobs, but by 1990 this was down to 22 per cent. This drop represented over two million workers being transferred to the payrolls of smaller (though usually still quite large) private businesses.

What are the implications of this dispersal? The detailed implications for social consciousness and political action are explored in later chapters, but here we should note that government employment has always been more secure than jobs in the private sector, and that jobs in large private companies are more secure than those in small businesses. Scattering the workforce out of large organisations has helped to make employment more precarious (see above). It is only large firms that can offer structured career opportunities, and on average very small firms pay less than large companies. There is another, related, difference: large firms' workforces are more likely to be in trade unions and to have collectively negotiated terms and conditions. Public sector employees are the most densely unionised of all.

Places of Work and Residence

Another dimension of the dispersal of the workforce has followed the spread of car ownership. This has reduced, if not eliminated, the advantages of businesses locating close to the hubs of public transport networks, usually in city centres. Sites on city outskirts, or in small towns, or completely greenfield sites, are often more accessible for car-borne workforces as well as for customers, suppliers and a business's own transport. All of Britain's major cities have lost jobs since the 1970s (Turok and Edge, 1999), and the consequences have been disastrous for inner-city residents without their own motor transport.

Car ownership has become essential to gain access to the full labour market, or, at any rate, to give oneself the same scope for choice as today's normal, motorised employee. Once people have acquired cars, these enable them to live farther from their workplaces than formerly. At the end of each working day, in most workplaces nowadays, the staff disperse in numerous directions. Correspondingly, most neighbourhoods' residents disperse to a variety of workplaces at the beginning of each working day.

An effect is that fewer people have the daily experience of travelling to work and being at work alongside large armies of others all doing similar jobs. Fewer people work and live among the same colleagues; this type of communality has evaporated. All classes have been affected, but the working class most of all, because, in the past (see Chapter 4), its ways of working and living were the most likely to be communal.

Workforce Composition

Jobs have changed, and so has the workforce. Its demography is different from that of the workforce of the mid-twentieth century. In terms of gender and ethnic composition, the workforce has become better-balanced, whereas in terms of age it has been compressed.

Age

Working life has shrunk. People at both ends of normal working life have been withdrawing from, or have been squeezed out of, the labour market. This is only partly in response to the economic and occupational changes reviewed above. There have been other causes, as with the other demographic trends considered in this section, but these, like the changes in the age composition of the workforce, have interacted with recent economic changes.

Irrespective of the economic context, there would almost certainly have been a trend towards prolonged education. Each generation of better-educated parents tends to seek even better education for its children. All sections of the population have become more aware of the importance of qualifications in fixing labour market chances, and the school system has become more effective in getting young people through exams. Higher education has expanded to accommodate roughly a third of all young people in England and Wales (compared with less than 15 per cent at the beginning of the 1980s), and somewhat more in Scotland. However, the decline of youth employment (nowadays less than 10 per cent of 16-year-olds become full-time employees compared with roughly two out of every three in the early 1970s) has been largely due to the tougher competition for jobs. A series of vocational education and training measures have been introduced basically in response to the youth unemployment problem.

Meanwhile, men have been retiring at younger ages than formerly. In 1979 two-thirds of 60–64-year-old men were in employment; nowadays two-thirds are not in work (Campbell, 1999). Once again, it is most likely that there would have been such a trend whatever the economic context. Despite people living longer, an increasing number would probably have used part of their share in the generally rising prosperity by shortening their working lives and enjoying prolonged retirements. But as with the removal of young people from the workforce, the tough labour markets of the late-twentieth century played a part in easing-out the over-50s (the men at any rate). There has been little change in the proportion of women aged 55–59 who are in employment. In this age group, as in others, the employment rates for the two sexes have converged. In the mid-twentieth century men either knew that they could look forward to retiring at age 65, when they became eligible for state and sometimes occupational pensions, or feared not being allowed to continue beyond age 65 in their former jobs. Nowadays men (and women) either wonder whether they will be able to hang on until what is still regarded as the normal retirement age, or whether they will be among the lucky ones who are offered generous severance and early retirement packages.

Working life cannot shrink indefinitely, and the trend may be reversed in the early decades of the twenty-first century. European Union governments are now worried about their 'dependency ratios' (the proportions of the populations that are neither earning nor paying taxes). There are also fears that the European Union could run short of labour. Some businesses in the UK, most notably certain mass retailers, have been deliberately targeting the over-50s when recruiting staff. Older workers have definite attractions; many are in excellent health, have relevant experience, and prove extremely reliable. However, the other side of this story is that the employees usually experience downgrading *vis-à-vis* their former jobs. Ageism in the labour market still normally works to the disadvantage of the over-50s.

There are class implications in the compression of working life. To begin with, people are spending smaller proportions of their lifetimes exposed directly to workplace relationships and cultures. Perhaps even more significant for the working class, Britain has lost one of the two former routes into adult political careers. One route, now the only significant route, is via student politics during an extended academic education. The other route, which now scarcely exists, was via employment-based trade union and related political activity, all accomplished prior to marriage, child-rearing, and the time squeeze that these life-stage transitions enforce. It is also the case that the trade unions have lost the now early-retired over-50s who once lent immense experience and provided leadership for younger members.

Gender

In gender terms the workforce has become better-balanced. The proportion of women who are in employment, and the proportion of all employees who are women, rose progressively during the second half of the twentieth century. Women are now close to 50 per cent of the UK workforce. In some parts of the country where the decline in male employment has been particularly steep (due to job losses from manufacturing and extractive industries) women are already the majority of employees. Women have shortened their career breaks, and more now take maternity leave instead of terminating their employment. As a result, the 'male breadwinner' family type (a male supporting a wife and dependent children) has become quite rare – less than 10 per cent of all households. Girls have been improving their achievements in education – doing better than boys nowadays – and they play a larger role in the labour market and in public life more generally, in parliament for example. This is the so-called genderquake and the basis for claims that the future is female.

Economic and occupational trends in the second half of the twentieth century were relatively kind to women. Some occupations that women have always dominated – office jobs, and public-service professions such as teaching and nursing – expanded. It was mainly men's jobs that were lost as a result of the labour shake-outs from manufacturing and extractive industries. There has also been an increase in the proportion of all jobs that are part-time, especially in consumer services. Part-time work has been considered especially suitable for married women, and nowadays nearly a half of all female employees are in part-time jobs (under 30 hours a week in government figures).

The disadvantage for women is that many are still trapped in part-time, secretarial and other female ghettos. Whether women have continued to be channelled into women's jobs mainly by their own preferences, or by their limited full-time opportunities, inadequate child care and traditional male partners, is a matter of dispute, but the outcome is not in doubt. Males and females still tend to be segregated into mainly men's and mainly women's jobs. Since the equal pay and opportunities legislation of the 1970s there has been some weakening, but no collapse of gender segmentation (see Box 3.4) in the labour market.

Young women (school and college leavers) are now obtaining better jobs than their counterparts in the 1950s, 1960s and 1970s. Meanwhile, the quality of young males' jobs has declined (Egerton and Savage, 2000). Although they still tend to enter different jobs, there is now only a marginal difference in the quality of the occupations (measured by earnings, for example) entered by male and female young singles. But all this still changes following parenthood. Most women returners do so on a part-time basis. The number returning full-time has risen, but they are still a minority (they tend to have professional or management positions). So among the over-25s, women in the workforce are still very much the disadvantaged sex. Despite the number of firms that now claim to be family

Box 3.4

Labour-market segmentation

The key observation here is that labour markets are divided into interrelated but non-competing (in the short term at any rate) sub-markets or segments.

This segmentation arises when workers become trained, skilled and experienced in specific industries and occupations. They are sometimes able to progress upwards through internal (to an occupation, industry or firm) labour markets, gaining benefits that are lost if they move outside. Conversely, outsiders can only enter at the bottom, which will usually involve sacrificing any progress that they have made in their existing or former labour market segments.

Which segments individuals enter depend on their places of residence and qualifications, and gender and ethnicity are often influential as well.

Some analysts (dual labour market theorists) claim that a major division cutting right across the entire workforce is between primary and secondary labour-market segments, and that labour-market segmentation disadvantages certain groups (women, ethnic minorities and the poorly qualified) because they are likely to become trapped in secondary segments.

Some Marxists have regarded labour-market segmentation as an employer strategy to undermine workforce solidarity; but trade unions and professional associations are often deeply implicated in maintaining segmentation thereby protecting their members' jobs and career prospects from outside competition.

friendly, many women still experience occupational downgrading following their career breaks. On average they still earn considerably less than men in general, in total and per hour, and even compared with men with equal skills and qualifications.

We have already noted (see Chapter 2, p. 42–9) that women's increased presence in the labour market has placed question marks against the validity of class schemes based on males' jobs, and against the conventional practice of classifying entire households on the sole basis of a male head of household's occupation. We have also noted how the increase in the number of dual-earner families blurs class divisions (there is more income overlap, for example), while, since like tends to marry like, inequalities between the higher and lower-income households are widened. Here we can add to the list. Traditionally, women's attachments to the workforce have been more tenuous than men's; women have tended to regard paid work as their secondary role. This may well be changing, but eradicating tradition entirely is most likely to take a long, long time. In the meantime, women's increased presence in the workforce must mean that the average strength of attachment between workers and their jobs will have decreased, especially in the jobs and occupational grades where women predominate, namely, office jobs, certain professions, and some non-skilled manual occupations.

In so far as women make inroads into formerly masculine enclaves, workplace cultures will be de-masculinised, and feminised in some instances. Many jobs are still gendered, and many occupational cultures are still sexist. Women doing men's jobs can be marginalised by the male small-talk, and sometimes made to feel uncomfortable by their colleagues' ribald references to women in general, and even to themselves in particular. Men who enter women's jobs can also be marginalised by the dominant girl-talk, but up to now they are less likely to have been subjected to barrages of sexual innuendo. Things will change. Employers who condone sexual harassment and who are found guilty of gender discrimination risk hefty fines. This means that the type of masculinity which has helped to strengthen many workplace cultures will be eroded. And for some female workers, for many years to come, the gender struggle for equal opportunities is likely to take precedence over the class struggle. All told, in our present time, the feminisation of the labour market will be tending to undermine traditional occupational and class solidarities.

Ethnicity

Like women, ethnic minorities have an increased presence in the UK's labour markets. This is a consequence of the immigration into Britain from the new commonwealth that peaked in the 1950s and 1960s, and the subsequent growth of the minority populations which has been due mainly to natural increase. Roughly 6 per cent of all employees are now ethnic minority. The proportion varies from place to place and from occupation to occupation, but, as explained in Chapter 2, there is certain to be a further all-round increase over the next generation.

Britain has numerous ethnic minority groups, each with its own ethnic characteristics. Over time, as they have lost the common status of recent immigrants, their experiences in Britain have become more diverse – in terms of housing, educational attainments, and the kinds of jobs that they obtain – but they continue to share one important characteristic in common, namely, an ethnic handicap in the labour market (see Box 3.5).

The principal concern here is not with the details of each minority group's experiences in the labour market (except to note that there are

---

Box 3.5

The ethnic penalty

All Britain's ethnic minorities have one thing in common – an ethnic penalty in the labour market (see Heath and McMahon, 1997). This is evident in two ways: compared with whites with equal qualifications, all the ethnic minorities have

- inferior career achievements, and

- higher unemployment (except Indians).

It is difficult to think of any possible explanation for this other than racial discrimination.

---

indeed ethnic differences), or the reasons, so much as the class implications. These are in many ways similar to the implications of gender and women's increased presence in the workforce. Both pose similar problems for class analysis. Can the minorities' positions be portrayed accurately using class schemes developed from the experiences of the majority white population? How should ethnically mixed households be treated? In the long run, the presence of ethnic minorities may not dilute, but it is certain to change workplace, occupational and class cultures. One possibility is that the workforce will become socially and culturally divided along ethnic lines, thereby challenging class unity. As with women, equal opportunities (in this case *vis-à-vis* the white population) has become the overriding aim of sections of the ethnic-minority workforce. Another possibility is that workplace and class cultures will be stripped of all national/racial characteristics; this will benefit racial integration and harmony, but at the expense of losing national sentiment (whether British, English, Scottish, Welsh or Irish) as a factor in class loyalty.

Summary

In this chapter we have seen how globalisation and new technologies have ushered in new, post-Fordist economic times, characterised by greater flexibility (of labour markets, jobs and workers); more precarious, non-standard employment (temporary, part-time and self-employment); higher unemployment; pressure on those in jobs to do more; and wider income inequalities.

Amid these linked waves of change there have been major shifts of employment: from manufacturing into services, and from manual into non-manual grades. Both shifts are continuing. Simultaneously, the workforce has been scattered spatially: out of the public sector, large private enterprises and city centres into self-employment, small firms and green-field sites. Meanwhile, car ownership has facilitated the separation of places of work and residence. There have also been parallel changes in the composition of the workforce: there are more women and ethnic minorities, and fewer under-25 and over-50-year-old workers.

Now if class depends on how people earn their livings, that is, on their occupations, changes in employment are bound to change the class structure. Old class formations have been undermined; this is beyond dispute, and is easily mistaken for a decline of class itself. Yet class inequalities (in market and work situations) remain very much alive. Indeed they are now wider than ever, certainly judged by income differentials.

Two class effects deserve underlining. First, the numerical decline of the manual working class and the expansion of the white-collar grades, with powerful implications for the demography of all classes. Second, a whole raft of trends in the economy, labour markets and in the composition of the workforce has tended to undermine older employment-based cultures and the associated solidarities, and has made it difficult for new solidarities to develop. These trends are:

* Greater flexibility and mobility (among men) in the labour market.

* People spending more time (as a proportion of their lifetimes) outside the workforce: in education when young, during spells of unemployment, and on account of earlier retirement (for men).

* Its rate of expansion means that a high proportion of the present-day middle class is first-generation.

* The spatial scattering of labour from local concentrations in particular firms, industries and occupations.

* Less uniformity within all occupational grades in terms of gender and ethnicity.

4

The Working Class

Introduction

Previous chapters have defined class, explained its continuing importance, adopted a class scheme as a guide, and examined the economic and occupational trends which have reshaped Britain's class structure in recent years. In this and the next three chapters we look in detail at each of the main classes, beginning with the working class. This chapter:

- describes the original working class that was created in Britain following the industrial revolution;

- reviews the debates of the 1950s and 1960s about embourgeoisement and the creation of a new working class;

- analyses how subsequent trends have disorganised the working class; and

- considers whether an underclass has been detached from the working class proper.

The Original Working Class

Roots

Britain's original working class was created in the nineteenth century. It was the world's first industrial working class: Britain was the first industrial nation. At the beginning of the nineteenth century four-fifths of Britain's population lived in rural areas; by the end, four-fifths lived in towns and cities. The countryside was depopulated. Towns and cities expanded and kept growing together with their mines, docks and factories. These new industries attracted workers escaping from rural poverty, in search of better living standards and more regular work. The countryside-to-town movement of people was augmented by migration, mainly from

Ireland, but also from the continent when Central and East Europe's Jews fled from pogroms (organised persecutions and massacres, at least tacitly condoned by the authorities). The expanding ports, textile, mining and engineering towns were unruly places at first, Britain's version of the Wild West. Employers found it difficult to induce 'green' labour to accept industrial discipline – regular and long hours of work, six days a week when required. This was the background to the nineteenth-century campaigns against drink and blood sports, and in favour of 'rational recreation' – playing modern sports, using libraries, visiting museums, and engaging in other so-called wholesome, edifying activities. A motive behind the drive for universal elementary schooling was to accustom children to industrial work routines.

In time, of course, the new workforces did settle, and industrial, urban cultures developed throughout the land. The major enterprises employed scores, often hundreds of workers. Except in textiles, the workforces were mostly male; the work was usually arduous, and power-driven equipment was introduced only slowly. The work was often dangerous – in steel works, engineering workshops, on the docks which handled imports and exports, in railway construction, and especially in the mines. Workers needed to cooperate in order to do their jobs, and were often dependent on each other for their physical safety. These are the origins of working-class comradeship, and the us–them frame of mind. 'They' were the people who imposed on 'us' what they would not have considered tolerable for themselves or their families. During the next century (the twentieth), experience in the two world wars, and especially the First World War, consolidated the us–them mentality. Mistrust and contempt for the officer class, who sent thousands of infantrymen 'over the top' to their deaths, survived the cessation of armed hostilities.

Interdependence in the workplace spilled into out-of-work life. Before the age of mechanical transport, it was necessary for workers to live close to where they were employed. This continued to make sense even when bus, tram and suburban railway services were introduced. Working-men's clubs, pubs, beer, football, chapel, brass bands, pigeons – the mixture varied from place to place – but these became the foundations of working-men's leisure. It was not necessarily edifying but there was usually no threat to law and order. People who worked together also played together. When pits and factories closed for annual wakes weeks, each town would empty and the inhabitants would travel together, and stay in adjacent streets and boarding houses in nearby coastal resorts.

Workplace and neighbourhood relations were mutually reinforcing, but homes and neighbourhoods were primarily the women's domains. It was mostly women who were at home throughout each day throughout each week. Sons often followed fathers into the same pits and factories, and usually continued to live locally. Daughters did likewise. Parents would assist their grown-up children to obtain accommodation of their own by speaking to the rent man. Prior to the Second World War, most working-class families lived in privately-rented dwellings. In the days when families with six and more surviving children were common, neighbourhoods became knit by numerous interlocking kin relationships. Relatives and neighbours would help each other in times of adversity and need. Factory lay-offs, and, less frequently, strikes, were occasions of adversity. The death of parents, or their disablement through accidents at work, were common sources of need. Risks of mortality during infancy, childhood and adulthood have always been higher, and remain higher to this day, among manual compared with non-manual workers and their families. Other needs were life-cyclical. Families usually lived in, or close to, poverty during the child-rearing life-stage, and their living standards would plunge again in old age, if they survived that long. It was hardly possible to cope with ordinary pressures of life without family and community support.

Needless to say, this communality was stronger in some places and in some sections of the working class than in others. Everywhere there was a distinction between the respectable and the rough. Respectable working-class families adopted some bourgeois habits, or, at any rate, habits that were being urged upon workers by some sections of the middle class – sobriety, saving, holidays, Sunday schools and, above all, regular work. Skilled workers had the most regular work, and the highest earnings, and were the most likely to be able to lead respectable lifestyles. Early sociological surveys of working-class districts distinguished strata of loafers and criminals. All the industrial cities had rough areas, usually where the most recent migrants settled, which were renowned for the residents' irregular work habits, their criminality, the gangs, and the street fights after closing time at weekends. Children from respectable families were warned never to venture into such places, and to avoid the children from them. The rough working class diminished in size throughout the twentieth century, after urban growth had ended, and was near-eliminated except in small pockets by the 1950s. The expansion of the respectable working class was a product of full employment (after the Second World War) and higher incomes, and, above all, the development of the welfare state and the rehousing of residents from slum areas, though some new council estates immediately became tarred with the reputations of the rough areas from which the residents had been rehoused.

Mateyness at work and communality in neighbourhoods were hallmarks of respectability, and acted as the soil from which working-class organisations grew. For as long as there have been factories, workers have seen advantages in 'combination' – to protect each other from arbitrary dismissal, pay cuts, and to express demands (for more pay for example) with which entire workforces have agreed. Workers have always appreciated the need to avoid competing against one another, and against workers doing similar jobs in other factories. They have wanted to prevent employers hiring the cheapest and sacking anyone with the temerity to ask for more. In medieval times, the various tradespeople organised themselves in guilds which then sought to monopolise the crafts. In the eighteenth and early nineteenth centuries, combinations of employees were usually unlawful and employers did whatever possible to smash them. Then, in the 1850s, skilled workers began to develop effective combinations, which is how they came to be called 'trade' unions. Employers began to recognise and negotiate with these unions instead of trying to suppress them; the workers who were combining were recognised as respectable and responsible. Subsequently, from the 1880s onwards, trade unionism spread among semi-skilled and unskilled workers, and by the First World War all the main industries and manual occupations had trade unions. At that time the working class amounted to three-quarters of the population. They had learnt that their strength lay in numbers; that 'the union makes us strong'. Their problem then, and ever since, has been to mobilise this potential strength: to achieve as close to 100 per cent union membership as possible, and to ensure that any collective action is truly collective. Achieving this has never been easy. The trade union movement did not cover the majority of UK employees until the 1970s (since when membership has declined). Activists have always understood the need for solidarity, and how elusive it can be; hence the stigma within the organised labour movement attached to free-riders, and to scabs or blacklegs. The trade unions were always strongest in towns dominated by single industries, and in large establishments, where workplace and community loyalties reinforced each other. Pit villages and dockland areas were sometimes almost ideal-typical cases.

The cooperative movement was another product of the capacity for effective organisation that the working class developed during the nineteenth century. The type of cooperative that turned out to be most successful was the consumers' cooperative: stores owned by the shoppers, and therefore able to pass-on any profits (the dividend) to their ordinary members.

The Labour Party, of course, was the other great product of the working-class's ability to self-organise. It was established in 1900, principally by the trade unions which had already learnt the limitations of industrial action. They needed political representation to gain legal protection for themselves, and to pursue benefits that could never be won through negotiation with employers. Throughout the twentieth century the trade unions were to remain the Labour Party's main source of financial support. The rise of the Labour Party was aided by the two world wars, and catastrophic splits in the Liberal Party after the First World War. From the

1920s onwards, Labour was the party that attracted most support from the working class, and the main alternative to the Conservatives, but it was not until 1945 that the UK had its first majority Labour government.

Working-class Values

It has become easier with the passage of time to identify core values that were institutionalised early-on in trade union practices and Labour Party policies, and which have always struck chords when expressed in any workplace or working-class neighbourhood. The culture of the British working class was never Marxist. Christianity was more influential – more likely to be preached from the chapel than the Church of England to working-class congregations. Britain's working class has never been truly revolutionary; its creed is better described as Labourist.

First, the working class was always more meritocratic than egalitarian. Workers have always believed that skill, effort, output and long hours should be rewarded. They have opposed only what, in their eyes, have been unmerited inequalities like inflated salaries, unearned profits and inherited wealth. A society where some drive Rolls Royces and sail super-yachts while others cannot keep their homes warm has been regarded as obviously unjust. Working-class parents have always wanted their children to get on, if at all possible, and this is not a recently acquired aspiration. Miners and their wives have not wanted their sons to go down the pits. Skilled workers have always put in a word, if they have been able to do so and if necessary, to secure apprenticeships for their sons, but the majority's preference has always been that their children should achieve better things. Working-class parents are more ambitious for their children than middle-class parents, maybe not in absolute terms, but relative to their own starting points. Hence the consistent and persistent pressure from the trade unions and the Labour Party for equal opportunities in education: for secondary schools and universities to be accessible irrespective of financial circumstances and family background. Mobility out of the working class was exceptional in the early twentieth century – inevitably so because most jobs were manual – but throughout the century more and more working-class families were able to realise the dream of seeing their children do well at school, sometimes progress into higher education, then into really good jobs (see Chapter 8).

Second, the working class has always recognised the need for solidarity – for workers to stand together and to settle contentious issues among themselves and with other parties, through negotiation, bargaining and, eventually, binding agreements. These have been cardinal values; collective bargaining and agreements have been seen as absolutely necessary.

Trade unions have sought to control bosses' rights to hire and fire; they have needed to prevent activists being dismissed; they have needed to ensure that anyone hired already belonged to, or was willing to join, the union. They have appreciated the need for everyone's terms and conditions to be collectively agreed in order to prevent employers favouring a minority, dividing a workforce, and inducing them to compete against each other for rewards that would only be offered to some. In working-class culture, collective organisation and agreements have been more than a means: they have been treated as ends in themselves.

Third, workers have wanted their organisations – the trade unions and their political representatives – to guarantee certain basics for everyone: decent housing, sanitation and other crucial services, burials, and adequate income in the event of unemployment, sickness, incapacity and in old age. In other words, they have sought security for all: the removal of the threat of abject want, poverty and destitution.

Fourth, the working class has favoured the removal of certain services – primarily health care and education – out of the marketplace altogether on the principle that benefits should be governed by need rather than ability to pay. Working-class culture takes offence at people being able to queue-jump for medical treatment, or receive better treatment, simply because they are able to pay, and likewise when some children receive an education that is denied to others who are unable to afford the fees or extras such as uniforms.

Fifth, the working class has always believed in economic planning: an end to the vagaries of the market. Instead of booms and slumps, overtime followed by short-time and lay-offs, workers have wanted someone to take control so as to ensure regular work and wages for everyone.

There is a danger here of endowing the working class with a nobility that it never possessed. Support for working-class values was always based on self-interest, and people were far more likely to be concerned about their own streets or neighbourhoods, or their own industries and occupations, than the welfare of the entire working class. Craft unions were always intent, above all else, on defending their members' own work and pay differentials. Loyalty to (white male) mates could be accompanied, indeed strengthened, by some particularly savage forms of racism and sexism. The working class was never truly united at neighbourhood or industry, let alone national, level. As explained earlier, presenting a semblance of solidarity was always difficult. It was never easy to mobilise support, and there was very rarely genuine (as opposed to coerced) 100 per cent support for any political or industrial action. Also, the organised working class did not always use its power in its own long-term interests. By the 1960s some trade unions had become among the most conservative organisations in the country, intent on defending rights that their members had won even when these included grotesque over-manning (so-called Spanish practices) which, in the long run, were bound to weaken the firms and industries in which the workers' jobs were based.

Nevertheless, all the above values still strike chords with any working-class audience, though the vibrations are weaker today because the old roots of the working class in occupational and neighbourhood communities have largely gone. And, of course, the working class is now much smaller than in the past. The working class would no longer be guaranteed electoral success if only all members turned out and voted the same way.

Nostalgia

Sociologists started to describe and analyse working-class ways of life only when Britain's original working class was already in decline. Until the Second World War, poverty was the big issue; material conditions rather than culture and values preoccupied researchers. For a time, in the 1950s, it was believed that poverty had been abolished, consigned to history. The working class was enjoying a type of prosperity that had been almost beyond the imaginations of prewar generations, and sociologists set about examining these changes.

Dennis, Henriques and Slaughter (1956) were able to study a Yorkshire coal-mining community (Featherstone) where workforce solidarity was as strong, and community life was as vibrant, as ever. But when Michael Young and Peter Willmott began their widely acclaimed research in Bethnal Green in the 1950s, this was to record a way of life that was then under threat. *Family and Kinship in East London* was first published in 1957, and ever since then sociologists have relied heavily upon it (either at first, second or third hand) for their knowledge about traditional working-class communities. This portrait of London's East End surprised much of middle-class England in the 1950s. It had been supposed that people disliked living in slum areas; conditions were supposed to be repugnant. Young and Willmott described an East End to which the residents were strongly attached, a way of life that was warm, and a community whose members were so supportive towards each other that the rest of the country was envious. The story-line in the book was about how Eastenders were being resettled to London's outskirts, on council estates with better dwellings, more spacious neighbourhoods and cleaner air, yet regretted deeply that they had been uprooted, isolated from kin and life-long friends.

Richard Hoggart's *The Uses of Literacy* was also first published in 1957. This book was based on Hoggart's knowledge of life in Hunslet (now a part of Leeds), where he had been brought up. His portrait of traditional working-class life was basically as in Young and Willmott's account, and came with the same message; that something of real value was being lost. In Hoggart's account, the main threat was not from bulldozers and urban redevelopment so much as the mass media – the press, radio, the cinema, and especially television, but most of all from the imported American culture which was seen as obliterating older sensitivities and forms of sociability, and replacing them with something more shallow, less authentic.

David Lockwood was able to draw on these accounts in his landmark 1966 article, 'Sources of Variation in Working Class Images of Society'. In this article Lockwood identified two traditional working classes. One as a deferential working class, which was said to have developed in agricultural communities and in small businesses where workers were bound into relationships of dependence on (personally known) employers. Lockwood argued that such contexts bred deferential attitudes, which were liable to spread into politics where the workers were quite likely to vote for the party led by their 'betters'. Lockwood's second and larger traditional working class was proletarian, and subscribed to a power-model, us–them view of society. It was the original working class described above. Lockwood's purpose in constructing these traditional types was to lay down benchmarks against which to describe a new working class that was coming into existence (as he and others suspected).

It is not just sociologists but the entire country that appears to share an abiding nostalgia for Britain's traditional proletarian working class. How else can we explain the popularity of *Coronation Street* and *Eastenders*? These television series portray a world that we have lost. In a similar way, the first generations in the industrial cities were nostalgic about traditional village life. A few people like Richard Hoggart (and myself) can still recall childhoods in more-or-less traditional working-class communities, but for most people today these are just powerful folk memories of an era when people had true mates at work, and when neighbours popped-in-and-out and chatted to each other on doorsteps daily. And, of course, the children all played safely in the streets.

It was never really like that, and village life was never really idyllic. The close-knit working-class communities could be claustrophobic; there was no privacy; it was difficult to prevent everyone knowing one's most intimate business. There were neighbourhood feuds; children (and sometimes adults) fought in the streets. These were risky places. And, of course, even though they may have regretted being separated from kin and existing neighbours, people were delighted when they were rehoused in places with bathrooms, hot water and gardens.

Times have certainly changed. It is possible today to be nostalgic about the power that the working class could still mobilise even as recently as the 1960s and 1970s. It was only when their roots were already weakening, that the main working-class 'political' organisations, the trade unions and the Labour Party, were at their strongest. Wildcat strikes triggered a royal commission in the 1960s. In the 1970s the coal-miners were able to strike and cause power failures which put the whole of British industry on a three-day working week, and provoked irate middle class Britain into 'writing by candlelight' to newspapers in protest. In 1978–79 the trade unions were able orchestrate a 'winter of discontent'. It all seems a very long time ago.

For the working class at the time it was less glamorous than nostalgia can make it seem. In 1926 the Trade Union Congress called a general strike which fizzled out after 10 days. Most set-piece, large-scale confrontations ended in defeat for the workers; and wildcat strikes disrupted the work and earnings of other employees. Harold Wilson, the Labour prime minister in the 1960s, noted that one worker's wage increase was another's price rise. The damage that industrial action could inflict, on one's own job among others, worried many workers. Strikes were always the resort of desperate men (and sometimes women), and even in its heyday, working-class power was difficult to mobilise. Remember, there was no majority Labour government until 1945, and at no time in the twentieth century did a Labour government serve two full terms in office.

Be that as it may, the original working class has certainly waned. By the 1960s groups of workers who took industrial action were unable to rely on the automatic, unreflecting, sympathetic solidarity of the entire working class. The coal-miners strike of 1984–85 split the National Union of Mineworkers, and the strikers found it impossible to mobilise effective support (which would have brought industry to a halt) in other sections of the working class. By then such sympathetic action (in support of workers in a different occupation, firm or industry) would have been illegal, which is another sign of how working-class power had waned. There are still pockets of industry and neighbourhoods where the old ways survive. Some of the brass bands are still playing. The old culture lives on in many trade union and local Labour Party branches; here the old values still strike powerful chords. The faithful's problem is that the old roots have gone.

The New Working Class of the 1960s

The Embourgeoisement Thesis

Sociology began to study the working class thoroughly only when it was believed (correctly as it has turned out) to be changing in fundamental ways, and the change alleged by most commentators in the 1950s and

1960s was embourgeoisement (the economic, social, cultural and political assimilation of manual workers into the middle class). This was in the context of the full employment, steady economic growth and regular pay rises that had been maintained since the Second World War. Manual earnings were rising year-on-year, and the earnings gap with white-collar salaries was closing. Goods and services formerly associated with the middle classes – soft home furnishings, television sets, washing machines, motor cars and holidays abroad – were being enjoyed by more and more working-class families. The claim was that as manual workers' incomes rose into the middle-class bracket, their ways of life, identities and politics would change accordingly. These claims looked plausible in the 1950s when the Labour Party was losing three successive general elections. It was claimed that as fewer and fewer manual workers lived like, and identified with, the traditional working class, then fewer and fewer would support a political party with a working-class image. Hence the argument that the Labour Party was in danger of becoming a permanent opposition unless it overhauled its constitution, policies and image, and broadened its appeal (Abrams *et al.*, 1960). This triggered a debate within the Labour Party that was not won decisively by the 'modernisers' until the 1990s. Many Labour activists felt, throughout the intervening years, that they had fallen victims to their own success in improving the lives of manual workers.

The embourgeoisement thesis never received much support from sociology. Its main exponents were political scientists and journalists (for example, Turner, 1963); the argument always sounded too simplistic for sociologists to be convinced. Ferdinand Zweig (1961) was probably as near a supporter as sociology produced. He interviewed 600 manual workers from five modern factories and concluded that the new working class, content with the system in which it lived and worked, was more concerned to boost its earnings within than to question let alone challenge the prevailing economic and social order. Zweig also drew attention to how affluence made nuclear families less dependent on kin and neighbours, thus weakening one of the roots of traditional working-class culture.

The research which interrogated the embourgeoisement thesis most thoroughly was a study conducted in Luton in the mid-1960s by John Goldthorpe, David Lockwood, Frank Bechoffer and Jennifer Platt. Their main book from this project (Goldthorpe *et al.*, 1969), is one of the best-known works in the history of British sociology. It was based on interviews with just 229 (male) manual workers at three establishments in Luton (a car manufacturer, an engineering company and a chemical plant). Fifty-four white-collar employees were also interviewed as a comparison group. It is remarkable that the findings from this small-scale study, or rather the interpretations that the researchers placed upon their findings, were to define British sociology's view of the 'new' working class for the next quarter century. One of the reasons for the study's impact was the choice of location. Luton was selected partly because it was not too far from Cambridge where the researchers were based, but mainly for its 'prototypicality'. Luton was not a traditional industrial town with a history of working-class organisation and an associated traditional working-class culture. It was an expanding town, and in the 1960s many of its employees had migrated from other places. Earnings in the town were well above the national average. The authors could claim, with justification, that if embourgeoisement was happening anywhere, it should have been evident in Luton. They might have broadened this to claim that if any new working class was being created, its birth was likely to be more advanced, and its characteristics clearer, in Luton than in most places. Another reason for the study's success was the sophistication with which ideal types of traditional sections of the working class, proletarian and deferential (see above, p. 88), were constructed. This enabled the investigators to pinpoint exactly how their Luton sample differed. Arguably, these researchers were less thorough in defining middle-classness, and specifying precisely its similarities and differences *vis-à-vis* the traditional and new working classes.

On the basis of their findings the Luton investigators rejected the embourgeoisement thesis, and as far as sociology was concerned the thesis lay dead and buried. With the exception of Peter Saunders (1978, 1981, 1990, see below), hardly anyone of note in British sociology has felt it necessary to take the embourgeoisement thesis seriously for over 30 years. The Luton investigators did in fact have excellent grounds for rejecting the thesis. First, the vast majority of their respondents identified with the working class. Second, they were nearly all not only trade union members but regarded trade union representation as indispensable. Third, 71 per cent had voted Labour in the most recent general election (a higher figure than for the working class nationally). Fourth, the manual workers had few if any white-collar friends. They were not rubbing shoulders with factory managers in local pubs or visiting each other at home. Kin and neighbours were the manual workers' main associates outside their workplaces. Unlike the white-collar respondents, they were not joining formal leisure-time associations, or developing wide networks of friends.

The Luton investigators had good grounds for asserting that the acquisition of a middle-class income did not lead automatically to social integration into the middle class, or the adoption of a middle-class identity, values and political preferences. They argued that a washing machine was basically just a machine for washing clothes rather than a middle-class status symbol, and that affluent workers were simply affluent members of the working class rather than middle-class. In terms of their work and market situations, the Luton sample remained emphatically working-class. They were on the receiving end of authority at work; they were paid per hour and according to how much they produced; they did not identify with their jobs or employers in the ways considered characteristic of the middle class. The Luton workers had no long career ladders to ascend. Their prospects of betterment depended, as ever, on making collective gains, alongside colleagues. There were no signs of the traditional class divide at work even fraying let alone collapsing.

A concurrent study of compositors endorsed this conclusion (Cannon, 1967). Print workers, although highly paid, homeowners, and so on, retained proletarian identities and loyalties due to the strength of their craft-based working lives and trade unions.

Privatised and Instrumental

The Luton investigators rejected the embourgeoisement thesis but they were still impressed by contrasts between the evidence from their sample and the ideal types of traditional working class that they had constructed. Two keywords signal these contrasts.

First, privatism: in Luton there were no deferential relationships of dependence on superiors, but neither was there much of the workplace mateyness associated with the proletarian working class. In their factories, employees were positioned at individual work stations, as along car assembly lines, separated from each other by noise and machinery. The work process did not require them to collaborate. In this sense their lives at work were privatised. Interestingly, since the 1970s many large firms have introduced teamwork and quality groups in an attempt to integrate workers more closely, and to persuade them to identify with company goals and strategies. However, there has been no reversal in the other area of life where the Luton team noted a spread of privatism. Few members of the Luton sample had plenty of kin living locally. Their houses did not open directly onto streets or common 'backs' but were separated by gardens. Kin and neighbours were the workers' main social contacts, but their lives outside work were basically home-centred. The affluent workers had been buying soft home furnishings, carpeting and, most crucially, televisions. At the end of a working day they did not hang around with mates. Nor did they go out to pubs to spend time with their mates during the evenings. If they did go out occasionally this would be as a couple or family group. The sample's life projects were nuclear family-centred.

In the Luton investigators' account, this lifestyle was spreading by choice. There was little of the sense of loss reported in the Bethnal Green study, or in Jeremy Seabrook's (1971) concurrent account of working-class life in northern cities. Maybe the difference was that so many of the Luton sample had chosen to leave their home areas of their own accord. However, neighbourhood life was collapsing throughout the length and breadth of the country at that time. More married women were taking paid jobs; they were no longer around all day to knit neighbourhoods together. More working-class children were getting on and leaving their home districts (see Chapter 8). Families were smaller so, in any case, there was less chance of a child remaining local. Above all, television was keeping people 'in', while the motor car was enabling them to go out in private, and was turning streets into thoroughfares rather than places for children's play and other forms of community life. Also, although this attracted little comment in Goldthorpe *et al.*'s (1969) *The Affluent Worker* study, Luton in the 1960s was becoming a multiracial town, and old working-class areas throughout the land were likewise being transformed into multiethnic inner-city districts.

It is necessary, here, to see these changes in their 1950s and 1960s contexts rather than from present-day perspectives. In the 1950s and 1960s more married women were returning to work; there were more dual-earning families, but at that time males' working-class jobs were not threatened. There was no equal pay or opportunities legislation. Women were recruited to women's jobs, generally at well beneath male rates of pay. The men were still the breadwinners, and (in public at any rate) could refer to women's earnings as pin money (for luxuries rather than essentials). In many towns and cities some working-class neighbourhoods were becoming multiracial, but this did not apply to all, or even to most, of the working-class areas. At that time the newcomers to Britain rarely qualified for council housing. They had to wait their turn on waiting lists, and often faced straightforward discrimination. The council estates were still overwhelmingly white. For most white workers, 'race' was still an issue that they read about in the press. Until 1968 race discrimination was not unlawful; it was not an offence for employers and estate agents to add 'no coloureds' to their adverts. Immigrants read such signs daily. 'Mother Britain' was less welcoming than its new commonwealth citizens might have expected. The first generations of immigrants were channelled into industries and occupations where there were labour shortages – on public transport in many cities, as hospital ancillaries, and on the night shifts in Lancashire textile factories, for example. The crucial point here is that by far the greater part of the white working class was hardly affected directly.

The second keyword in the typification of the new working class in the Luton study was instrumentality. The workers' lives were home and family-centred, and all their engagements with the outside world tended to be instrumental, means to ends, rather than ends or values in themselves.

This certainly applied to their orientations towards work. These were pecuniary. The workers were not worried if their jobs were not intrinsically satisfying, or if they were not bound into fraternal work groups. None of this was either sought or expected. Many of the sample had been attracted to Luton by the well-paid jobs, and if the pay was right the workers were satisfied. The Luton investigators queried whether their respondents could be regarded as alienated at work if their jobs were offering what they wanted. They worked in order to earn the wages to support home-centred lifestyles. Homes and families were the places where the workers had emotional investments.

There appeared to be a similar instrumentality in the workers' attachments to trade unions and the Labour Party. They supported trade unions because this was the best way of obtaining and protecting even fuller pay packets. In other words, they endorsed collective means in pursuit of private objectives. In a similar manner, their support for the Labour Party seemed to have a calculative base; they judged Labour to be more likely than any of the alternatives to implement policies that served their private interests. Their support was pragmatic and, by implication, fickle, rather than solidaristic.

The Affluent Worker ended with an insistence that the new working class could be persuaded to support a radical political programme, but there was little sign of this in the rest of the book, or in Goldthorpe's (1969, 1979) concurrent or subsequent work in which he attempted to explain inflation and persistent industrial action in terms of groups of workers all pursuing sectional interests, unregulated by any wider morality. Ferdinand Zweig (1976) incorporated the findings from the Luton study into an updated diagnosis of the new acquisitive working class, dedicated to self-interest or, at best, the interests of the workers' immediate bargaining groups, rather than a broader class or nation. In this book, Zweig re-endorsed the embourgeoisement thesis (unlike the Goldthorpe team, Zweig believed that affluence was at the root of the changes), and claimed that only 20 per cent or so of manual workers had been left behind in the wake of this development.

False Diagnosis?

The new working class thesis did not win instant acceptance in British sociology. At the time of the book's publication, the near revolutionary (on the continent) events of 1968 were still fresh in mind, and the spirit was still in the air. Wildcat strikes and cost-push inflation were the big issues in Britain's industrial relations. Governments were trying, unsuccessfully, to curb shopfloor power. Trade union activists appeared to be more militant than the national leaders, and it was not wholly implausible to imagine capitalism being toppled if only the working class received radical leadership. How wrong can you be?

Some critiques of *The Affluent Worker* study queried whether a 'new' working class had been discovered. It was argued that instrumental, pecuniary orientations towards work were in fact long-standing. Workers had always been concerned about their earnings. Many had always been most concerned about 'number one', and sometimes their immediate families. The tidyness with which the Luton researchers had distinguished deferential, proletarian and new working classes was queried. It was shown that agricultural workers were not consistently deferential (Newby, 1977), and that shipbuilding workers were not as consistently proletarian in outlook as the typology suggested that they should be (Brown and Brannen, 1970). It was counter-argued that, in practice, all sections of the working class were more likely to hold muddled mixtures of radical and conservative, rather than coherent views about their own circumstances and the wider society (Abercrombie and Turner, 1978; Mann, 1970, 1973; Nichols and Armstrong, 1976).

A related criticism was that there had always been Lutons – expanding towns attracting migrant labour, when, at the stage of the cycle in question, there was no tradition of local community life or workplace organisation. Given time, it was argued, Luton would change. Luton has indeed changed, and its affluent workers were re-studied in the 1980s (Devine, 1992). By then many had kin who had joined them in the town, or family ties had developed locally with the growth of a second generation. Extreme privatism in the 1980s, when it occurred, was due to constraint rather than choice – long and unsocial hours of work, or financial constraints which prevented people from socialising in the local pubs and clubs. The privatism of the Luton workers in the 1960s was partly misunderstood. At that time privatism was accentuated by so many of the workers being migrants, usually from other parts of Britain. Prioritising the home as a site for emotional investments, and consumer spending, need not be incompatible with an outgoing social life. 'Going out' can be a highlight in basically home-centred lifestyles. By the 1980s Luton had ceased to be a growth town: its major employers were reducing rather than expanding their workforces, and the population was more settled. Most of Devine's sample did see friends and kin regularly. However, Luton had not become another Bethnal Green. The older type of community seems incompatible with the motor car, television, and married women holding paid jobs.

From the 1960s onwards architects and town planners were trying to design and build communities rather than just houses. Earlier council estates were criticised for being soulless and facility-bare; the overriding aim, earlier on, had been to get people into decent dwellings. Subsequently, community centres and other neighbourhood facilities were built in from the start, and blocks of houses were designed around communal space whereon, the intention was, the residents would become friends. This test of architectural determinism was an abject failure; there has been no resurrection of the older working-class communities.

Another point made against the new working class diagnosis was that the cash nexus was likely to prove more brittle than the analysis suggested. It was argued that workplace and local community loyalties may have inhibited the spread of class-wide solidarity and political action in the past (Westergaard and Resler, 1975). Throughout the 1970s many sociologists continued to believe that the working class was but a short step from becoming a truly revolutionary force. Whether workers really were satisfied with assembly-line jobs, provided they were well-paid, was also queried. It was argued that the Goldthorpe team had underestimated the resentment, anger and the dehumanising character of the work, testified by the cheers that would ring through car plants whenever a line broke down, and the sabotage that ensured that breakdowns occurred reasonably frequently (Beynon, 1973). In other words, the so-called new working class was believed to be capable of developing a radicalism from within (see also Moorhouse, 1976). In retrospect, this seems less plausible than in the aftermath of 1968. And even at that time it was being argued that workers needed to be somehow protected from the barrage of dominant (upper-class and middle-class) values and world views propagated by the mass media and political parties if they were to develop then consolidate their own oppositional dispositions and alternative political agendas (Parkin, 1971). The older communities seemed to provide this protection. The working class appears to need such shelters if it is to develop its discontents into a political programme.

The reason why the Luton study and its diagnosis of a new, non-traditional working class enjoyed an extended life in sociology is really quite simple: at the time the diagnosis was basically correct.

Prototypical?

In contrast, the claim of prototypicality for Luton's working class of the 1960s proved short-lived. This is not a criticism of the team that conducted the 1960s study. They expected more and more sections of the working class to become more and more like the Luton respondents, which seemed entirely reasonable at the time. We now know how unreasonable it is to expect any sociologists to make sound future predictions.

By the mid-1970s, New Times had arrived, though few realised it then. During the 1970s unemployment in Britain passed the million barrier and rose towards two million. At the time this was attributed to the oil price spirals and Britain's long-term (relative) economic decline which was to be remedied by, well, the proposals varied but they all envisaged a resuscitation of British manufacturing. It was not until the 1980s that analysts began to proclaim a process of fundamental restructuring, and we learnt about post-Fordism, and so on. However, even in 1983 Paul Thompson was predicting that the recession combined with employers' offensive tactics would push the working class into transformatory politics. The old spirit was still alive, in parts of sociology at any rate. But by the 1980s the industries in which the old labour movement was based were shrinking dramatically in terms of employment and, in some cases, were almost disappearing. Attention therefore shifted from affluent workers to the unemployed and the working-class poor.

The new working class of the 1960s rarely surfaced in the sociological literature of the 1980s and 1990s. The entire analysis may now appear outdated, but in fact the new (1960s brand) affluent working class has not disappeared. Britain still has car plants, oil refineries and so on, some with thousands on the payrolls in what are now called 'quality jobs', mostly full-time and permanent, and usually paying well above the national norm for manual labour. The employees are in trade unions, and terms and conditions of work are collectively bargained. These workforces must be examples of strong instrumentality, and they are expected to do more than in the past. All slack has been shaken out of the companies. The employees are usually expected to be multi-skilled, to aim for continuous improvement in their performances, and to do everything just-in-time and to get it right first time, every time. Why do they do it? They appreciate what they have to lose; they are well-paid by working-class yardsticks; they have cars, homes of their own, foreign holidays, satellite television and so on – the same family-centred lifestyles that were developing in the 1950s and 1960s.

Present-day Britain not only still has affluent manual workers; there is a new aristocracy of labour. The original aristocrats had craft skills, and most of these occupations have now been deskilled or multi-skilled. The new aristocracy is composed of technicians and technologists, usually part-time educated up to HNC or higher-level NVQs. They do design and maintenance work, and monitor their firms' technical systems. They are usually salaried rather than hourly paid, and their normal workstations are more likely to be in laboratories or in front of computer screens than on factory floors. These are not dirty-hands occupations, and there has been much uncertainty within sociology as to whether these occupations should be placed in the working class or in the middle class, or in between (Carter, 1985; Smith, 1987). Many of the employees believe that they ought to be treated as managements' equals, and the same individuals usually feel resentful and frustrated at being denied this recognition. In practice the majority interpret their positions using the culture acquired from their (mainly) working-class homes, and their early career experiences on shop-floors. They are well-disposed towards trade unions and are usually well-organised, just like the earlier aristocracy of labour. Britain's affluent working class is certainly not extinct.

In the 1980s the embourgeoisement thesis was revived, albeit mainly in political science rather than sociology. The Conservatives were then in the process of winning four consecutive general elections, and the skilled working class, the so-called C2s, were deserting Labour in droves. At the time, the Conservative government was forcing local authorities (some enthusiastic, others recalcitrant) to sell council houses to sitting tenants at heavily discounted prices. This policy was opposed by the Labour Party at the time but it was popular among the purchasers. Peter Saunders (1978, 1981), from within sociology, took seriously the possibility that home ownership might be changing manual workers' class identities and poltical partisanship. Even if it was not lifting those concerned into the middle class, it may still have been changing their views on their positions in society. They were acquiring assets which (they hoped at any rate) could be passed down the generations. At the same time, a series of pop-ular privatisations (popular at least in the sense that shares were marketed to the public-at-large) was making some, admittedly a minority, but still some, manual workers into share-owners. The relevant research did not find that becoming the owner of a former council house was changing people's class identities or politics (Saunders, 1990); however, the crucial point here is that Britain still has manual workers who remain basically working-class in terms of their identities and politics, despite their relative prosperity, relative, that is, to other present-day manual workers and to working-class standards of living in the past.

One of the detailed studies of the relatively affluent working class in the 1980s was in fact the re-study of Luton, with a smaller sample than in the 1960s, but including women as well as men and using depth interviews (Devine, 1992). The respondents in this study still had well-paid jobs in objective terms, compared with typical manual earnings, but they did not feel particularly prosperous. By the 1980s they felt vulnerable; they knew that their jobs would not necessarily last for ever. Unemployment had become an issue in Luton; local employers were no longer scouring the country in search of labour, hiring anything warm, and retaining anyone who could stand the pace. Advertised vacancies invariably attracted shoals of applicants, and the sifting process had become almost as rigorous as the graduate 'milk round'. Holding on to their jobs and living standards required the workers to do more in some way or another. The dual-earner family had become the norm, often juggling pairs of unsocial shifts, and, no-one regarded the women's earnings as pin money: family's standards and styles of life depended on two incomes. These people certainly did not feel that they had become part of the middle class. As in the 1960s, they continued to identify with the working class, but many had become sceptical about the labour movement – trade unions and the Labour Party. They had not personally turned against trade unionism or working-class politics; rather, in their eyes, they had been let down by those who were supposed to represent and protect them. This feeling has been widespread, even, apparently, among the relatively advantaged, as well as within the sections of the working class that have manifestly lost during the economic restructuring since the 1970s.

Does Money Matter?

It was the embourgeoisement thesis that initially triggered sociology's search for a new working class, but very early-on money was tacitly discounted by most sociologists even as a base for the emerging new working class's distinctive features. According to the original Luton investigators, it was not their affluence but the nature of their jobs or, more specifically, the kinds of social relationships in which they were involved at work, and the absence of powerful local kin and neighbourhood ties, that were separating the new from the traditional working classes. Maybe money was discounted too readily, out of enthusiasm to end all talk of embourgeoisement. Money matters in all sections of the working class, old and new; in fact it was the high earnings that had attracted many of the respondents to Luton in the 1960s, and which held them into their jobs. It was their earnings that enabled them to make their homes attractive and comfortable. In retrospect, though, as Ferdinand Zweig observed much earlier, it is fairly obvious that postwar affluence itself was making nuclear families less dependent on kin and neighbours, and giving them wider consumer choices. They were no longer restricted to spending evenings in the local pub or club if they chose to go out. They were no longer limited to holidays at the most convenient, the nearest, seaside resorts. The more people have to spend above and beyond the necessities, whether these are defined materially or culturally, the less likely it becomes that common ways of life and aspirations will be sustained within any group.

It is equally clear this side of the turn of the century that affluence itself is simply unable to bourgeoisify the working class. Something only has to become normal within the working class for it to lose any middle-class associations. This has happened successively to holidays at the English seaside, on the Costa Brava, television sets and washing machines, and council houses. The families that were rehoused to suburban council estates in the 1950s were regarded, and regarded themselves, as moving up, but before long being a council tenant had acquired entirely different connotations, and the same has now happened to owner-occupation.

The class implications of relative prosperity are always likely to depend on the context. In the immediate postwar years working-class affluence set those concerned apart from and, in everyone's eyes at the time, above what had hitherto been mainstream working-class culture. Since the 1970s affluence has been a condition for integration into the rather different, new mainstream working-class culture of the age. Nowadays it is the workers in the firms that offer the remaining quality manual jobs, and the new aristocracy of labour, who are most likely to be in trade unions. It is they who can afford what has come to be regarded as a normal working-class lifestyle including car ownership, holidays abroad and so forth. Rather than the integrity of the working class being threatened by sections of the manual workforce being lifted above and out, the greater threat in more recent times has been 'dropping down' into unemployment, low-quality jobs and a new kind of privatism imposed by poverty.

Disorganisation

It is only at this point that we encounter the economic trends reviewed in the last chapter – globalisation, new technology, labour-market flexibility, more non-standard employment, spatial scattering, job insecurity and unemployment. The digression into history has been necessary, first, because, albeit in a partial way, the history is part of the memory of the present-day working class, a template for experiencing and evaluating current conditions, and second, because the post-1960s economic trends have not created a totally new working class but have reshaped what already existed.

Myths and Real Trends

We need to be clear about exactly what has happened to Britain's working class since the 1970s. First, there has not been a steep decline in the number of manual jobs. Rather, a long-term slow decline has continued. Second, unskilled jobs have not been especially vulnerable. In fact the steepest decline has been in the skilled manual jobs in manufacturing and extractive industries which used to be filled by men. The idea that jobs which require no formal educational qualifications or extended training are disappearing is plain bunk.

The main trends have actually been a shift of manual employment from extractive and manufacturing industries to services, from large to small establishments, from city-centre locations and older industrial estates to out-of-town greenfield sites, and increases in the proportions of women and ethnic minorities in the manual (as in the non-manual) workforce. In themselves these trends would not have automatically wrought an improvement or deterioration in the overall quality of manual jobs; what has been decisive here has been the context in which the trends have occurred.

Labels and Explanations

Applying labels such as post-Fordism, and invoking globalisation and new technology, has limited explanatory power. As we have seen in Chapter 3, post-Fordism and globalisation are useful terms for describing the several interrelated trends and tendencies grouped beneath each label. Technology is also important in its own way, that is, as a mediator, but sociology dispensed with technological determinism ages ago. Technology does not come into existence of its own accord; its development and uses are always shaped by human beings with specific interests. Likewise, globalisation has not just happened: a condition has been governments opening their borders to trade in goods and flows of capital. Organisations and work-forces have been made flexible by owners and senior managers, not through the force of an impersonal law of history.

From the point of view of any individual worker, the new technologies that have been installed are brute facts of life to which the person simply has to adjust. Likewise, from the point of view of any company, globalisation is simply a condition from which there can be no escape, and competition may well oblige a firm to make itself flexible or die. The same can be true even for countries. It is sometimes said that all these developments are good for business, which begs the question of exactly whose business. The owners of businesses and their senior managers must have been chuckling all the way from their stockbrokers to their banks.

We will not find the causes of the ways in which manual employment has changed in recent times within the working class. For causes we must wait until the recent reorganisation of the upper class is dealt with in Chapter 7. The working class has felt the effects of changes in which capital and its owners have been the prime movers. A condition for these changes has been the weakness of the working class as a cultural and political entity, and part of the background to this weakening (of the original working class) has been sketched in previous sections of this chapter. During the last quarter of the twentieth century, this permitted developments which would have been unthinkable earlier on, and these developments have led in a circular fashion to a further weakening, the disorganisation, of the working class.

Country Specifics: The UK Context

Countries still make a difference, even in an era of globalisation. Labour is still organised in national trade union movements, and political parties organise nationally. The UK economy is far from fully converged and synchronised with continental Europe. So although many of the trends in Britain have occurred elsewhere in Europe, and in North America and in the Far East's new industrial states also, there are ways in which the British experience has been distinctive.

First, Britain is less regulated than most other European Union economies. Regulation here means by 'corporatist' agreements between governments, trade unions and associations of employers, and by law. Britain was the first industrial nation. Countries that developed later were faster to regulate. In recent times, the cross-national trend has been deregulation, and here Britain has been at the forefront (Lash and Urry, 1987). This is despite the minimum wage and the ceiling on compulsory working time that were introduced, somewhat reluctantly and half-heartedly, in Britain in 1999. The minimum pay is extremely low, and the ceiling on working time is easily breached. The other indicators of Britain's unregulated state are the relatively low rate of trade union membership, and the low proportion of the workforce covered by collective agreements, especially national agreements (see below); few restrictions on employers' ability to hire, fire and to declare redundancies without consultation or negotiation; and the similar prerogative claimed by employers to run their businesses as they see fit, legally subject only to their shareholders. Since the 1970s British governments have stood at arm's length from economic life. 'Lame ducks' have been allowed to sink; owners and managers have been told to do their best or face the consequences.

A second, related feature of the British experience has been the radical reforms to trade unions and industrial relations that were implemented in the 1980s and early 1990s. These required trade union officials to be elected periodically, banned the closed shop, required ballots prior to industrial action, banned most forms of secondary (sympathetic) industrial action, made the unions responsible for the actions of all their officials, including shop stewards, imposed heavy restrictions on picketing, and placed the unions' funds at risk in the event of any breaches. Some of these reforms were actually popular among most trade union members – an indication of the distance that had arisen between the organisations and their grassroots. These reforms have made it easier for employers to opt out of national bargaining, and to limit workplace negotiations to matters of their own choosing like basic rates of pay and hours of work, but not working practices or incentive systems let alone investment decisions. The industrial relations reforms were possible only because organised labour was unable to resist effectively, and have in turn led to a further weakening of organised labour, indicated by the decline in trade union membership from just over a half to a third of the workforce between the 1970s and the 1990s. Trade union membership declined across Western Europe, but more steeply in Britain than in most other countries. In Britain the proportion of the workforce covered by collective agreements declined from 70 per cent to 47 per cent between 1980 and 1990, while in Germany it was 82 per cent throughout this period (see Ebbinghaus and Visser, 1999; Traxler, 1996).

The decline in trade union membership and in the collective regulation of working life has occurred mainly in the private sector, and manual workers have been the most affected. The profile of organised (in trade unions) labour has changed in a way that was unpredicted, and which has attracted surprisingly little comment. By the 1990s the trade union movement had been lost to the British working class in the sense that managers and professional-grade employees were more likely to be members. The present-day trade union movement is no longer rooted in the working class.

A third feature of the British context has been the substantial shift of employment from the public to the private sector. This has been partly due to the series of privatisations – steel, oil, British Airways, gas, electricity, water, telecommunications, the railways, coal and others. A subsidiary source of the shift has been the outsourcing of non-core functions from public services – catering, cooking and laundering from schools and hospitals, for example. Also, instead of performing direct works, local authorities are now more likely to contract-out. This has happened to refuse collection and the management of some local authorities' leisure services. An outcome is far fewer blue-collar public-sector jobs. Managers and professional staff are still employed directly by schools, hospitals, universities and so on, which is the main reason why, across the country, these grades are now the most likely to be unionised. Roughly two million jobs have been shifted from the public to the private sector. The employees have found themselves in smaller, often non-unionised firms, in more competitive environments. Some sections of the privatised workforces have done rather well; train drivers, for example, are now among the country's best paid manual workers. Elsewhere, pay and other conditions of work have been degraded, and privatised jobs are invariably less secure (see Davidson, 1990; Nichols and Davidson, 1993). Until the 1970s public-sector employment was expanding and, in some ways, in times of full employment, set the standards that private businesses had to match. Nowadays the public sector is more likely to be 'market tested' against private-sector efficiency and practices.

A fourth aspect of the British context has been the high unemployment (compared with the 1945–70 period) that has prevailed since then. Levels have fluctuated, as ever, but have never fallen beneath a million. Official figures are generally accepted as underestimates (see Chapter 3, p. 61). They do not include young people who remain in education or training because they are unable to find jobs, others on government schemes, the early retired, or the unemployed who have taken the initiative in having themselves classified as unable to work on health grounds. Fieldhouse and Hollywood (1998) investigated what happened over the next 10 years to a sample of over 1000 individuals who were employed as coal-miners in 1981. By 1991, only 42 per cent were still in full-time employment; just 12 per cent were unemployed; but a larger number, 14 per cent, were (for benefit purposes) permanently sick. Twenty-five per cent were retired, although many of these had still to reach the normal retirement age.

In recent years Britain has had lower unemployment than most European Union countries, but Britain has a somewhat longer history than most countries of unemployment at 'modern' levels. The level in Britain peaked with the shake-outs from manufacturing industries in the early-1980s. So for many years now, in the parts of the country where most employment was in manufacturing and extractive industries, there have been gross surpluses of labour in the relevant labour-market segments. Over time it has become clear to all concerned that the only hope of displaced workers regaining employment has been to accept demotion, sometimes into so-called 'Mickey Mouse jobs' (see Bottomley *et al.*, 1997; Daniel, 1990). There has been more and more state pressure on the unemployed to accept whatever is available. The administration of the Job Seekers' Allowance and government Welfare-to-Work measures have pressured the unemployed to take part-time and temporary positions. Over time, there has been persistent downward pressure on the quality of jobs that the unemployed working class can realistically expect.

Old Jobs, New Jobs

There was an original working class whose core members worked in coal, shipbuilding, docklands, steel and other metal industries. Most of these workers were men; they had full-time, long-term jobs, and they worked in large, unionised establishments. There are still some such 'quality' jobs, but far fewer than in the 1960s. Where has the work gone? Much of it has been exported; capital and orders flow internationally more easily than labour. Other jobs are now done by machines instead of humans. Members of the original and new (1960s-type) working classes have experienced the changes with mixed feelings. Overall the UK workforce has been upgraded. Working-class parents always wanted their children to get on, if possible, rather than spend their working lives down the pits, on the docks, or in the steel mills, and prospects of ascent have improved (see Chapter 8). However, it has usually been impossible for the workers directly displaced from older industries to find jobs with banks or in computer software companies. And despite the overall upgrading, around 40 per cent of men and 30 per cent of women are still manual workers. So, given the zero-change in relative mobility (see Chapter 8), most working-class children must still remain in the working class.

Most of the manual jobs that have been created during the last 30 years are in service sectors. There are more high-level jobs in services, and computer software is one example – everyone has heard of Bill Gates. There is also money to be made in music – everyone has heard of Richard Branson. But the service sector contains a lot of low-level, part-time and casual jobs (see Walsh, 1990). The new working class is employed in shops, or more typically supermarkets and hypermarkets, in restaurants and hotels (the hospitality industries), and other businesses connected with leisure, sport and tourism. There is more work in call-centres, in security firms, and with contract cleaners. Some of these jobs look attractive to working-class school-leavers, especially those in hairdressing, fashion and music where work and leisure interests can be fused. Once in these industries, individuals are most likely to find that their work is mundane and low paid, though some young people still enjoy their associations with the industries in question. Many of the new jobs require an emotional input; the work is often demanding, though not skilled in the traditional sense. Employees are required to market themselves and to supply 'aesthetic labour'. Their appearances and demeanour in shops and restaurants are part of the services that the businesses offer. This also applies in air travel (see Tyler and Abbott, 1998). Such work can be stressful, and demeaning, it requires tacit skills rather than formal qualifications and training. There is still plenty of straight 'donkey work' but many of the new working-class jobs require the occupants to appear human, interested, and committed to the customers' satisfaction.

Most of the new service-sector jobs are in small establishments (compared with shipyards and steel plants). The new working class is fragmented, and these employees are rarely in trade unions. The work is quite likely to be at odd, variable hours, and many of the jobs are part-time. Workforces in consumer services need to expand and decline alongside consumer demand. Many of the businesses themselves are fragile, unable to offer security let alone long-term careers. For the new millennium working class, the kind of leisure society that has been created is not one in which they work shorter hours, for more pay than in the past, and have acres of free time and the money to enjoy it; it is one in which they service other people's and sacrifice their own leisure routines, and cannot afford to become high-spending consumers when they have free time (see Seabrook, 1988).

Labour market participation by working-class (and middle-class) women has continued to rise. So there are now more dual-earner working-class households than in the 1960s. Most of the new manual jobs created since the 1960s have been in occupations, or on schedules, customarily considered suitable for women. As regards their own labour-market opportunities and responses, for working-class women the trends of the 1950s and 1960s have continued. But it has been different for working-class men; most of the working-class jobs that have been lost have been men's jobs. Hence the higher rate of unemployment among men, especially working-class men. In some households the woman has become the main breadwinner, though rarely the sole breadwinner on a long-term basis (if she is living with a male partner). Families can usually live almost as well, and sometimes just as well, on state benefits as on a woman's wage. Since the 1970s women have possessed the legal right to equal opportunities, but real progress has been slow. There are still mainly men's jobs and mainly women's jobs. On average women are still paid less than men, mainly because women's jobs tend to be lower paid, but some women have been entering what were formerly male enclaves. At first there were so-called 'token women', who often felt uncomfortable on car assembly lines, in the oil fields, and in garage workshops, but nowadays women have more than a token presence in most occupations. The age of the trail-blazers has passed. There has been a trend towards men taking what were formerly women's jobs, but this trend has been weaker than the inroads that women have made into what were formerly men's occupations. There are fewer attractions for men in breaking down gender divisions at work. The jobs on the other side – as care assistants, in word processing, cleaning and so on – are not powerful magnets. Some of the occupations that are now recruiting 'new men' may have their status enhanced, eventually. In the short term the men who have taken these jobs have often felt de-masculinised; they have known that the jobs will not enable them to act as family breadwinners. There has been talk of a crisis of masculinity among young working-class males: unable to obtain men's jobs, unemployed while their female peers are earning, unable to take out a girlfriend, let alone support a family.

So are the women alright? Not really. Overall they are still paid less than men. Working-class women's earnings are rarely sufficient to support a home and family, yet they now face a shortage of working-class male breadwinner partners. More women have been experiencing single parenthood, and hitherto normal patterns of working-class family life have been undermined by economic restructuring. Government advice to impoverished working-class women has been to get off welfare and into employment. Governments are usually keen to reduce their welfare spending, if this can be done painlessly, but a problem in this case is that single women with dependent children and women with unemployed male partners are unlikely to improve their standards of living substantially – not on a woman's wage. Even dual-earner working-class families are unlikely to be able to afford child care at commercial rates. Government advice at this point has been to urge people to train, acquire more skills and climb the occupational structure into better jobs. Fine when the strategy works, but it cannot work for everyone where roughly a third of all jobs are lower-level (working-class). The male breadwinner model once worked (admittedly with problems) for working-class men and women, now it must seem to many that nothing works satisfactorily. Its current disorganisation and weakness become manifest when problems are defined (in the political system) in ways that offer no solutions for substantial sections of the working class.

At this point it is necessary to stress the difference between disorganisation and all-round immiseration. There are still plenty of working-class men in well-paid jobs in car plants, construction and chemicals, for example. Earnings have risen faster than prices for people in such 'quality jobs'. In the 1980s many working-class families who were council tenants were able to become home-owners. Some bought shares and made windfall profits during the privatisations of nationalised industries, and those with savings are likely to have gained further windfalls during the conversions of building societies into banks. To repeat, the affluent worker is not extinct.

Inequalities within the working class have widened. Not all council tenants were able to purchase, and some did not want the millstone of the particular dwellings that they occupied. High-rise flats were unpopular with tenants, and were left largely in council ownership. 'Sink estates' have been created where few properties have been privatised, and where most of the rent-paying families are on social security. These estates are characterised by their sky-high rates of unemployment, single parenthood and crime. Residents in these districts have above-average rates of criminal conviction and victimisation.

The general upgrading of the occupational and social class structures since the 1970s has been accompanied by a general rise in children's and young people's educational attainments. This is exactly what any sociologist would have predicted, but this has not prevented governments using the trend as a sign that their particular educational policies are succeeding. The schools that have not shared fully in the educational success story tend to be those that recruit most of their pupils from neighbourhoods populated by the more disadvantaged sections of the working class. 'Sink estates' containing 'sink schools' do not surprise sociologists, but successive governments have reacted by castigating the teachers.

The proportion of ethnic minorities in the working class, as in the country as a whole, has risen since the 1960s. The last chapter explained that all the minorities (except Indians) have above average rates of unemployment, but the majority of adults in all the minority groups are in fact in work. Since the 1960s the minorities have been dispersed – throughout the occupational structure and all types of housing. However, they are now overrepresented on most of Britain's 'sink estates' and in run-down inner-city areas. Indeed, in government statements, 'inner-city' has become a euphemism for multiracial.

Britain is a far more prosperous country now than in the 1960s, but a substantial section of the working class has not shared the benefits. The country as a whole is now spending much more on motoring and holidays, but roughly a third of all households are car-less and take no holidays away from home.

Even for those manual employees who have hung on to decently paid jobs, life at work has become tougher. In the larger firms which still offer quality jobs, managements have been asserting their right to manage. Even if the workforces are unionised, the trade unions are not necessarily consulted. Personnel management has been replaced by so-called human resource management. Businesses have made themselves lean and mean: no slack is carried. 'Featherbedding' and heavily racheted overtime rates have been eliminated on the docks, in coal and in print. None of these are 'the greatest game' any longer; not for the employees at any rate (see Prowse and Turner, 1996; Turnbull and Vass, 1994). Managements have asserted themselves not out of malice, but because they have been exposed to stronger competitive processes (a result of globalisation), and the availability of new technology has magnified the potential rewards for revamping the entire labour process. The Fleet Street bosses never wanted to carry excess staff in their print works, and computer technology made it possible to off-load the lot. Firms have embraced total quality management; which means expecting top standards from everyone, all the time. Customers are prioritised; costs are reduced wherever possible; and workers have little choice but to acquiesce. They know that their own jobs could go in the next round of downsizing, delayering or outsourcing. Labour market conditions have meant that a typical route into such 'quality' jobs has been to succeed against hordes of fellow applicants, often for positions that are initially temporary or part-time, then hope to be made full-time and permanent.

It is sometimes said that customers, the consumers, benefit from all this, implying that the changes are in everyone's interests because we are all consumers. But some can afford to consume much more than others. Inequalities at work – the gap between top and bottom earnings – have widened dramatically. The working-class features of working-class jobs have been accentuated; the employees have zero authority and negligible genuine autonomy at work, and their market situations are pathetically weak. Yet some still claim that class is dead, and that we are all in the same class now.

Has this been a one-sided, overly pessimistic account of how the working class has fared since the 1970s? I think not. There has been little unequivocally good news for Britain's working class. The advice of governments to working-class parents and their children has been basically correct: get qualified and get out. Unfortunately, in a society where over a third of all jobs are still working-class, it is impossible for everyone to follow this advice.

Disempowerment and Devaluation

To repeat, the working class is still a substantial class in terms of numbers. It is still the largest single class accounting for roughly 4 out of 10 male, and 3 out of 10 female employees. The working class is in long-term numerical decline, but this was not the main reason for its loss of power in the late-twentieth century.

The working class has lost the trade unions in the sense that most manual workers are no longer members, and they are no longer the section of the workforce that is most likely to be unionised. In the 1990s the working class lost the Labour Party: the leadership made it clear that it did not wish to be associated with any particular class, and that it valued its links with employers as much as its relationship with organised labour. The co-op has become just another retailer. Working men's clubs and other community, free-time organisations have been largely replaced by television and commercial leisure. The workplace and neighbourhood communities from which the original working class acquired solidarity have gone. The new working class of the 1960s is not extinct, but fewer manual workers today are even instrumentally attached to trade unions and a Labour Party which, they can realistically hope, will deliver what they want. The net result is a disorganised working class which has lost not only its capacity to act collectively but even to develop shared knowledge of its interests and common aspirations.

Most manual workers still identify themselves as working-class. This has not changed. Maybe those who never knew the original working class do not realise how the label has been devalued. Identifying with the working class is no longer associating oneself with a powerful group, or a way of life with features that others should envy. Beverley Skeggs' (1997) ethnographic study, conducted over 12 years among of a group of 83 young women from working-class backgrounds in an industrial town in north-west England, found that working-classness was treated as a stigma. The young women's abiding concern was to become respectable. This was expressed in their concern about dress, accent, and the places where they preferred to be seen. Skeggs appears to believe that, for women, to be working-class has never been respectable, but this is simply not true. The original working class constructed its own version of respectability. Skeggs' findings need to be set in the context of the post-1970s disorganisation of the working class, and the substantial absolute volume of upward mobility into the intermediate and middle classes among present-day young working-class women (see Chapters 5 and 8). Those who remain working-class nowadays are likely to feel that they are being left behind. Skeggs' evidence may not be generalisable; males may be different; so may young women in other parts of the country. Nevertheless, the signals from Skeggs' study must be worrying for anyone who hopes to rekindle working-class culture and politics. Maybe there is no longer a working class with which young people can identify, or want to be identified. Yes, there are still working-class jobs, but the trade unions and the Labour Party have been lost. There is no longer a working-class project. Traditional working-class values are ridiculed and declared outdated by virtually all public figures.

The working class at the start of this new millennium would like to get on, as was always the case, but many of its members' real concern today is to cling on and avoid descent into the ranks of the really poor, the long-term unemployed, the welfare dependents. These groups appear to be held in much lower regard by the employed working class than they are by more socially distant sociologists and other professional commentators.

The Underclass

Excluded Groups

Let us be clear at the outset here: as yet the best reason for having an underclass in class schemes is to maintain the (sociological) purity of the working class. Recognising intermediate classes serves much the same purpose in enhancing the sociological purity of the middle class. If lower-level office staff and the self-employed are excluded, our chances improve of identifying the characteristic life-chances and forms of consciousness of the remaining middle class (salaried managers and professionals), and similar arguments apply in the case of the working class. But in the latter case, the groups excluded, those who are left out and deemed beneath the working class, come nowhere near, as yet, to comprising an underclass which passes the standard class tests.

At present we have a series of what are best described as 'excluded groups', the most disadvantaged sections of a generally disorganised working class. One such group is the very poor who are mostly either retired and dependent wholly on state benefits, or child-rearing families where no-one is employed. Most of these families are single-parent, and such families can be found in all parts of the country. Another excluded group is often, though not necessarily, seriously poor, but is characterised primarily by its chronic unemployment, either long-term or recurrent. This group is concentrated in parts of the country where the original industries have closed or downsized radically, and is composed mainly of older displaced workers on the one hand, and, on the other, young people who are unable to establish themselves in the workforce. Another excluded group is composed of persistent criminal offenders with long court records and, in some cases, histories of judicial custody. An overlapping group comprises people who seek their livings from crime or in various unofficial economies. Another overlapping group is composed of people with serious alcohol or drug dependency problems. There is obviously a great deal of unofficial remunerative work in Britain given the scale of illegal drug use. Other excluded groups are composed of people with serious physical, mental or psychological disabilities which make it difficult for them to participate successfully either in employment or other normal social practices.

In the 1950s and 1960s it was realistic for probation and rehabilitation officers to aim to establish their clients in employment as a first step towards their full social integration. This first step was generally regarded as absolutely essential. Subsequently, in tougher labour market conditions, the job prospects of the groups in question have become bleak. Employers have become less willing, because they have less need, to take a chance and to carry 'passengers'. This applies even with employers who, in research interviews, express support for the principle of assisting marginalised groups to obtain employment (see Roberts *et al.*, 1997).

It is possible that an underclass will form in Britain if poor and/or unemployed parents rear low-achieving (in education) children, who fail to obtain proper jobs and develop careers in crime and other forms of unofficial work, then start rearing a further generation of disadvantaged children, thus repeating the cycle. This may happen if the levels of unemployment which have prevailed in Britain since the 1970s persist for another 30 years or so, but it has certainly not happened yet. What has happened is that sections of the working class have been detached: cut off from normal, respectable (1960s-type and subsequent) working-class ways of life.

Charles Murray

At the beginning of the 1990s the underclass debate in Britain was hijacked by Charles Murray, though the hijacking was not entirely his fault. Murray is an American social scientist with wide-ranging interests. In America his original reputation was based on *Losing Ground* (1984), an analysis of how inner-city blacks had been left behind despite the increasing prosperity of

America, and despite the expansion of a black middle class since the equal-rights legislation and affirmative action programmes of the 1960s. Alleging the existence of this heavily disadvantaged group in America was not controversial (see Wilson, 1987), but not so Murray's explanation, which was over-generous welfare.

In the early 1990s Murray was hosted in Britain by the *Sunday Times* (a Thatcherite newspaper at that time) and the Institute of Economic Affairs (a right-wing think-tank and publishing house). Murray was invited to consider whether an underclass similar to the one that he had discovered in America existed in Britain. His initial verdict was that a British underclass was 'emerging' (Murray, 1990). Four years later he found that 'the crisis' was deepening (Murray, 1994). Terms such as 'rabble' littered Murray's description, and he argued that Britain's emergent underclass was characterised not so much by its lack of work and poverty as by its attitudes and lifestyles in which the unemployment and poverty were rooted. As evidence of an emerging underclass, Murray cited persistent unemployment among able-bodied young men, a rise in crime, especially violent crime, in high unemployment districts, and high rates of single-motherhood among young women in the same areas. Murray's emerging British underclass was composed mainly of native-born whites, though one would expect the black population to be overrepresented within any such class given its disproportionate tendency to remain stuck at the bottom of the class structure (see Chapter 8). Just as in America, Murray decided that over-generous welfare was the original cause of the formation of a British underclass.

Murray is a provocative and potentially persuasive writer, and it was impossible for sociology to ignore him. Indeed, for a time anyone using the term 'underclass' was suspected of being a Murray sympathiser. This was despite the term having been used previously in British sociology (Giddens, 1973; Rex and Tomlinson, 1979; Runciman, 1990). Previously the suggestion that an underclass was forming had been contentious, but the arguments had not been heated. Murray changed that.

Murray heated up the underclass debate by offering a crystal-clear (whether correct or incorrect) analysis, and spelling out the implications for social policy. It was this that generated all the heat. The underclass issue was drawn into social policy debates, and into the division of opinion as to whether the best way to attack poverty and unemployment was by being tough or tender. Immediately, a left-right division opened among those who believed that Britain did indeed have an emerging underclass. The left saw the underclass as victims of circumstances – of a society that failed to offer decent jobs for all, and to supply adequate welfare in the absence of employment (Field, 1989; Westergaard, 1992). The right claimed that the rest of the population were victims of 'workshy scroungers' or 'idle thieving bastards', sometimes but not always in more temperate language.

There has been a similar split over the causes of, and the appropriate policy response to, social exclusion. The left-view is that unemployment leads to poverty which excludes the victims from normal leisure and other social patterns, and eventually leads to political exclusion as those concerned become disillusioned with all the political alternatives, and because politicians with aspirations to office are reluctant to be identified too closely with the least advantaged. The right-view simply adds lack of qualifications, skills, motivation and appropriate attitudes to the head of this list.

Whether it is the disadvantaged's circumstances or attitudes which are responsible for their predicaments is really a fruitless, chicken-and-egg, argument. There was a similar inconclusive debate in the 1960s about whether a culture of poverty was the cause or consequence of the predicament. Even if the original and continuing background cause of social exclusion is a lack of work, it could still be the case that the culture developed in adapting to this situation becomes an additional impediment to the social and economic ascent of those concerned.

It has been pointed out that fear of the mob has a long history, as does the tendency of the privileged to blame the victims for their poverty, or at least to try to distinguish between the deserving and the undeserving poor. Murray's underclass theory is in some ways comforting for the already comfortable. It assures them that they are not to blame, and that spending more of their taxes on welfare will actually be contrary to the best interests of the recipients (Bagguley and Mann, 1992; Mann, 1991).

There are advantages in pulling the underclass issue out of the social policy arena, at least temporarily, and situating it within class analysis, then asking whether the underclass 'hypothesis' passes the normal class tests. These are: first, whether those concerned occupy distinctive work and market situations; second, whether they are a demographic entity with characteristic life-chances; and third, whether they have developed a characteristic type of consciousness and political proclivities.

Work and Market Situations

The underclass hypothesis has little difficulty with the first test. It is not difficult to demonstrate that there are indeed people whose work and market situations differ from those of all the (literally) working classes (Buckingham, 1999). The distinctive work situation is having none. The distinctive market situation is so weak that the people concerned are unlikely to obtain employment. The weakness may be due to their own attitudes and labour market behaviour – not looking for work seriously, and seeking to avoid rather than to obtain regular, official employment – or to personal or social characteristics which repel rather than tempt employers – disability of some description, criminal records, evident drug use or alcohol problems, or just long records of joblessness.

Simply being unemployed is insufficient to pass this class test. Around a third of the UK population appears to have experienced unemployment at some time during every five-year period since the 1970s. Many people's unemployment is one-off, or on just a few occasions during their working lives. School and university leavers often have spells of unemployment prior to commencing their careers. These periods are not spent in an underclass.

For other people, unemployment is recurrent. Most who register as unemployed leave the register within six months, but in many cases this is for temporary jobs or places on government schemes. Sometimes these positions act as stepping stones, but in other cases the 'black magic roundabout' leads back to unemployment. Then there are those who never join the 'roundabout' or who dismount and never try to 'ride' again. Very few people never work during their entire lives, but others spend prolonged periods without permanent, regular, official jobs.

Characteristic Life-chances

It is with the second class test that the underclass hypothesis stumbles. The long-term out-of-work, and the recurrently unemployed, are a variety of distinct groups with very different reasons for their prolonged or repeated unemployment. There are displaced workers who are nearing the normal retirement age. Then there are lone parents. Then there are convicted repeat offenders. Then there are people with chronic disabilities. Does it help in diagnosing any of these groups' situations to lump them all together?

It can also be argued that there is in fact no clear division between the long-term unemployed and the rest of the working class, but that the reality is a continuum ranging from those who are continuously and fully employed (though they may change jobs) at one end, through various types of sub-employment (occasional or recurrent spells out of work) to those who stay workless throughout their entire adult lives. People with these different experiences live side by side in the same working-class neighbourhoods (Byrne, 1995; Morris, 1992; Morris and Irwin, 1992). Does it make sense to try to draw a class boundary among them?

Now it is in fact possible to rescue the underclass hypothesis from what might appear to be a hopeless situation. First, the existence of a clear division is not a normal pre-condition for distinguishing any class. All class boundaries are blurred. The crucial issue is whether the people inside each boundary are a 'clump' (see Chapter 1) with a core whose work and market situations are qualitatively different from those of the cores in other classes. In the case of the underclass, it can be argued that there is indeed such a distinction between people who experience occasional spells out of work during careers which are spent primarily in regular, official employment, and people who never rise above short-lived temporary posts and spells on schemes of various types.

The criticism that the alleged underclass consists of disparate groups can also be disarmed. It can be argued that any class that is in formation (the middle class, for example) is likely to recruit members from various origins via many different routes, and that the crucial demographic test is not how the existing members arrived but the life-chances of those who are born into the class in question. Here there is strong evidence that multiple disadvantage does run in families. A 1970s study by Rutter and Madge (1976), which was conducted in the context of a contemporary 'cycle of disadvantage' debate, is often cited. This study found that only approximately a half of all children who were reared in extremely deprived circumstances became similarly deprived adults. The authors used this evidence to argue that a deprived background did not need to be a lifetime handicap, and that whether individuals escaped depended on the job opportunities that were available to them, and the assistance that they received. However, if just a fifth of children are reared in heavily disadvantaged circumstances (and the real figure was well-beneath this in the 1970s), a 50 per cent rate of inter-generational continuity represents heavily skewed life-chances.

Everything that we know about relative rates of social mobility and their rigidity across time and place (see Chapter 8) must lead us to expect that exceptional disadvantages will tend to be passed down the generations. There is in fact a wealth of evidence that unemployment tends to run in families (Payne, 1987, 1989), but this does not mean that all children or even most of the children born to parents in all the groups that pass the underclass's work and market situations test, will occupy the same positions as their parents. Much will depend on whether the shape of the class structure remains stable, or whether the underclass expands or contracts. It simply means that if Britain's workless groups do not diminish in size, then it is probable that over time there will be a core within the 'class' that is inter-generationally immobile.

Consciousness and Related Matters

On the third test the underclass hypothesis looks completely hopeless. There is large-scale survey evidence showing that the unemployed, even just the long-term unemployed, are just as keen to work as the employed population, and that the only difference in their political proclivities is that the unemployed are even more likely than those in employment to support the normal working-class choice of party, namely, Labour (Gallie, 1994). Studies of the long-term unemployed have found that most are ready and willing to seize any opportunity to work regularly, and that if given the chance they have little difficulty in adjusting to work routines (Marsden, 1982). These studies have stressed how unemployed adults typically struggle to maintain 'respectable' lifestyles, and to ensure that a work ethic is inculcated into their children (Allatt and Yeandle, 1991; Coffield *et al.*, 1986; Wright, 1994). Studies of young blacks have recorded some spectacularly high unemployment rates in inner-city districts, but have consistently found that their work aspirations and political views are thoroughly conventional (Connolly *et al.*, 1991).

Now it can be argued that members of an underclass are less likely than anyone else to feature in formal surveys because they are less likely to have permanent addresses and telephone numbers, and to be on electoral registers. It can also be argued that, up to now, most of the unemployed adults with normal work attitudes and political orientations have had prior histories of regular work. These are fair points, but they still do not amount to positive identification of an underclass.

There is case-study evidence from particular districts of the development of distinctive social practices and knowledge among some chronically unemployed groups of young people (and adults as well in some cases): detailed knowledge of the benefit system which enables individuals to ensure that they claim all their entitlements, sometimes coupled with a reluctance to 'sign-off' for fear of being unable to qualify again (Jordan and Redley, 1994); treating fiddly (unofficial) jobs as a normal way of topping-up benefit (MacDonald, 1994), and, in some cases, developing criminal skills and knowledge, and relying on these for a livelihood (Craine and Coles, 1995); and high rates of single-motherhood among unemployed young women. But while all these may be good examples of sociocultural differences *vis-à-vis* most of the population, they are neither common throughout the long-term unemployed nor political. It is possible to envisage common and distinctive political orientations developing over time – extreme radicalism and extreme apathy are equally plausible predictions. Some members of the hypothesised underclass may become involved in claimants'-rights groups; ethnic minority members could regard ethnic community organisations as their main political representatives. But all this is plain conjecture at present.

Verdict

A British underclass is at best a future possibility. The present reality is that a variety of disadvantaged groups have become separated from 'respectable' sections of the working class, which is only to be expected given the levels of unemployment since the 1970s and the deterioration in state benefit entitlements. The root cause of the re-creation of non-respectable groups has been the same economic restructuring that has disorganised most of the working class. The people did not suddenly change of their own accord in the 1970s and lose a former will to work. The explanation cannot be that non-employment became more attractive due to changes in the state benefit system because the changes have been in the opposite direction to what would have been required.

So can we bury the underclass concept? No, because it is a real future possibility. Before the mid-twenty-first century there could well be a British underclass if recent levels of unemployment persist, and if the state welfare regime is unchanged. To repeat, an underclass will be created if poor parents rear low-achieving (in education) children who leave school then become chronically unemployed themselves. The creation of an underclass will require those concerned to interact with one another more than they interact with members of any other classes, which is likely if they are concentrated within particular districts, and in doing so they are quite likely to develop a distinctive culture. This may tolerate and transmit skills required for criminal activities and work in the unofficial economies, and lifestyles which the wider society rejects. The consolidation of an underclass will require the second generation to rear yet another generation of heavily disadvantaged children by when the class will be a demographic entity with characteristic life-chances. At present its politics are difficult, really impossible, to envisage. Even so, the above future-gazing is not pure guesswork, it is based firmly on our knowledge of the normal conditions for, and processes of, class formation.

Summary

This chapter has described how Britain's original working class, then composed of the working masses, the bulk of the workforce, was created following the industrial revolution. Its culture arose from people's firsthand experiences of interdependence at work and in their neighbourhoods. Working-class culture became the 'soil' in which working-class organisations developed – brass bands, the co-op, trade unions and the Labour Party. The values that became enshrined in these organisations were rewarding merit, the right to work, solidarity, state guarantees of basic welfare, and the removal of key services – health care and education – from the marketplace.

The chapter has then discussed the debates (within and beyond sociology) of the 1950s and 1960s about the effects of the spread of affluence and other postwar changes on the working class. The embourgeoisement thesis was rejected by most sociologists; rather, it was argued that a non-traditional, privatised and instrumentally-oriented working class was being created.

The impact of the post-1970s economic changes, examined in detail in Chapter 3, on the working class was then examined. The changes have been bad news for Britain's working class. It has shrunk in size and it has been disorganised by the spread of unemployment and job insecurity; the loss of (mainly males') jobs in extractive and manufacturing industries; the loss of members and erosion of trade unions' rights which were both cause and effect of the industrial relations legislation of the 1980s and early-1990s; by ethnic diversity; and the crisis of working-class masculinity. The good jobs that remain have become less secure and the workers in these jobs are now under greater pressure in the workplace. Meanwhile, sections of the working class have been impoverished. They are concentrated in the inner-cities and on 'sink' council estates which have spectacularly high levels of unemployment, single parenthood and crime rates, and low educational standards.

Has a separate underclass been created? Not yet, but a series of 'excluded groups' have been separated from the working class proper, and during the twenty-first century it is possible that these groups will congeal into an underclass, especially if recent levels of unemployment and the gap between state benefit levels and average earnings are allowed to persist.

5

Intermediate Classes

Introduction

All other things being equal, one would expect class formation to be weak in the intermediate classes. This is partly because they are intermediate; neither at nor very close to the top with clear advantages to defend (like the middle class), and not at the bottom (like the working class) with everything to gain, so it might appear, from radical change. If classes are small, this will also work against their demographic integrity. One would expect high absolute rates of both inward and outward intergenerational mobility. In other words, the core memberships with intergenerational continuity should be quite small. Moreover, both the inflows and outflows from intermediate classes are most likely to be both upwards and downwards. It is different in the working class where, if we discount the alleged underclass, the only way to move is up. Conversely, in the middle class the characteristic concern is to avoid descent, and mobile recruits have nearly all moved up (the exception being those who descend from the upper class). Such tidiness is less likely in classes which are literally in the middle.

All told, therefore, we should not expect to discover well-defined lifestyles, forms of consciousness and political orientations. But all this assumes that all other things are equal, and in the real world this never applies.

Just two intermediate classes are examined in this chapter – lower non-manuals and the petit bourgeoisie (the self-employed and owners of small businesses). These classes are very different from each other; they have little in common except that both are intermediate – neither working-class nor middle-class. The lower non-manuals are a large, mainly female occupational group; they are demographically unstable intergenerationally, and socially amorphous with no distinctive lifestyle or political proclivities. This was the case in the past, remains so, and is most likely to be so in the future. The lower non-manuals' most significant class characteristic is arguably that they have not been absorbed into either the working class or the middle class. The petit bourgeoisie is small, but currently growing, mainly male, and has impressive intergenerational continuity. Its members

119

have not just a very distinctive work situation (working for themselves), but also a distinctive work-centred lifestyle and political enthusiasms, and they play important ideological and organisational roles in Britain's (and in other countries') politics.

It is possible to argue that additional intermediate classes could be identified and examined. The two main candidates are, first, foremen, chargehands and other supervisors of manual employees, and second, technicians and technologists. Deciding not to treat either of these groups as separate intermediate classes is consistent with conventional, present-day sociological practice, but as Chapter 2 recognised, there are always arguments about the classification of specific occupations, and groups of occupations. An embarassing (for sociology) fact of this matter is that we know little about the class characteristics of either of the candidate groups. Neither supervisors, technicians nor technologists are listed in the main sociological dictionaries where the petit bourgeoisie (or the self-employed) and non-manuals (or white-collar workers) are always present. Maybe supervisors and technicians have been unjustly ignored. Or maybe they are less significant than lower non-manuals and the petit bourgeoisie in not amounting to distinct classes of occupations.

In this book (as in the new official class scheme) supervisors of manual workers have been subsumed within the working class – part of the old and present-day aristocracy of labour. There are strong arguments for this placement. Supervisor is rarely a career-long status; supervisors of manual workers are usually ex-workers; and it is most likely that those concerned will regard themselves as having risen within, rather than out of, the working class when their working lives remain shopfloor-based.

Technicians and technologists are treated differently in this book: they are disaggregated (also as in the new official classification). Some, like laboratory workers, are grouped with the lower non-manuals. Others are treated as part of the working class – another section of the aristocracy of labour – with better-paid jobs, which usually require vocational qualifications, and where there is no grime. Computer technicians, and personnel who control production processes from computer consoles, and who maintain such technical systems, are treated in this way. Other technical grades are merged into the middle class. These include research and development, and other occupations into which university graduates may be recruited prior to gaining full professional status or rising to management positions.

As already admitted, we have only limited evidence about the class characteristics of these occupational groups. It is possible that this book is mis-locating them; there are always unresolved issues in sociology. That said, another fact of this matter is that the relocation of any of the groups would make little impression on the apparent overall shape of the class structure, or the character of any of the main classes. The locations of supervisors and technicians are not critical issues for class analysis, which will be the main reason why the occupations have not been studied more thoroughly.

Lower Non-Manuals

This intermediate class accounts for approximately 40 per cent of women employees (if they are classed by their own occupations) and 20 per cent of men. It is not a small class, if women are placed by their own occupations. There are more women in these jobs than in any other class of work, whereas there are more men in both the middle class and the working class.

The present size of the lower non-manual class is the result of the growth of this type of employment which began before the end of the nineteenth century, then accelerated throughout the first technological revolution in the modern office when typewriters, various types of calculating machines, duplicators and other mechanical aids were introduced. This wave of new technology did not reduce office employment; the effect was the exact opposite. The technology enabled offices to provide enhanced services for managers and customers, and the mechanised office facilitated the growth of large corporations. The offices coordinated everything, or enabled managers to do so. This was the era when big firms grew bigger, when central and local government were increasing their functions and the size of their bureaucracies. The result was armies of office workers who flocked into city centres every weekday morning and departed in the late-afternoons. Large organisations appeared to have insatiable appetites for qualified school-leavers who could fill these positions, and, following the 1944 Education Act, an expanded secondary school system delivered the labour supply that was needed.

We are now well into the second technological revolution in the modern office. Ours is the age of electronic information technology – the computer, word processor, fax, E-mail and photocopier. Some jobs have been lost but, up to now, just as many new office jobs have been created. Once again, the overall effect has not been to decimate employment but, in some organisations, to intensify administration and enhance the service. It is now possible to despatch thousands of standard but personalised letters during few minutes at a keyboard. Airlines can now profile individual passengers' travel routines and send out offers accordingly. Prior to the technology being introduced, these operations would not have been mounted. Nevertheless, some types of work have been withdrawn from offices; I am personally keying-in this text for example. It was different before we all had PCs; manuscripts used to be written by hand then typed-up by secretaries, and making alterations was labour-intensive. Nowadays we generate more output but have fewer secretaries in the department office. Elsewhere, as in universities, managers and professional-grade staff can often do it themselves just as conveniently as through an office. It is as easy to check one's own E-mail as to ask someone else for a print-out. Some organisations have found that customers can be enabled, and may actually prefer, to serve themselves, using automated cash machines rather than dealing with human bank staff, for example. So some organisations, including the major banks, are now reducing employment in their office grades. Up to now there has been no overall contraction, but the growth of office employment appears to have ended. The current expansion is higher up, in the management and professional grades.

It is not easy to specify exactly what all lower non-manuals have in common. They are not all in offices. This is just a convenient shorthand though the office is the class's most common workplace. The lower non-manuals include laboratory staff, customs officers, nursing and teaching assistants. Some non-office occupations were demoted into the working class during the twentieth century; this happened to gardeners, domestic cleaners, ancillaries in hospitals and other care establishments, and most shop and supermarket staff. The character of the jobs (their work and market situations) changed, and hence how the jobs were regarded in society at large, and in sociology's class schemes. It is a long time since anyone in sociology treated the non-manual label literally. All jobs involve some physical activity, but measuring the extent to which jobs are manual and non-manual is not part of the process of placing them in any of the current class schemes. This makes it quite remarkable that the terms manual and non-manual remain part of everyday discourse. People seem to know intuitively which group most occupations fall into. Sociologists can argue that lay people are responding to differences in occupations' work and market situations that they experience without knowing exactly what it is that makes the difference. That said, the lower non-manuals are the class that is defined by what it is not rather than by what it actually is. The occupations have some middle-class features, like hierarchical relationships at work so that most staff are senior to someone else, and have at least modest career ladders to ascend. These features separate the occupations from the working class, but the occupations are clearly not management or professional.

Actually it has only been during the last half century that we have been able to say 'clearly' not management or professional. At the beginning of the twentieth century most future managers and professionals started in the office, usually at age 16, then worked up. At that time clerks were definitely part of this milieu – perhaps lower middle-class, but definitely middle-class. At that time, attempts to define the middle-class usually settled upon style of life, attitudes and culture. Non-manual jobs were too heterogeneous to supply definitive characteristics. This was at the time when most jobs were manual. The working class was by far the largest class, and, in a sense, the most important feature that other occupations had in common was that they were not working class. By the 1940s and 1950s the middle class was generally perceived as threatened: by higher taxation and the material advances that were being achieved by the working class which were seen as undermining the middle class's way of life and status, and also by the expansion of the white-collar grades which was creating diversity and specialisation (Lewis and Maude, 1949). Most commentators at that time deplored the threat to the English middle class, just as, later-on, the passing of the original working class was regretted. It was at this time that a clearer division was opening between the new middle class proper of managers and professionals on the one hand, and other non-manual grades, those that have subsequently become clearly intermediate.

Office work is very different today than it was 100 years ago, but we need to digress into history in order to understand the current class locations of office staff. The grades were initially placed in modern organisational hierarchies at the same time when the original working class was being formed, and the grades have tended to remain where they were initially placed. There is a parallel in the working class: the original working-class culture has weakened but it is still not extinct.

The Blackcoated Worker

No-one talks about the blackcoated workers any longer, except in sociology. The term has lived-on in sociology because it was the title of a book by David Lockwood, first published in 1958, but still a standard reference. Even in 1958 the blackcoated worker was almost extinct. The phrase refers to the standard working attire of male middle-class employees in the nineteenth and early twentieth centuries. They wore black jackets and striped trousers – a modified version of the morning suit (still often worn at weddings). By the 1950s the attire was worn for work only by a few bank staff in London and by some city solicitors and barristers. Other men were wearing the dark 'lounge suit' which remained normal male office attire until 'dressing down' began to spread in the 1990s. By the 1950s it had become more common to describe the relevant staff as 'white-collar' rather than blackcoated. 'White-collar' was appropriate because the men all wore white shirts and ties. The white shirts usually had detachable starched collars which would be changed every day while the shirt might be worn all week. People had less-extensive wardrobes than nowadays, and, before the days of automatic washing machines, clothes were not usually washed after being worn just once. Office dress codes are somewhat different today; even when men are still expected to wear suits, their shirts can be coloured, so white-collar has become another dated term. Do we need a replacement? Probably: dress remains a way in which people signal their class positions.

It has puzzled some, and annoyed others, that office workers have always tended to locate themselves above the working class (though nowadays they are just as likely to describe themselves as working-class as middle-class). Things have changed in this respect, but it still holds that despite their employee status, and, in many cases, lower than average manual earnings, many still regard trade unions as not for them and fail to support the working class's normal political choice, the Labour Party. Marxists used to dub these people as falsely conscious.

This was the context in which David Lockwood (1958) conducted his historical study of modern office work and workers. His book, now regarded as a sociological classic, charted developments from the nineteenth century up to the time of writing in the 1950s. The book's argument was that office workers who regarded themselves as middle class were not falsely conscious, but were responding to objective features of their market, status and work situations. Until the 1950s, few (non-Marxists) doubted that office workers were part of a single, if not solidaristic and completely homogeneous, middle class. They were described by others, and mostly described themselves, as lower middle-class, definitely not working-class (Crossick, 1977; Lewis and Maude, 1949; Wright Mills, 1956). In a sense, Lockwood provided a sociological justification/explanation for this.

It had always been the case that, just like manual employees, office staff sold their labour power. But Lockwood pointed out that recruits into offices had required additional, scarce skills; namely, the standards of literacy and numeracy needed to handle correspondence and to keep ledgers by hand. Their rewards for these skills were not necessarily higher pay, but greater security, fringe benefits such as sickness pay, holiday leave, and sometimes pensions, that were not offered to manual workers. In other words, office staff had distinctly superior market situations.

Lockwood argued that the status situation of the blackcoated worker was also rather different to the manual employee's. Future office workers were likely to be educated separately, in secondary schools. Normal street attire (like black coats) could be worn when going to and from work, and while at work. Hours of work were shorter in the office which was usually physically separate from 'the works'. With their superior rewards, office workers were able to live in better, respectable districts, and do respectable things like spend annual holidays away from home. Lockwood argued that office staff had not been deluding themselves if they believed that their status was superior.

The typical work situations of office staff were also different. Most worked in small offices, counting houses in the businesses that handled cash. Even in large organisations, the white-collar employees would be scattered across numerous small offices, all performing specialist functions. There would be cost clerks, sales clerks, wages clerks, and so on. In these office environments, workers would experience personal relationships with superiors, and sometimes, in the smaller businesses, with their employers. Office staff were invariably graded; there was always a hierarchy. So newcomers could anticipate promotion, which was more or less certain to come their way in time. Their dream was that eventually they might become so experienced and knowledgeable about their bosses' affairs as to be considered indispensable, and offered partnerships. This rarely happened, but office staff did rise progressively in seniority. Usually everyone in an office would have a different rank, signalled by job title, amount of working space, and maybe physical proximity to the employer. Promotion was a normal expectation, and a normal part of the office worker's experience, unlike in the works where it was exceptional.

Lockwood noted that during the twentieth century, superior clerical occupations had been created in some large businesses such as banks and insurance companies, and in central and local government. These positions offered higher pay, but there was no possibility of partnership, the dream of office staff in smaller enterprises.

Of course, all this was most typical in the early part of the period about which Lockwood wrote, before the Second World War and earlier in the twentieth century. *The Blackcoated Worker* told the story of how, over time, the market, status and work advantages of office staff had been gradually eroded. The work situation in offices was changing; open-plan designs had become increasingly common from the interwar years onwards, creating situations similar to factories where large numbers of employees, all on the same grade, did very similar jobs. Also, machinery had entered the office – the first technological revolution was well-underway by the 1950s. As a result, many office staff were being treated in much the same way as manual employees; as appendages to machines – the mechanised office bore a resemblance to the factory production line. Over time, the status advantages of office staff had also been eroded. After 1944 everyone attended a secondary school; manual workers were being rehoused to suburban council estates, and they were receiving better treatment at work; they were being provided with washrooms and industrial clothing at the workplace which enabled them to journey to and from work in normal street clothes, if they wished. The office worker's market advantages had been eroded also. The standards of literacy and numeracy that mechanised office jobs required had become near-universal; the welfare state had made pensions, sick pay and holidays into universal entitlements. Finally, office staff were encountering the kind of promotion blockage than had always existed above the working class. Large organisations had begun recruiting higher education graduates directly into their management grades and as professional trainees. So lower-level office staff were facing earlier or tighter career ceilings. In other words, their prospects were deteriorating.

But Lockwood was at pains to stress that these changes were not from one extreme to another. There had always been office recruits who had been fast-tracked up the hierarchies. In the past these individuals had sometimes been exceptionally qualified, but they were more likely to have been relatives, or sons of friends, of the owners. Non-privileged staff might have felt resentment, but there was no resistance. They continued to emulate rather than display antagonism to those ahead of themselves, and there seemed to be no reason why increased graduate recruitment should change this.

Nevertheless, as the above changes had occurred, office staff had become more likely to join trade unions. By the 1950s there were already high levels of unionisation among central and local government staff, in some other public services, and in banking and insurance. It was possible to envisage the entire office grades coming to regard their jobs as basically working-class, and themselves as part of the labour movement, available for mobilisation by the Labour Party. So even if manual workers became a minority of the workforce, as was imminent in the 1950s, there would still be a working-class majority. However, Lockwood pointed out that trade unions had become common among office staff only in some business sectors, reflecting, in his view, that although many office staff had lost some of their former advantages, the occupation was far from fully proletarianised.

Lockwood also noted (he could not have failed to notice) that as the relative position of office staff had deteriorated, the occupations had been progressively feminised. At the beginning of the twentieth century, the typical office worker had been a male clerk – the blackcoated worker. At that time women were permitted only limited inroads. Very early-on the job of typist was deemed suitable for women, but by the 1950s very little was still deemed unsuitable and there was a clear female majority. Office work had been largely feminised. What difference, if any, was this making to the class location of the employment?

White-collar Proletariat

Between 1979 and 1981 Rosemary Crompton and Gareth Jones (1984) conducted another major sociological study of office staff. This was not a historical investigation; it was a 'What's happening now?' type of enquiry. It was a study of office jobs and staff in a bank, an insurance company, and a local authority in a city in south-east England. The business sectors were chosen because they had been responsible for much of the expansion of office work over the previous 20 years.

Crompton and Jones' verdict was that, by the 1980s, in the organisations that they examined (and by implication in many others also), in a strictly technical sense clerical work had been thoroughly proletarianised. Most recruits were early (16-year-old) school-leavers, and neither exceptional ability nor qualifications were really necessary. The jobs were at best semi-skilled. Recruits were expected to acquire the necessary skills on a learn-as-you-go basis, and there was nothing akin to apprenticeship or professional training. Newcomers were expected to be on the job and earning their salaries virtually from the start. Promotion prospects were limited; individuals had realistic chances of progressing into more skilled and senior clerical jobs, and possibly into supervisory posts in the offices, but not into management. Earnings in the office grades were usually inferior to those of skilled (mostly male) manual workers. Even so, Crompton and Jones did not accept that clerical employees were clearly separate from what Goldthorpe had described as the service class (the middle class in this book). Clerks were, after all, still in offices, not the works.

Needless to say, by the time of the Crompton and Jones enquiry, the feminisation of office work was even more advanced than in the 1950s. The vast majority of the employees who were studied were women. Now in recent times a politically correct reaction to this has been to say, 'So what?' However, Crompton and Jones realised that the sex of the staff was making a difference. It has often been said, in respect of women's work, that men would not stand for it. Crompton and Jones were certain that the employers would have been unable to fill their office vacancies with equally qualified males. They were able to seek, and obtain, 16–18-year-old females with good qualifications (for their age). As we shall see in Chapter 8, women with most levels of qualifications have tended to obtain inferior labour market returns to equally-qualified men. Young men with the qualifications preferred of office staff by banks, insurance companies and local authorities might nowadays seek apprenticeships, jobs in which they will be trained up to professional status, and, at the time of the Crompton and Jones study, they were more likely than young women to remain in full-time education taking three or more A-levels, then seek places in higher education.

Notwithstanding all this, Crompton and Jones did not attach undue significance to the gender balance and divisions within the offices that they studied. They noted that males and females tended to perform rather different tasks, and that the males were more likely to study for further qualifications, and to receive promotions, but only to the higher rungs of the clerical grades. For both sexes, there was a technical base for the development of proletarian attitudes, but also good reasons why this was unlikely to happen, in the short term at any rate.

In their book, Crompton and Jones speculated as to why the employers wanted well-qualified recruits in their offices. The jobs did not appear to require this, at least in a technical sense. Crompton and Jones noted that qualifications were a way of sifting out the less-reliable, less-compliant (the well-qualified would have been 'good pupils' at school), and others who might be unacceptable in office environments. They also noted that the qualifications that were demanded defined the jobs as superior to others that 16-year-old school-leavers might seek.

Female recruits into such jobs in the early 1980s, and today also, are likely to be only too willing to believe that they themselves, and the jobs that they are entering, are a cut-above. The main alternatives for 16–18-year-old females are still in factories and shops. Office jobs are superior in all respects – the pay, security, prospects, being able to dress up for work and having a clean environment to work in. Office staff have mostly performed better at school than female contemporaries who take jobs in factories and shops. In this sense, for young women at any rate and given the gender segmentation that persists in the workforce, it remains as true today as in the period covered by David Lockwood's study that there are objective grounds for office staff continuing to regard themselves and their jobs as rather better.

Trade Unions

Since the 1970s the significance of trade unionism in debates about office (and other) workers' class locations has been reassessed. Previously, ever since white-collar trade unions had been studied, from the 1930s onwards in practice, the prevalence (density) of white-collar trade union membership had been taken to indicate the extent to which an occupation had been proletarianised, and the extent to which the workers identified themselves as working-class and with a broader labour movement. So David Lockwood noted the growth of white-collar trade unionism as evidence of a trend, but stressed the trade unions' limited inroads as a sign that office work was still well-short of full proletarianisation. By the time of Crompton and Jones' study, the levels of trade union membership in banks, insurance companies and local authorities (high in all three) were regarded as only marginally relevant to the workers' class locations and identities.

During the intervening years the meaning attached to trade-union membership in the wider society had changed. In the 1960s Kenneth Prandy (1965) had contrasted two types of occupational associations – professional bodies and trade unions – that recruited professional-grade employees. He argued that professional bodies were basically status organisations – they tried to advance their members' interests by raising their status in the eyes of employers and the public at large. Trade unions, he argued, were class organisations which operated through bargaining strength. Prandy argued that professional organisations could possess some class features, and that white-collar unions could possess some status characteristics. This line of thought was developed by Robert Blackburn (1967) in a concurrent study of bank clerks where he argued that a high level of trade-union membership had been achieved only by a loss of unionateness, meaning characteristics hitherto associated with blue-collar unions such as willingness to strike and engage in other forms of collective action.

It is now clear with hindsight that things were changing. Just as it only takes enough manual workers to purchase washing machines and foreign holidays for these to cease to be middle-class status symbols, so, in a similar way, it is necessary only for enough non-manual employees who regard themselves, and are regarded by others, as middle-class, to join trade unions for the behaviour to lose its working-class connotations. By the 1970s, researchers were noting that white-collar trade-union membership levels were responsive to much the same circumstances as blue-collar membership. White-collar employees were most likely to be unionised when they were employed in large concentrations, and when in both objective and subjective senses they were separated from management. It was also noted that white-collar trade-union membership rose when unions were recognised by employers, and when the political climate was favourable, meaning when collective bargaining was being encouraged rather than discouraged by the government of the day (Bain, 1970). By the 1970s, trade unionism had come to be, and was recognised as, something that could be linked to various types of consciousness and used for a variety of class and other social objectives. It could indicate proletarian circumstances and outlooks; or, alternatively, trade union organisation and militant action could be used by white-collar workers to prevent their proletarianisation, or in attempts to improve their standing *vis-à-vis* other non-manual groups (Roberts *et al.*, 1972, 1977).

Already in the 1970s there appeared to be a convergence in the significance of trade unionism within working-class and non-manual occupational groups. Manual workers' attachments to their unions had often become instrumental rather than solidaristic (see Chapter 4), motivated by a desire for personal or sectional rather than class-wide benefits. White-collar trade unionists usually have exactly the same motives.

Demographics

Most office jobs are filled by men and women from working-class back-grounds (Goldthorpe, 1980; Marshall *et al.*, 1988); they greatly outnumber the intergenerationally static and those downwardly mobile from the mid-dle class. This will be a product of the changing shape of the class struc-ture. The working class was by far the largest class up to the Second World War. Subsequently there was a sustained expansion of office jobs and it was structurally inevitable that most of these positions would be filled from outside, in practice from beneath since the working class was the largest, and a contracting, class. Throughout the twentieth century, obtain-ing an office job was the main way in which girls, and rather fewer boys, from working-class homes were able to 'get on'. In the latter decades of the century, office work was a step upwards for girls from ethnic-minority backgrounds.

The outflow picture has been a little more complicated. Here there has been a clear difference between the life-chances of boys and girls whose fathers occupied lower-level white-collar positions. Very few such boys have entered the same type of employment; they have either moved up into the middle class or down into the working class. Ever since the Second World War it appears that routine non-manual fathers have con-sidered their type of employment unsuitable for their sons. Dale's (1962) study of clerks in industry found that only seven out of the 208 who were interviewed wanted their sons to become clerks. The occupation was per-ceived, accurately from all the evidence that we have, to be declining in attractiveness. Fathers who were spending their own careers in the office grades appeared to feel that their sons would be better advised to train for skilled manual work if they were unable (as the fathers would usually have preferred) to qualify for management or professional careers.

The situation with girls has been rather different. The daughters of lower-level white-collar fathers have entered office jobs themselves, and risen into the middle class proper, in roughly equal numbers (around 40 per cent each). Far fewer daughters than sons have descended into the working class. There has been much more intergenerational continuity between lower-level white-collar fathers (and presumably mothers also) and their daughters, than between the parents and sons. The intergenera-tional step upwards from the working class into the lower non-manual grades appears to have been more secure for females than for males. In the next generation the males have been the more likely to step backwards, though neither the fathers nor the sons have necessarily have seen it this way. The explanation will be partly that there have been far more women's than men's jobs in the office grades, partly that there has been an outlet into apprenticeships in skilled manual trades for males, and partly because parents, teachers and others may well have taken the view that a job in an office is fine for a reasonably qualified girl, but less so for an equally qualified boy.

Times may be changing in this respect, though probably not to the extent suspected by most people in higher education. It is certainly true that girls with good academic qualifications are now more likely to go to university than to leave education at age 16 or 18 and take a job in an office. The girls no doubt hope that higher education will lead to professional or management positions, but in practice many still find that their initial jobs are in the intermediate grades. Some work in call centres; the graduate secretary has become more common – a status symbol for senior managers; and what about the two-thirds of all girls who still do not enter higher education? After age 16 they are less likely than boys to study technical subjects; in the sixth forms they tend to read arts or social sciences. On vocational courses they are most likely to study 'care' or business/commercial options. There are still plenty of young women entering office jobs.

Class and Gender in the Office

Since office work was feminised, the interest of class researchers has waned, excusably if it is only male occupations that matter as far as class is concerned, but this argument is far from won (see Chapter 2). There have been plenty of studies of women and employment over the last 20 years, but these have paid much more attention to how their situations are gendered than to their class positions. Beverley Skeggs' (1997) study of young women in north-west England, and Valerie Walkerdine and colleagues' (2000) study of girls growing up in London, are rare exceptions. In studies of women at work, there have been occasional pieces on office staff (see, for example, Truss, 1993), but far more on the smaller numbers of women who enter management, engineering and other professions. We have learnt about how these women have been obtaining post-entry qualifications, opting for nearly-unbroken full-time careers, still encounter disadvantages, but are nevertheless breaking through former glass ceilings and pressuring males' promotion prospects (see, for example, Crompton and Sanderson, 1986). Males with intermediate, ambiguous class locations have received more attention than secretaries. In addition to the self-employed, technicians and technologists have been the subjects of some enquiries into whether they are a genuinely intermediate group, or best regarded as a new aristocracy of labour, or part of an enlarged middle class (see Bain, 1972; Carter, 1985; Smith, 1987). As explained above, the view taken in this book is that the class location varies from one technical occupation to another.

Maybe all that needs to be said about female office workers has already been said. Office jobs were initially designed for men, and, by agreement among all commentators and the men themselves, the jobs were then on the fringe, but definitely part of the middle class. Those were the days when office workers gained an intimate knowledge of their employers' businesses. They needed to be trustworthy and rewarded sufficiently to secure their loyalty. Then came office mechanisation, a vast expansion of office employment, and an influx of women. A gendered division of labour was established very quickly; men managed and supervised while women operated the machinery, and took on other feminine tasks, including customer-care in recent years (see Halford and Savage, 1995). The gendering has been strongest in the manager–secretary/office wife relationship. The latest generation of new technology has been absorbed into relationships that were already gendered. At first computers were considered masculine, but very quickly this was restricted to systems analysis and programming, and women were left with the operating.

In their study, Crompton and Jones (1984) chose to stress how all clerks, males and females, had limited promotion prospects. These prospects were being squeezed by the growth in the number of clerks, and the simultaneous growth in overhead recruitment into management and professional careers. Crompton and Jones proceeded to discuss the possibilities, and the impediments to, the development of a proletarian consciousness throughout the clerical grades. Yet it was already known that men and women in lower-level white-collar jobs were usually performing rather different tasks, and were in somewhat different career situations. The males were, and still are, administering, and were, and still are, by far the more likely to be promoted, because women in the grades who become mothers (the majority) rarely pursue full-time continuous careers. This is why, in respect of the males, the Cambridge class researchers (see Chapter 2) have argued that it is possible for lower-level non-manual occupations to be proletarianised, but not the incumbents (Stewart *et al.*, 1980). It can be argued that, rather than occupying distinctly intermediate locations, males in lower-level non-manual occupations are better conceptualised as located on the lower fringe of the middle class proper, as in the days of the blackcoated worker. It has been different for women. They have been more likely to occupy intermediate positions for life. This could change as career breaks shorten, if more of the women return to work on a full-time basis and claim their equal opportunities to be trained for career progression. But is this really likely? Young males and females with all levels of educational attainment, and who enter all types of occupations, may be equally career-minded (Bynner *et al.*, 1997; Roberts and Chadwick, 1991), but the current and likely future career rewards of those in ordinary office (and manual) jobs, and the relative (to earnings) costs of child care, are very different from those of women and their partners in middle-class occupations. Lower down the class structure, the male bread-winner model has been, and remains, a more rational family strategy (Creighton, 1996).

The continuities since David Lockwood wrote *The Blackcoated Worker* are startling. There are still superior office jobs in banks and insurance companies; the difference is that the old prospects of partnership in other firms, and of promotion to management from the basic entry grades in the superior jobs, have all but disappeared completely. And the other change, of course, is that most of the employees are now women. There is no reason to expect anything to change while 16–18-year-old female school-leavers still face the same basic choice – if not higher education, then shop, factory, office or, nowadays, a 'care' occupation. As in the past, office work will be considered attractive by those with the necessary qualifications, from working-class homes. Valerie Walkerdine and colleagues (2001) and Beverley Skeggs (1997) have both emphasised how keen these young women are to leave the working class. The office occupations that they enter are intermediate par excellence. There is no distinctive consciousness, lifestyle or politics. Ethnic diversity has simply added to the variety rather than broken up a distinctive culture linked to lifestyle and politics. The class identities that women office workers adopt continue to depend heavily on their fathers' or husbands' occupations, types of housing and so on. They are never likely to align overwhelmingly and unambiguously with either the working class or the middle class, or to develop a characteristic consciousness and politics of their own.

The Petit Bourgeoisie

Growth

Until the 1970s the petit bourgeoisie was in long-term decline. As Marx had predicted, small enterprises (pre-capitalist relics) were being squeezed out of the market or absorbed by larger companies. This process was most evident in retailing, the business sector with by far the largest number of small enterprises. By the 1970s the march of the supermarkets was already well-advanced, and in retailing the decline in self-employment has in fact continued. National chains selling clothing, toys, computers, carpets and so on have filled the new city-centre shopping precincts and out of town retail parks. Their advertising shapes consumer demands. Sometimes their bulk purchasing power enables them to pass-on lower prices to customers, and smaller independent shops have been unable to compete. We all deplore the demise of the small retailer; we would love the convenience of being able to pop out to the corner shop. But we still do our main food shopping by car, at more distant supermarkets, and head for the major stores at other times. Shopkeepers are still the largest, albeit contracting, single occupational group among the self-employed, but in other business sectors there has been a turnaround. The number of small enterprises has grown steeply. The self-employed now amount to 13 per cent of the UK workforce, just over three million people, roughly double the number and proportion in the 1970s. There has been a similar recent upward trend in all the advanced industrial countries, and Britain still has a lower rate of self-employment than most European Union states. This is due mainly, though not entirely, to there being fewer small farms in Britain. The prospects for further growth in the number of small enterprises in Britain are rather good, with most of the factors which have led to the recent growth still operating.

One reason for the growth of self-employment has been unemployment-push (see Bogenhold and Stabler, 1991). People who have been made redundant have sometimes used their lump sums (redundancy pay-offs) to establish their own companies. Many individuals who have been unable to find jobs have taken the initiative in creating their own, and there has been a great deal of survival self-employment. It has not always been the entrepreneurs' first choice. In the 1980s and early-1990s a government-operated Enterprise Allowance Scheme provided modest financial assistance for the unemployed who qualified and who wished to start their own businesses, but many of these businesses struggled. Robert MacDonald (1996) found that only 14 out of 86 young entrepreneurs who had been first studied when they were setting-up in the late 1980s were still in business in 1995. The young unemployed who try to create their own businesses have an extremely high failure rate (Kellard and Middleton, 1998), and well under 10 per cent of all the unemployed exit for self-employment (Metcalf, 1998). This does not mean that it is always inadvisable for the unemployed, even for the young unemployed, to try self-employment. Britain has probably the world leader among organisations that aim to assist disadvantaged young people to become self-employed – the Prince's Youth Business Trust (see BMRB International, 1997). The secrets of its success are being highly selective over who to assist, and providing continuing support throughout and following the start-ups.

Government policies have assisted new businesses, not just with the Enterprise Allowance that was available to the unemployed at one time, but also with the various support services – advice centres and suchlike – that have been created. In the 1980s the government claimed to be fostering an enterprise culture and cited the growth in the number of small businesses as evidence. In practice there was no evidence of cultural change.

Self-employment is a very old dream, especially within the working class. Nevertheless, the government in the 1980s did create a favourable ideological climate for, and offered modest forms of material assistance to, business starters. Enterprise was taught in schools and on Youth Training schemes. Taxes on incomes and wealth were reduced. A climate was created in which there was no shame, but pride, in being able to flaunt success and money. All governments have continued to be supportive towards small enterprises for one very good reason – they have realised that it is such businesses that have been responsible for most of the new job creation and net employment growth in recent years.

Unemployment-push has certainly not been the only factor in the growth of small enterprises (see Meager, 1992). New technology has been another, and it is an underlying and continuing factor in this growth. The latest generation of new technology has two important relevant features – it is small and cheap. This means that it is no longer necessary to be a giant company to do things the cheapest way and to obtain top-quality results. Quality publishing is now possible in any office, even from home. Small independent companies can produce recorded music of the same quality as the multinationals; and new technology has applications in most industries and occupations so that the effects are pervasive. Typists, design engineers and even radio broadcasters can do it from home.

Outsourcing (see Chapter 3, pp. 71–2) by large companies has been another engine behind the growth of small enterprises. This has been a way in which big businesses have made themselves flexible, and it has created new business opportunities, sometimes for staff displaced from the larger enterprises. People with office, craft and professional skills have often discovered that they can earn more in total, and provide themselves with greater security, by going self-employed and obtaining contracts from a number of businesses rather than by working full-time for any one of them.

Demographics

Small businesses and their proprietors are clearly a very mixed bag. There are many types of businesses, and even when the various kinds of professional consultants are excluded and placed in the middle class, we still have a motley collection of cleaning and security firms, shopkeepers, garages, builders, other service businesses, and so on. Should they all be grouped together? An alternative, in class analysis, is to return all concerned to the classes in which employed members of their occupations are located. The case for grouping them together is that they have such a distinctive, and common, work situation; namely, working for themselves, being the boss.

The businesses vary in size, turnover, profits and solidity. There are much higher annual birth and death rates among small businesses than among large companies. Some new businesses never grow beyond the micro-fragile stage. Others are quite substantial concerns with employees and turnovers in millions of £s. Some are long-standing 'family businesses'.

The amazing thing is that the proprietors, if not the businesses, do in fact share a great deal in common. First, they are mostly men. Over four-fifths of the people who are self-employed as a main occupation are male (Taylor, 1994). This is one of the two classes (the active section of the upper class is the other) which are most dominated by one sex (men in both cases). There are niches in business for women – in hairdressing, typing and fashion, for instance – but generally the business culture is masculine. As we shall see, the self-employed pride themselves on masculine values such as competitiveness, independence and individualism. And their work schedules are usually too long, and the hours are too varied, to be compatible with major domestic responsibilities.

Second, young people are underrepresented. Self-employment is usually not career-long. Most people who start businesses, especially those who then stay in business, do so having gained some experience in someone else's. The main exceptions are when children join family businesses, but even in these cases they are most likely to start off as employees rather than bosses.

In terms of ethnic mix, the self-employed are less dominated by whites than any other class. Indians, Pakistanis and Bangladeshis are overrepresented (Taylor, 1994). Britain's ethnic minorities have transformed the restaurant trade, and have also made a major impact in retailing. Business is one of the ways in which members of these ethnic groups are achieving individual and collective upward mobility in Britain.

What about mobility flows? Here, the Goldthorpe survey in the 1970s (Goldthorpe *et al.*, 1980) and the Marshall survey in the 1980s (Marshall *et al.*, 1988) produced broadly similar results from their nationally representative samples. Roughly a third of self-employed men have fathers who were also self-employed. This is a very respectable rate of intergenerational continuity; more than three times the level that would occur in an equal life-chances society. It is likely that the motivation, and some of the skills, that are needed to run a small business successfully will be passed down the generations in business families. Of those who are recruited intergenerationally from outside, there are roughly three times as many from the working-class as from the middle-class. There are roughly as many self-employed people with working-class as with business (self-employed) family backgrounds, and relatively few whose fathers were managers or professionals.

The outflow picture is rather different. There are broadly similar numbers of sons of business fathers who themselves run businesses, who enter the working class, and who enter the middle class. Intergenerationally, setting up in business is more likely to be a step upwards, or at least an attempted step upwards, from the working class than a step down from the middle class, no doubt due partly to the fact that the middle class has been expanding and the working class contracting over recent generations, and this trend is continuing. However, in the subsequent generation, the children of business fathers are just as likely to fall back into the working class as to continue their families' intergenerational ascent. We have seen that this applies also to males in the other intermediate, lower non-manual, class. All the evidence shows that intermediate positions are less secure than positions in the middle class proper. This is one justification (there are several others) for separating a middle class of managers and professionals in sociological class schemes, rather than lumping all non-manuals plus the self-employed into a single middle class.

Consciousness and Politics

It is all the more surprising given their diverse occupational make-up, the variations in the size, stability and longevity of the businesses, and the mixed origins of the self-employed in terms of social class and ethnicity, that they tend to share a very distinctive consciousness and political proclivities. With the exception of the ethnic minorities (see Chapter 9), the petit bourgeoisie is the most Conservative of all the social classes except possibly the upper class (Marshall *et al.*, 1988). Conservative here has a capital. The self-employed are not conservative in the sense of being content with the status quo. They tend to be angry, sometimes radical, Conservatives; but Conservatives they nearly all are. They have been the Conservative Party's infantrymen, providing cash and organisational inputs at local levels, just as big business has at the national level.

The self-employed have a distinctive set of values (see Bechoffer and Elliott, 1981; Blanchflower *et al.*, 1987; Nugent and King, 1979): they are individualistic, and proud of it; they believe that people should stand squarely on their own feet; they believe in independence; they also believe in hard work and discipline; and they are low on gambling spirit. Success is believed to follow hard work and enterprise, not pure luck. These values are likely to have driven the self-employed into, and are probably sharpened by their experience in, business.

The petit bourgeoisie have little time for government or most politicians, and they discriminate among politicians in their own preferred party. In the 1980s Margaret Thatcher was their hero, and the self-employed were among the staunchest Thatcherites in the country (Edgell and Duke, 1991). Thatcher appealed not just because she was a grocer's daughter but also for her evident determination to clamp down on state spending and reduce taxes (though she achieved neither), and to disempower the trade unions (where she was more successful). Usually the self-employed do not like government. They object to the number and levels of the taxes that they have to pay, and they also object to the torrents of paperwork that the government requires – for income tax, national insurance, VAT and so on. They resent all the health and safety, equal opportunities and other regulations that are liable to trip them up.

The self-employed do not like big companies. They are scathing about salaried managers and professionals (and civil servants, of course) with their inflated salaries, cushy jobs, security and pensions to follow. Many depend on trade that is put their way by large firms, but they dislike the way in which these customers will pay no more than rock-bottom prices, then pass on fantastic mark-ups. Then there is the speed, the leisurely speed, with which big firms tend to pay their bills. What is just normal bureaucratic delay in big companies means heavier interest charges on small businesses' bank overdrafts.

Needless to say, the self-employed have no time for trade unions, and their own workforces are rarely unionised. Many of these employers are adamant that they would not let trade unions through the door. Their view is that everyone should be independent and prove their own worth. Collective representation (for others) is anathema.

Nevertheless, the self-employed are not adverse to having their own interests collectively represented by trade associations, chambers of commerce and the Institute of Directors, for example. All these organisations confirm that the self-employed are difficult to organise. The business community does not like to be regimented, but it sees clear advantages in having its voice heard in local councils and at national government level.

Intolerance of others is a personality trait associated with self-employment (Blanchflower *et al.*, 1987). Of course, bosses can afford to be intolerant, within their own enterprises at any rate. This character trait will be nurtured in business, though it could also be the case that some of the self-employed would never have been comfortable working under someone else.

It must be said that the self-employed have grounds for feeling that they themselves earn everything that they receive. They do have a distinctive, work-centred lifestyle: they work long hours, and homes are usually workplaces even if the businesses have bases elsewhere. Every small business has hordes of competitors. Actions by central and local government, and by big companies, over which the self-employed can exert little control, can make a crucial difference. The withdrawal of a large order can be crippling, and a new competitor can always open across the street. A new road, or new parking restrictions, can decimate a business's custom. New parking charges, or failing to provide sufficient car parking space in a commercial district, can blight all the local businesses. Hence the small business community's perpetual vulnerability. They know it, and they feel it.

The Significance of the Contemporary Petit Bourgeoisie

The self-employed are not a historical relic, and they play an important role in the contemporary class structure. Thirteen per cent is not a negligible proportion of the working population. They are never going to be the main targets for political parties' election campaigns or in consumer advertising, but to begin with they employ more people than their own numbers, and the proportion of employees in small businesses has been growing. Over two-fifths of all employees are in establishments with under 50 on the payrolls. The petit bourgeoisie have not been the prime-movers, but they have been deeply implicated in the processes that have disorganised the working class. Small might be beautiful for some employers, but this is rarer for the workers (see Rainnie, 1985). Wages are lower than in large companies; the workforces in small enterprises are unlikely to be unionised; the jobs are often chronically insecure; there is no chance of a career; and working conditions are, well, varied. These are the employees who are most likely to have benefitted from the statutory minimum pay and ceiling on compulsory working time, and their employers are quite likely to have been vocal in their opposition to these examples of government interference and the burdens imposed on small businesses.

Second, the petit bourgeoisie are the people who keep the Conservative Party in being, financially and organisationally, throughout the country. The party would no doubt survive without them, but everyone would notice the difference.

Third, the petit bourgeoisie play an ideological role by their very presence. They are the living proof, or so it can be said, that we live in a society where anyone with talent and enterprise can make it.

Summary

The intermediate groups prevent the class structure becoming polarised. Rather than 'clear sky', the two main classes are separated by 'muddy water'. The character of the intermediate classes also prevents the population coalescing into a middle mass: the classes that are intermediate are distinct from the working class on the one side, and the middle class proper on the other.

Lower non-manuals, now mainly women, have held their intermediate position throughout their expansion and all the technological changes since the nineteenth century. Roughly 40 per cent of women's occupations are in this class, yet the class is demographically unstable and has never developed a separate and distinctive subjective class identity, lifestyle or politics. Most members of this class are in cross-class households, thus further blurring the class divisions beneath and above their own occupations.

The petit bourgeoisie is currently expanding rather than contracting. Most of the self-employed are men, and they have arguably the most distinctive of all work situations – working for themselves. They also lead distinctive work-centred lifestyles, and are the source of a distinctively angry and radical brand of conservatism. A third of the sons of business fathers remain in the petit bourgeoisie – an impressive level of intergenerational continuity for a class that accounts for just 13 per cent of the working population. The petit bourgeoisie has an ambiguous relationship with the working class. On the one hand, they are the suppliers of some of the poorest jobs. On the other hand, these are the employers who are closest to their workers, and not just in terms of working alongside them. Few manual workers can realistically hope to become managers or professionals, whereas self-employment is a realisable dream. It is most likely to involve hard work for modest rewards, maybe failure, but there is the possibility of real success, a high income, wealth accumulation and a status position in the local community.

Both of the intermediate classes, albeit in rather different ways, play highly significant roles in the overall system of class relationships in present-day Britain.

6

The Middle Class

Introduction

Previous chapters have described the economic and occupational changes that have reshaped Britain's class structure in recent years. We have looked in detail at the implications for the working class and the intermediate classes, here we turn to the middle class.

*   First we deal with its recent growth (very rapid) and current social composition (extremely diverse).

*   Second, we consider the middle class at work, and its members' typical reasons for both celebration and discontent.

*   Third, we examine divisions within the middle class: by levels, between those in the public and those in the private sector, between managers and professionals, and by lifestyle. The key issue here is whether the divisions are sufficiently severe to make it unrealistic to bunch everyone into a single class.

*   Fourth, we look at the typical preoccupations, and the types of consciousness and related political action, that characterise the contemporary middle class.

The Rise of the New Middle Class

Growth

The middle class is now Britain's second largest; it is pressing on the heels of the working class and accounts for roughly a third of the population. During the second half of the twentieth century the proportion of the workforce in middle class occupations more than doubled. Some time during the twenty-first century the middle-class could become Britain's largest.

141

The present-day middle class needs to be distinguished from an older middle class whose core members were self-employed professionals and proprietors of businesses. The present-day middle class is newer: in fact it is Britain's newest class, even though its origins can be traced back to the nineteenth century. The Northcote Trevelyan Report (1853), implemented from 1870 onwards, was a landmark. This report recommended that recruitment to government employment should be on the basis of competitive examinations (previously positions had been filled by patronage and the purchase of office). Civil service and army reform acted as a catalyst, but also reflected broader cultural changes. During the same period some older craft guilds and new aspirant professions began to tighten their entry requirements and adopt the examination system. The universities, likewise, introduced matriculation (entrance) examinations which were rationalised after the First World War into a national system of secondary school examinations, from which our present-day GCSEs and A-levels have developed.

The reformed civil service adopted the 'army model' of a separate officer (administrative) class, but this type of career organisation was slow to spread. Industry's production managers and engineers continued to be drawn mainly from shopfloors. Individuals who progressed gained any further qualifications through part-time study, in technical colleges, on the so-called 'alternative route'. This is how twentieth century Britain came to have (apparently) undereducated leaders of industry compared with competitor countries. Until the Second World War Britain's university system was tiny and there were very few occupations that required a university qualification. This was necessary in order to enter directly into the civil service's administrative grades, to become a medical doctor, or a secondary (but not an elementary) school teacher. University was also a common route into the Anglican ministry. In contrast, all types of engineers, accountants, solicitors, bank clerks, journalists and social workers normally started work on completing secondary school then worked their way up. Anyone with a university degree joined the normal career streams rather than a separate grade. This was the era when clerks (lower non-manuals) were definitely part of the middle class (see Chapter 5). Some organisations have retained the single-grade entry system to this day: banks and the police service, for instance, though nowadays both allow university graduates to be fast-tracked.

In the first half of the twentieth century the growth of government employment was a main source of growth in the new middle class. The functions of central and local government were extended, so there were more jobs in administration (management) and in public sector professions – education, housing, social work and health care, for example. The economy was becoming dominated by large companies (the number of small businesses was then declining, while large firms were growing forever larger), and these businesses began to seek bright secondary school and (more rarely at that time) university leavers to fast-track into management positions and professional occupations. However, it was not until after the Second World War that the growth of the new middle class really took off. The newly-nationalised industries adopted versions of the civil service model (ever since the Northcote Trevelyan reforms, paper qualifications have been more vital in public than in private sector employment). Higher education expanded. It became normal for large and even medium-sized companies to recruit designated management trainees, and more and more occupations became closed to non-graduates. Business and management schools were established in universities from the 1960s onwards; initially their courses were postgraduate, but since the 1980s business/management has become the most popular undergraduate subject.

During these developments the new middle class expanded rapidly, and the core members of the old middle class – business proprietors and independent professionals – became peripheral. Genuinely middle-class occupations became more distinct from the lower non-manuals. That said, Britain's managers and professionals are still poorly educated compared with their counterparts elsewhere. This is a legacy of history, and also a feature of Britain's relatively unregulated labour markets (see Chapter 3). The 'alternative route' is still open: it remains possible for individuals to rise to management without gaining any particular qualifications provided they can demonstrate the necessary ability. People in some 'professional' occupations, in financial services for example, can be completely unqualified. Everyone must have heard of Nick Leeson.

Social Composition

Nowadays men are only slightly more likely than women to be in middle-class occupations, but men are still much more likely than women to reach the higher levels. Women have tended to stick lower down, and this is still the tendency, even though times are changing in this respect. The professions may have been designed originally by and for men (Witz, 1992). Nevertheless, these are the occupations in which more women are now getting in, gaining post-entry qualifications, and pursuing long-term, scarcely broken, full-time careers. Glass ceilings have been cracking in most businesses and professions. The proportions of women in some senior positions are increasingly spectacularly in percentage terms, but from very low baselines, like just 2 per cent of university professors being women in the 1970s; there are now roughly seven times as many, around 14 per cent.

Britain's ethnic minorities are no longer underrepresented in the middle class. The main contrast today is not between whites and all the minorities, but among the latter. Indians and the Chinese are much better represented than Afro-Caribbeans, Pakistanis and Bangladeshis (Abercrombie and Warde, 2000). Within the middle class the minorities are currently more likely to be in professional than in management positions. In the professions the entry criteria are clearer, and paper qualifications rather than less formal judgements of suitability play the major role during the initial entry stages at any rate, but up to now ethnic minorities have remained much better represented in lower-level than in higher-level grades. Also, as explained in Chapter 3, the minorities are sometimes channelled into specific niches, like work in the 'inner cities'. Equal opportunities policies have been in operation since the 1960s, and the current ethnic composition (like the gender composition) of the middle class is most likely to be in a fluid, intermediate stage, perhaps en route to full equality. Political initiatives to accelerate this process are somewhat compromised by the minorities' underrepresentation at higher levels in the government's own departments, and in politics itself.

The expansion of the middle class has been responsible for the gradual rise in the absolute rate of upward social mobility from the working class which occurred throughout the twentieth century and is still ongoing (see Chapter 8). A consequence of the rate of middle-class growth is that its current members have varied origins. As we shall see in Chapter 8, roughly two-thirds of the present-day middle class have been upwardly mobile. Those with middle-class parents are quite likely to feel that they themselves needed to earn their positions by obtaining the necessary qualifications; they will know people from similar backgrounds to their own who have experienced social demotion. The composition of the present-day middle class cannot but tell those who are 'in' that entry has been possible whatever an individual's starting point. Unless they have studied sociology, they are unlikely to feel that they are beneficiaries of an unequal opportunity society.

The trend in the twenty-first century will be towards a growing proportion of the middle class being recruited from within. The intergenerationally-stable core will grow, and, as this happens, a characteristic consciousness and politics may become clearer. At present, the best that we can hope to see are indicators. Simultaneously, in the twenty-first century people who start life in the working and intermediate classes will have improved chances of reaching the middle class. These developments might appear incompatible, but Chapter 8 will explain in detail how both are possible. Once people are in the middle class, they personally are unlikely to experience demotion, but there are significant, even though diminishing, chances of their children failing to maintain their positions.

Hence the middle class's concern about their children's opportunities and progress in education.

The middle class has always been vocal and politically active, but the class is now more numerous than ever before. We shall see that the middle class has already become culturally and politically dominant. Its concerns already shape political agendas.

The Middle Class at Work

Congestion

Can it really be true that a third of the workforce have good jobs as professionals and managers? There have been suspicions of these ranks being artificially inflated by people being given symbolic rewards in the form of job titles when in reality they are just sales, office and laboratory staff. Some call-centre staff are called 'banking consultants'.

As far as we can tell, these incidents have not been happening recently to any greater extent than may always have been the case. We know that around a quarter of the people classed as managers and administrators say that in practice they do not have any management duties, but there are almost as many people in other classes of occupations who say that they do manage (Rose and O'Reilly, 1997). How many people are crystal clear about what management is? Does a manager have direct control over other staff, or a budget? Can a university head of department be described as a manager? A fact of this matter is that in large organisations management is a process; most decisions are governed by rules or taken by committees. It is a function of particular grades of occupations, rather than specific individuals within them.

We know that jobs classed as management and professional have not become less onerous. Reported skill and qualification requirements have risen in recent years at all occupational levels, including management and the professions (Gallie and White, 1993). In most organisations there is a clear division between the offices and laboratories (the intermediate grades) on the one hand, and management-level grades on the other. The jobs differ not just in titles but also in the salary scales, the overall composition of compensation packages, and promotion prospects. All the evidence suggests that the normal rewards of middle-class status still accompany the job titles.

To recap, middle-class occupations have privileged work and market situations. These employees are not closely supervised at work but are trusted to use initiative and discretion responsibly. The decisions taken by middle-class staff, individually or collectively, and even decisions taken by those outside the main lines of command, have implications for the work of others. Middle-class employees also have superior compensation packages, especially when account is taken of all the fringe benefits and, in particular, the promotion prospects. The jobs are distinguished by the opportunities for progressive careers. There is considerable distance between the bottom and top rungs in the management and professional grades, not least in terms of salaries. And career ascent is still a normal and realistic expectation. As ever, the opportunities are greatest in expanding firms, professions, business sectors and regions. In recent times, south-east England appears to have acted as an escalator region; people have been able to move in, and possibly out again at a later career stage, having reached a higher level than they would probably have attained had their intervening years been spent outside the south-east (see Savage *et al.*, 1991).

However, there is a sense in which a degree of 'proletarianisation' has been inevitable. Clearly, when a third of the workforce is in the middle class, it is impossible for them all to enjoy well-above average status and salaries. Things were rather different before the Second World War when less than 15 per cent of the workforce was in the professions or management. Nowadays it is inevitable that many middle-class careers will start off on below-average earnings, and that many will never progress far above the average. The growth of the middle class has not been accompanied by a corresponding expansion in the room at the very top – on boards of directors of large companies, for example. So the growth of the middle class has led inevitably to an increase in career congestion.

There is also increased congestion at the points of entry to middle-class careers. Nowadays the normal preparation for such a career is higher education, and although this is now the most common, as already explained, it is not the only route in. There are still plenty of 'non-credentialled' managers and formally unqualified people in 'professional' occupations. It is still possible, though rare, to start in the working class, then to progress through the skilled to the technologist and into the professional grades. Likewise, there are still promotions from the office grades into management. In Britain a third of all young people now enter higher education: too many for them all to be recruited into the middle class, or, at any rate for them all to spend their entire working lives in middle-class occupations. So there is more competition, more scrambling, for entry positions in the management and professional grades, then, once in, there is equally intense competition to progress up the career ladders.

Discontents

In recent years the mathematically inevitable consequences of the expansion of higher education and middle-class employment have interacted with two independent developments. First, the drive to cut costs, boost labour productivity and reduce staffing levels which began among manuals has spread through offices and has infected the management and professional grades. Here there has been delayering, and pressure on the remaining staff to do more, often reinforced by target-setting and staff appraisals. Second, mergers and takeovers have sometimes led to site closures, rationalisations and redundancies, and sometimes to businesses taking on new functions or widening their product ranges. For example, most banks and building societies have become multipurpose financial service providers. An outcome has been the creation of new management and professional specialisms, which has required staff to adapt, and created dangers of becoming trapped in contracting niches. A net result of these developments has been that recent studies of the middle class at work have uncovered widespread unhappiness. This is despite the fact that the long-term growth of the middle class has meant more jobs and, overall, more opportunities to get ahead.

The Institute of Management has found that its members have been making more job changes than in the past, and that more of these changes have been enforced rather than voluntary. 'Enforced' here includes cases where individuals have jumped before being pushed. Also, more of the moves have been sideways or downwards rather than upwards. The 'onward and upward' view of management careers is said to be outdated (Inkson and Coe, 1993).

Building society managers have also been griping. Until the 1980s most branch managers 'expected to stay' until the normal retirement age, but by the 1990s the normal expectation was 'hope to remain'. The managers were under new pressures. Their employers were marketing wider ranges of financial products, which the managers were under pressure to sell, and they were being set performance targets. They knew that staff of their level and seniority had been offloaded during previous bouts of reorganisation, and that they could be next. Delayering had made promotions less frequent. Organisational pyramids had been flattened and this had led to more career congestion in the upper, as well as at lower, career levels (see Redman *et al.*, 1997).

Research and development staff in the pharmaceutical industry complain about deprofessionalisation. Competitive pressures, rationalisation, drives to cut costs and demands for measurable results have created a sense of autonomy being lost and promotions becoming more difficult (see Randle, 1996).

Kate Mulholland's (1998) research among managers and professionals in privatised electricity and water companies has portrayed an all-round loss of commitment among staff who would once have been loyal organisation men. In these businesses the staff recognised a split between 'survivors' and 'movers and shakers'. The 'survivors' (from the days when the organisations were nationalised utilities) were typically in their 50s. They were fully aware that employees such as themselves had come to be regarded as a cost, and that all costs had to be cut wherever possible. They knew of scores of former colleagues who had either jumped or been pushed, and they knew that their own positions were vulnerable. They believed that their experience and technical expertise were still valuable, but felt that this was no longer recognised by their employers. Since privatisation they had been joined by new, younger colleagues, the 'movers and shakers'. These were not all accountants by profession, but they were all part of the accountancy-led cost-cutting culture. They knew that they were expected to deliver – to find ways of reducing costs, in which case they could expect to get on. They also knew that failure meant that they would have to move on. So the recent recruits to the businesses were uncertain of their own career prospects. They were all constantly reading job adverts and looking for their next career moves.

Some large organisations appear to have been stripped of commitment. Manual employees feel vulnerable, and it appears that this is equally the case nowadays in many offices and even in the management and professional grades. Investors remain only while they can expect a better return on capital than is available elsewhere (see Chapter 7). Organisations recognise no long-term commitment to any grades of staff and the feeling is reciprocated. This is how the large organisations that were reliable fixtures on the Fordist landscape have been drained of solidity.

New Careers?

Let's be clear: there has been no decline in middle-class career opportunities. The distance between the bottom and top of management and professional hierarchies has widened, and middle-class employment is still expanding. The trends in these grades are not basically the same as in the working class; the change in the middle class has been in the social organisation of careers. New technology and globalisation have played a part, as in the restructuring of manual employment. Organisations and professions themselves have also lost much of their former solidity; careers are not as predictable as formerly, and promotions are no longer regular, like clockwork. But overall there are more opportunities, and the higher-level middle-class jobs are better rewarded than ever before.

Halford and Savage (1995a) have looked in detail at employment in banks and local government. They confirm that there has been no overall decline in the statistical chances of middle-class employees in these fields experiencing career advance. But in both banking and local government some old career paths have closed, and new, often more specialised, career tracks have been created. There are no longer as many distinct layers in the organisational hierarchies, or on career ladders. All employees' performances are now systematically monitored; people have targets, they are appraised regularly and have to apply for promotions; which are no longer simply delivered. Then there is the new possibility of redundancy. Also, women are now competing for promotion with men, and many jobs have been redefined socially in ways that advantage feminine rather than paternal qualities. Sales has been re-imaged as customer care (Halford and Savage, 1995b). These are the reasons for the middle class griping. There are losers, but also winners; some 'new' managers and professionals have been able to make spectacular progress.

It may be useful to unpack some of the principal changes in middle-class careers. In real-life situations the changes are always merged and coloured by firm, industry and occupation specifics. However, one general trend has been towards more regular and formal staff appraisals, thus making everyone more 'accountable', and giving rise to feelings of loss of autonomy and control. Second, promotions are now less likely to be automatic: people have to apply and compete with one another. Third, many middle-class careers have ceased to be linear and now involve more retraining and repositioning. The rewards available in middle-class careers have not shrunk, but the 'rules of the game' have changed.

Studies that have concentrated on the downside have been complemented by those that highlight the upside, and which have identified new types of management and professional careers (see Arthur *et al.*, 1999; Martin, 1998; Watson and Harris, 1999). These studies have portrayed new bricoleur professionals, flexecs, wandering troubadours, who treat jobs as projects in which they can extend their competencies, their portfolios of skills, and add to their CVs. Image and reputation within professional and management networks are now vital career assets. These people are said not only to create their own careers, but to develop every job that they take, and sometimes create new businesses of their own – management consultancies and professional partnerships in leading-edge fields such as IT and advertising, for example. The flexecs are not all young. There are examples of 50-somethings who have quit large organisations, jumped prior to being pushed in some cases, then thrived. However, it is important to bear in mind that as many small enterprises flounder as prosper.

Whether the entire middle class can become successful flexecs and bricoleurs is still not clear. All the studies in large organisations (which is where most of the middle class still work) find far more evidence of old careers disintegrating than new careers being created (McGovern *et al.*, 1998). The graduates who initially struggle to get in are less likely than in the past to find secure career plateaux from which they can make regular, if unspectacular, progress. There are no longer any secure plateaux in many organisations, and any upward movement needs to be won.

Divisions

Recent research on the middle class has sought to identify, first, how their work and market situations are changing, and second, whether they any longer have a typical class situation from which a characteristic type of consciousness and politics could develop. Some analysts have stressed the divisions that exist within the contemporary middle class or classes. Growth is said to have led to greater diversity, and four types of divisions have been highlighted: by occupational level, between those who work in the private and public sectors, between managers and professionals, and by lifestyle. The disorganisation of the working class combined with an alleged fragmentation of the middle class may be seen as adding up to a death of class. However, differences, which there most certainly are, need not amount to divisions, or, at any rate not to so basic a division as that between the working class on the one side, and an allegedly fragmented middle class, on the other. Also, differences do not necessarily imply disorganisation. Actually, the middle class today is better organised than ever.

Levels

There is obviously a great deal of inequality among managers and professional employees; more so than among manuals. Some junior managers and professionals earn less than the average in the present-day UK; others have telephone number annual salaries. Are they all in the same class? Of course there always were inequalities, but these have widened considerably in recent years. Hence the plausibility of suggestions that a clear division is being created between upper-level and 'proletarianised' layers of the middle class.

In Goldthorpe's original class scheme, the lower level of the 'service class' was described as a cadet grade through which entrants could rise into the service class proper. So junior hospital doctors eventually become consultants, junior managers become senior managers, and so on. Things are really more complicated than this. Some professions are higher than others. On the one hand, there are well-established professions – law, medicine and accountancy – which have been largely successful in retaining high proportions of jobs in the upper ranks, and have avoided the degree of career congestion that is now found in the basic grades in banks, among teachers, social workers, and so on. There are also graduates who are recruited into fast-track trainee posts with blue-chip multinationals and firms of consultants. Access to these positions tends to be restricted to young people who achieve good degrees (firsts or 2.1s) from older universities (preferably Oxford or Cambridge), who performed well in the A-level and GCSE examinations, and who can also survive days of personality and role-play tests to prove that they are the right type of person. These selection processes tend to favour individuals from established middle-class families who are privately educated, or who attend other selective schools. This leaves the lower middle-class positions to be filled by the upwardly mobile, from state comprehensives, new universities, and with lower-class degrees from older institutions (see Brown and Scase, 1994). It has been argued that the professions and management positions into which women and the upwardly mobile are recruited have been seriously degraded, and that men from elite family and educational backgrounds have gone into the financial sectors and high-tech fields where the rewards are considerably greater (Walkerdine *et al.*, 2001). True, but is this creating a class division among professionals and managers?

There are two problems, or at least qualifying points, that have to be entered against this diagnosis. First, it understates the amount of intermingling that occurs in schools and higher education, and in the early career stages, between eventual high-fliers and also-rans. Some graduates from older universities do not become high-fliers. There are wide inequalities within the established professions; there are small-town solicitors who depend on conveyancing and legal-aid work as well as big city firms that handle the business of large corporations. The same applies among accountants, and in medicine. There are people from modest backgrounds who have made fortunes in the city, and in E-commerce.

Second, there is the matter of gender. As feminist critics note, although times are changing, the high-level middle-class positions still tend to be occupied by men, while women are still far less likely to reach these same heights. This is despite the fact that more women in middle-class occupations are pursuing full-time, scarcely broken careers. What must also be said is that most of these women marry middle-class men. There is a powerful tendency for like to marry like, so there are now more middle-class households than formerly that benefit from two middle-class salaries. Neither salary needs to be particularly large to provide the base for a standard of living that is entirely different from working-class ways of life. The new middle class buys services, including domestic services, from the new working class. The former hires live-in nannies (in some cases), nursery child-care (in rather more instances), gardeners and cleaners (see Gregson and Lowe, 1993). And members of the middle class are able to pay to have their cars repaired and serviced, and their houses decorated and renovated. The new middle class is also able to afford to use out-of-home services in restaurants, hotels and theatres. There are more and less successful and prosperous managers and professionals, but are the differences among them really as basic as between the household cleaner and her employer?

Public and Private

The argument here is straightforward and arises from the prominence of taxation as an issue in British politics in the 1980s and 1990s. Managers and professionals who work in the private sector are said to have vested interests in low levels of taxes on incomes, enabling them to keep more of their earnings in their pockets or bank accounts, and a corresponding willingness and ability to accept the inevitable cutbacks in state services and benefits because they are able to buy alternatives privately. Public-sector managers and professionals are said to have entirely different interests: their jobs, salary levels and career prospects are at risk. No surprise, therefore, that the public services' white-collar employees have been at the forefront of campaigns to defend the National Health Service and state education. A new political cleavage can be envisaged between working-class users together with public-sector managers and professionals on the one side, and the private-sector middle class on the other.

There are several problems with what might initially appear a persuasive argument. First, there is nothing new about this division of interest, or between the trade-off between higher top earnings in the private sector and greater job security in state employment. Nothing has changed here. Second, in the 1980s, and presumably before and since then, both white-collar and manual public-sector employees have been more likely to vote Labour, or at least anti-Conservative, than their private-sector counterparts, but this difference has been small compared with the main divide in voting, which has been by social class – working class versus middle class – ever since the franchise was extended to manual workers (see Figure 6.1).

Third, there are just as good reasons as ever why the public–private sector split is unlikely to become as clear as the longer-standing class division. Public sector professionals may have been keen (and largely successful) in protecting the state services in which they are employed (education and health, for example) but they have not saved the nationalised steel, coal, railways, gas, electricity and other industries which had larger blue-collar workforces. Nor have public-sector professionals and managers prevented the contracting-out of the cleaning, laundering and catering from their schools and hospitals. Moreover, the state services that their middle-class employees are keenest to protect are used by managers and professionals

Figure 6.1 Class, sector of employment and voting

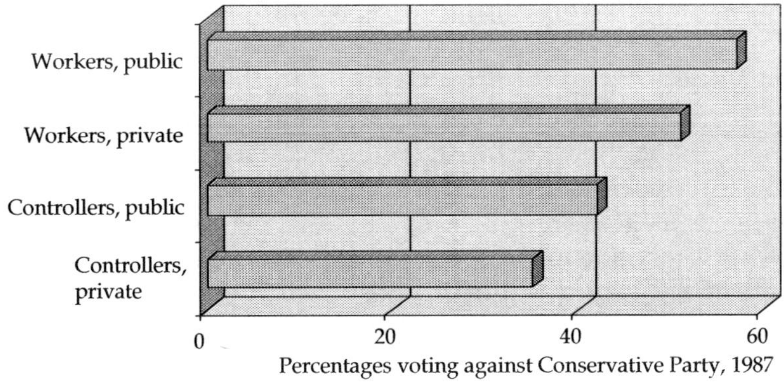

Source: Adapted from Edgell and Duke (1991).

in public and private-sector employment, as well as by the working class. There are more middle-class children in state schools than are educated privately. Very few middle-class pensioners are able and willing to meet all their health-care costs from private resources. Finally, doctors who work in the National Health Service and senior civil servants are not all adverse to having their children educated privately, or using private medicine. Many are no doubt as keen as anyone to have taxes on their incomes kept as low as possible, and to have government spending held down, provided only that their own jobs are not threatened.

Professionals and Managers

These words are nearly always coupled when describing the middle class. They can be treated as different types of occupations which share common middle-class characteristics. Alternatively, they can be treated as having distinct work and market situations; maybe sufficiently distinct to create a class division between them, or at least to prevent the middle class developing common and characteristic types of consciousness and politics.

The latter point of view has been developed by Mike Savage who has constructed what he calls an asset-based, realist theory of middle-class formation which explains how middle-class groups are able to become real entities which can act causally. Such middle-class groups, according to Savage, can have bases in three types of assets – in property, bureaucracy or culture (Savage *et al.*, 1992). Various mixtures are possible, but Savage's view is that the main sections of the contemporary middle class are based primarily on either one or another. The propertied middle classes can be set to one side for the time being; they are the petit bourgeoisie (see Chapter 5) and the upper class which will be considered in Chapter 7. For present purposes the crucial distinction is between bureaucracy and culture, which are said to be the bases of the managerial and professional middle classes respectively.

Now it is very easy to make stark contrasts in terms of ideal-types in which managers are shown to owe everything to their positions in organisations (bureaucracies) and the control that they exercise over organisational assets. Managers are portrayed as acquiring particularistic skills and knowledge (specific to the organisations). Their entire (ideal-typical) careers are said to be spent within the same organisations where they may well become indispensable on account of the detailed knowledge that they acquire about the organisations' working methods, suppliers, customers, various departments, and so on. These are the archetypal organisation men (see Whyte, 1957) whose working lives, careers and prospects are inextricably bound to the organisations in which they work. They depend on their organisations, and the organisations depend on them. Managers' loyalty is rewarded with security and career progression.

The careers of ideal-typical professionals and their claims to middle-class status and treatment are based on culture, meaning, in practice, skills and knowledge that are certified and validated by professional associations. The core functions of professional associations are to restrict entry to those properly qualified, and to regulate professional conduct. Professions are based on expert knowledge and related practices, which, it is claimed, are so esoteric that the only competent judges of whether work is of a satisfactory standard are other professionals. This creates situations where occupational groups can elevate their status in the eyes of the public, including actual and potential customers, thereby elevating the rewards that they can command, through professional organisation. Professional associations distinguish the competent from quacks, and may discipline and ultimately expel any members who do not matchup to the standards set by the professions. People who embark on professional careers need to invest initially in acquiring the appropriate cultural capital (qualifications); thereafter their main loyalty is to their professions. Their careers will often involve movement between numerous employers, but they always have a wider loyalty, namely, to their professions. They may work in professional organisations which are, in effect, controlled by the professionals (hospitals and universities, for example), or they may work in smaller professional practices. The crucial point is that they have options.

Studies which compare managers and professionals invariably find that the latter are the relatively advantaged group, and since the 1970s the advantages of professionals appear to have increased. Hence the claim that the professional–manager divide is deepening. Mike Savage believes that property and culture have always been more secure bases for middle-class positions than organisation-based assets, and that in post-Fordist times the latter assets have been devalued even further. This is said to have occurred during the waves of mergers and takeovers, rationalisations and delayering which have rendered many packages of particularistic skills and knowledge completely redundant (Savage *et al.*, 1992). Professionals appear to have been less vulnerable. They have been less likely to experience demotion (Fielding, 1995), and, moreover, it appears that cultural capital is more easily passed down the generations. Professionals' children are more successful in education than the children of managers and, therefore, are more likely to avoid socioeconomic descent (Egerton, 1997).

The problems with the neat manager–professional division only become apparent, but then become glaringly obvious, when we move from ideal-types into the real world. First, managers' careers have always had a cultural base. Initial positions on management career ladders are typically awarded partly on the basis of qualifications, and, although this may be nit-picking, the particularistic knowledge and skills that make managers valuable to their organisations are 'cultural'. Conversely, professionals often pursue careers in professional organisations in which they climb bureaucratic ladders. Also, many non-professional organisations like to develop their own professionals who can combine broader-based skills and knowledge with a deep acquaintance with company culture.

Second, professionals' careers often criss-cross between line management and professional positions. University academics may move into academic management; some become vice-chancellors (chief executives). Doctors in hospitals do likewise. Accountants, engineers and so on often move into line management posts in their companies (Mills, 1995), some finding that this move is necessary in order to keep their careers advancing. Out in the real world, the distinction between managers and professionals has always been blurred. According to Watson and Harris (1999), few managers embark on their careers with the set aim of becoming managers; they explain how they simply drifted into management, often from professional backgrounds, and stayed because they found that they could 'swim'.

Third, the respondents who are identified as professionals in surveys are sometimes distinguished from managers basically because the former are the better-qualified rather than on account of their membership of professional bodies. The well-defined lifestyles that can be distinguished, mainly within the professional middle class (see below), probably owe much more to their higher education, higher social origins, and higher incomes than to their membership of professional bodies.

Fourth, it can in fact be argued that, rather than widening, the distinction between managers and professionals is currently weakening, though qualifications (cultural capital) are undoubtedly becoming more important than ever as a base for middle-class careers. On the one hand, more careers in management are being launched on the basis of higher education, and there are more management qualifications available. There are MBAs and a variety of qualifications in marketing, personnel and other management fields. Some managers have always been able to benefit by possessing skills and knowledge applicable across entire industries rather than specific to one firm. So there have been oil men, car-makers, and so forth. Nowadays there seem to be more cases where people can claim generic management skills and move between organisations in entirely different industries, often moving upwards in the process. Some claim that management itself is now a profession, and a high status profession judged by the popularity of higher education courses with management in their titles.

Meanwhile, there are ways in which professionals are becoming more like managers. The traditional high-status professions – medicine, law and accountancy – are no longer typical. These occupations developed a public-service type of professionalism, not because their members necessarily worked in the public sector, but on account of their strong professional associations which set great store, in theory if not always in practice, on prioritising the public interest. The present-day professional is more likely to practise a commercial type of professionalism (Hanlon, 1998). The commercial professional is a certified expert who hires out skills to deliver whatever customers want, which is invariably plain expertise rather than moral guardianship. The clients of these professionals are usually organisations rather than individuals, and the customers set the ground rules. Professionals who are able to deliver, profit from this. Their strictly professional reputations (in the eyes of peers) are of secondary importance to their reputations in the eyes of customers.

Janette Webb (1999) has noted the development of such a division among public-sector middle-class employees. On the one hand, there are those who have embraced an entrepreneurial ethic; they are intent on making their departments lean and efficient, and on getting-ahead in their own careers. These public sector 'entrepreneurs' tend to be males, in higher-level positions. On the other hand, there are staff, mainly females in lower-level positions, who still subscribe to a traditional, caring, public service ethic. Note that the contrasts found by Webb were within the public-sector middle class.

Of course, there is a difference between the better and less-educated sections of the middle class, and between those who commit their careers to specific organisations and those who move between employers while remaining in the same occupations. There are differences between those who become high-fliers and those who stick at lower levels, and between those who work in the public and private sectors. In class analysis it is important not to lose sight of the crunch questions. These are, first, how the differences within the middle class compare with the division between the entire middle class and the working class, and, second, whether the differences within the middle class are sufficient to prevent the development of a characteristic type of consciousness and political proclivities.

Lifestyles

Its relevance to class analysis is not self-evident, but some researchers have identified a series of distinct lifestyle groups within the middle class – usually within the professional or better-educated sections of the middle class. In terms of eating, spending and other habits, the lifestyles of managers, or the less well-educated, appear best described as simply undistinguished (Warde, 1995). The sources and types of evidence vary. Sometimes it is quantitative data on spending or leisure-time use from large samples. Sometimes the evidence is from case studies in specific places, usually places of residence or where leisure-time is spent. On the basis of this varied evidence researchers have identified a series of lifestyle groups: healthy ascetics who play sport and take other forms of exercise, and who are careful about diet; a group that is into art, theatres, concerts and wine; a country set or sets; and inner-city gentrifiers (Butler, 1995; Cloke *et al.*, 1995; Savage *et al.*, 1991; Wynne, 1998).

Some of the researchers seem to believe that they are charting new, even postmodern phenomena. Actually, all that is new is the existence of researchers who have the inclination and resources to do the studies. There have always been middle-class minorities who have been into sport, and others who have been into the arts. There used to be a glaring difference between the (visible) lifestyles of educated professional gentlemen and the middle class that made its money from muck.

Middle-class lifestyles really need to be set in their broader social context. The present-day middle classes are distinguished by the fact that there are so many lifestyle variations among them, some related to age, gender, ethnicity and education. Working-class ways of life are more uniform, more basic, and more television dominated (Ophem and Hoog, 1998). Social background, education, and the tastes nurtured in these milieux, play a part in creating this class difference, but so does money. The poorest sections of the population – the long-term unemployed and the retired who depend entirely on state benefits, for example – have the most basic and uniform ways of life of all. Nowadays the middle class collectively do more of most things, except watching television. They take more holidays, play more sports, make more visits to theatres and the countryside, and eat out more frequently. They are typically 'omnivores' rather than highbrows – into popular music and football as well as visits to art galleries and museums (Peterson and Kern, 1996). It is their omnivorousness rather than any specific tastes that sets the contemporary middle class apart from the working class.

Now the fact that the working and middle classes share many similar tastes, and also dress in similar (typically casual) ways on most occasions when they go out, tends to blur class divisions, but class differences are not eliminated. So we have to ask which is the most significant: the lifestyle differences within the middle class, or the contrast between middle-class choice, variety and individuality on the one hand, and working-class relative uniformity on the other.

The existence of numerous lifestyle groups may make it unlikely that the entire middle class will become communal and solidaristic, aware of a common way of life and associated interests, but this does not mean that they cannot be considered a class. Up to now our only examples of (imperfectly) solidaristic classes in modern British history have been the original working class whose distinctive way of life developed under the constraints of poverty, and the upper class (see Chapter 7).

Descriptions of middle-class lifestyles have a self-evident descriptive value. The evidence becomes potentially significant when considering possibilities of class formation only when it is claimed that the lifestyles of these groups are becoming principal sources of identity, identification with particular sections of the population, and political proclivities, more likely to be expressed through participation in or support for 'new social movements' (see Chapter 9) than the older parties with their class-based politics.

Some lifestyle groups which have been identified do appear to share political dispositions and have similar social origins as well as occupations. For example, the gentrifiers of Islington and Hackney (in north London) in the 1990s tended to be politically left-of-centre, and were more likely to be from middle-class families than upwardly mobile (Butler, 1995). In contrast, the countryside appears to have a variety of meanings for the middle class (and other) people who live there or who spend leisure time there regularly (Cloke *et al.*, 1995), and they appear to share no distinctive politics.

Consideration of whether politics is still largely class-based can be postponed until Chapter 9, but here we can note a number of grounds for doubting whether lifestyles are likely to replace social classes as bases for interest formation and political action. First, distinct lifestyles appear to develop within, rather than straddle, class boundaries. The main exceptions are youth (or young singles) sub-cultures in which involvement is a temporary life-stage matter. Second, the lifestyles that have been identified are confined to far too few people to become politically potent. Third, lifestyles are characteristically unstable. They tend to draw together people in specific life stages, such as young singles or childless couples. People change their types of housing, and the districts where they live, more frequently than they change their types of occupations. Cars, clothing, hair fashions and musical tastes can be changed even more frequently. Sports participation drops steeply, as does involvement in most non-family forms of out-of-home leisure, when people become parents. Lifestyles are never likely to challenge occupations, or lifelong class trajectories, as sources of identity (people's views on, and feelings about, who they are, and their positions in society), or their views on features of the status quo that they wish to challenge and those that they wish to defend.

Consciousness and Politics

The Traditional and New Middle Classes

It is still too early, historically, for a precise and confident verdict as to whether the new middle class(es) will develop common and characteristic forms of consciousness and politics and, if so, what their key features will be. We have seen that the middle class grew steadily throughout the twentieth century, but especially from the Second World War onwards. It more than doubled in size, and a consequence is that most current members have been recruited from beneath. Collectively they have very mixed origins. But it is important to recognise that this will not continue indefinitely; the intergenerationally stable core will grow in size, and the rate of middle-class expansion will decline even if the trend continues (see Chapter 8).

At the beginning of the twenty-first century we are in a similar position *vis-à-vis* the middle class in trying to identify its likely political and societal impact, as analysts were *vis-à-vis* the working class at the time of the First World War. During the nineteenth century the working class had been created as an economic entity, and working-class cultures had developed throughout the land at local community and workplace levels. Trade unions and the Labour Party had been created. Even so, it was impossible in the early twentieth century to be certain as to the extent to which working-class power would be mobilised, or the uses to which such power would be put. Revolutionary, reformist and conservative (a domesticated, quiescent working class) prognoses were equally plausible.

It is important to recognise that during its twentieth-century growth the middle class was reconstituted; today's middle class is not simply a swollen version of the middle class at the beginning of the twentieth century. Up to the Second World War, the core members of the traditional middle class were proprietors of businesses and self-employed professionals. Other white-collar workers identified with this middle class core. Their market, work and status situations may have encouraged this, but the various sections of the traditional middle class were drawn together basically by the threat of working-class power. Middle-class griping is not new, but until the 1950s the characteristic gripes were quite different from those that we hear today. The recurrent and unifying concern earlier on was the advance of the working class, which threatened to erode the middle class's advantages. It threatened to tax their incomes to provide the working class with services that the middle class already enjoyed. So the middle class applauded everything that the working class was believed to be against: individualism, enterprise and independence. The traditional middle class was opposed to trade unions and the so-called 'nanny state'.

The new middle class is different. Its core members are salaried managers and professionals, and many of them work in the public sector. They are simply too numerous for them all to feel privileged, and for the defence of middle-class privileges to be an overriding common concern. Moreover, working-class power has waned. The middle class has been organising – joining trade unions, for example – but the working class is now disorganised, it is no longer a threat. If the present-day middle class is concerned about what is happening beneath, the worries are less likely to be about militant trade unions and a socialist Labour Party than the effects of unemployment and poverty on crime, the costs of welfare, and the general quality of life in their towns and cities.

Preoccupations

Up to now we have no national congress of professional associations or white-collar trade unions. There is no political party with policies that make an explicit, and provenly effective, appeal to specifically middle-class interests. The Conservative Party had the support of the traditional middle class, and retained this support for as long as Labour was regarded as a working-class party, and a threat. We now know that Thatcherism did not solidify new middle-class support for the Conservatives. New Labour was successful in the late-1990s in developing policies, or at least an image, that appealed in all classes. At the end of the twentieth century the Conservatives were unsure of how to regain even their traditional, once taken-for-granted, middle-class support.

It is impossible to say which policies will appeal, but it is possible to identify three preoccupations which are specific to, and resonate throughout, the new middle class. As one might expect, these arise from the middle class's typical work and market situations.

First, the middle class expects a 'service' relationship with employers. Managers and professionals expect to be trusted, to be given responsibility, autonomy and discretion; otherwise they feel misemployed and underutilised. They are willing to play their parts in the service relationship, to 'put in the hours' without overtime payment, for example. They may complain about the stress and strains imposed on family relationships, but they are just as worried if their employers have no need for such commitment. It is not usually fear of the sack that motivates managers and professionals to work 50-plus hours a week at the office, and to carry more work home in their briefcases. They are more likely to be, or want to be seen to be, work enthusiasts, and are keen to demonstrate their indispensability and promotability. They accept that relocation to another part of the country may be part of the package despite the additional strains on personal relationships, especially between dual-career couples.

The service relationship that the middle class seeks is rather different from the more widespread desire for 'interesting work'. The characteristic middle-class preoccupation also goes beyond vocationalism – pride in, and identification with, professional or craft skills. The middle class is willing to give more, and expects to give more, and those concerned are most likely to feel entitled to all the rewards that accrue. They are quite likely to approve of higher taxes on the rich but unlikely to place themselves in this category.

The conservatism of the middle class, in so far as the class is conservative, stems partly from the service relationship sought with employers. This makes the middle class unlikely to recognise any basic division of interest *vis-à-vis* a class above. The middle class depends on employers for its advantaged work and market situations, just as employers depend on salaried managers and professionals to protect and secure returns on their capital. The rewards that successful managers and professionals receive from work in the private sector are, in part, shares in profits rather than straightforward payments for work done. Middle-class salary levels are difficult to explain in terms of contributions (functional importance) to society, or with classical economic theory. They are easier to explain in terms of the value of the work to their employers. The higher echelons of the middle class are effectively integrated into the upper class. Top managers (at director level) are usually rewarded with share options. They may not become major shareholders in the companies, but the managers become wealthy individuals with vested interests in the returns that accrue to their own capital investments. Middle-class careers can be a route into the upper class. This is neither a normal career destination nor the most common route in, but it is a possible, and a highly attractive, reward for a successful middle-class career. A broader section of the middle class has been able to become personal share-owners as a result of the privatisations and building society conversions of the 1980s and 1990s. Approximately a half of all managers and professionals now own shares (Saunders and Harris, 1994). Also, it is the middle class rather than the working class that has been able to take most advantage of the government-provided tax shelters for savings – TESSAs, PEPs and subsequently ISAs. The really wealthy have off-shore tax havens, and the middle class has something similar. Upper and middle-class interests are far from identical (see Chapter 7), but the two classes are so interdependent that neither is likely to confront the other.

'Career' is the second distinctively middle-class preoccupation. The middle class seeks and expects careers. Managers and professionals expect to advance progressively in their organisations or professions, and may achieve this by following structured career routes or by forging new careers, but they all expect to advance. If necessary, they will switch employers and localities. These are accepted prices that may need to be paid in order to get on. The middle class is willing to undertake additional study and training, and to top-up qualifications, in order to keep its careers moving. Managers and professionals are far more likely than any other occupational group to receive post-entry, often recurrent and ongoing, training, and to engage in qualification accumulation. They are often willing to do whatever is possible and necessary to position themselves directly beneath promotion opportunities. They are equally concerned that their children should do well. Middle-class children are taught by their parents that school work is important. These are the parents who shop around, relocate if necessary, and sometimes pay for private education in order to give their children the best possible starts. For their part, the children become aware of their parents' financial and emotional investments. Failure becomes unthinkable – the ultimate act of family betrayal (see Walkerdine *et al.*, 2001).

A common middle-class gripe nowadays is about career blockages. Many present-day managers and professionals are dissatisfied with their career progress and opportunities, which is a reason why more have been joining trade unions (see Redman *et al.*, 1997). The present-day middle class is anxious rather than complacent and comfortable, but this does not necessarily or normally lead to a challenge to class divisions. The normal middle-class response is to try even harder, to seek a personal solution: hence the willingness to train, move house, top up qualifications, and so on. Otherwise the frustrated middle class tends to increase its psychic investments in out-of-work life. Those concerned may become home and family-centred (psychologically at any rate), and adopt instrumental, calculative approaches to their jobs (Scase and Goffee, 1989), just like the 'new working class' of the 1950s and 1960s.

The third characteristic middle-class preoccupation is meritocratic, of a specifically middle-class type. The middle class believes that positions and rewards should be earned, largely though not entirely on the basis of qualifications. They are opposed to virtually every other form of discrimination – by gender, race, religion, social background, country of origin, nationality. The one type of discrimination that the middle class endorses is according to qualifications. On qualifications they are arch-conservative rather than radical. According to Milner (1999), a qualification meritocracy which may well be deemed classless is the dominant ideology of contemporary intellectuals. Members of the middle class expect their own qualifications to be appropriately rewarded and will defer only to those who are even better qualified.

Middle-class Preoccupations and Working-class Values

These are no longer diametrically opposed as they were when the middle class had a 'traditional' core. It is realistic nowadays for politicians to seek to appeal simultaneously to both the working class, including the poor, and the middle class (or middle Britain, as they usually prefer to say). However, middle-class and working-class aspirations are not identical; it is still possible to address one set while ignoring, or at the expense of, the other.

The new middle class is not particularly conservative in either party political or broader social and economic terms. As the shape of the class structure changed during the second half of the twentieth century, with the working class diminishing in size, the proportion of the popular vote commanded by the Labour Party gradually declined. At any rate, this was the long-term trend from the 1950s until 1997 (see Table 6.1). It is less often noted, though more remarkable, that over the same period the Conservative Party failed to become more popular as a result of the expansion of the white-collar classes. The proportion of white-collar workers voting against the Conservatives, though not necessarily for Labour, increased gradually, then shot upwards in 1997 (see Chapter 9).

The socio-occupational profile of the non-Conservative middle class is well-known. They tend to be well-educated (university graduates), usually in arts or social sciences, employed in the public sector, in welfare professions (education, social work or medicine), or in intellectual private sector occupations such as journalism. The nature and sources of the radicalism of this section of the middle class are discussed below. For the present, the crucial point is that the present-day middle class is just as anxious to change the world as the working class. The changes that these classes desire are not diametrically opposed, but neither are they identical. Indeed, their aspirations have less in common than initial appearances may suggest.

Table 6.1   Percentages of total vote
received by Conservatives and Labour

	Conservatives	Labour
1945	40	48
1950	44	46
1951	48	49
1955	50	46
1959	49	44
1964	43	44
1966	42	48
1970	46	43
1974	38	37
1974	36	39
1979	44	37
1983	42	28
1987	42	31
1992	42	34
1997	31	43

Both favour meritocracy, but in rather different senses. For the middle class merit = qualifications. They expect returns on their investments in education and training; and they still feel this way even though it is no longer as obvious as in previous years that extended education requires the deferment of gratifications. This is because earlier school-leavers are unlikely nowadays to move rapidly into well-paid jobs (see Roberts and Parsell, 1991). In the working class merit is equated with effort, skill and the number of hours worked. It is measured in terms of the value that people produce, the output, rather than the quality of the input. From within the working class, inflated middle-class salaries do not appear justified on grounds of merit.

The working and middle classes have equally good, albeit different, reasons for responding favourably to and also for opposing proposals to replace the vagaries of the market with planning. The middle class could then become the planners, the distributors; the type of 'new class' that was created by state socialism. This strengthening of the middle-class role would not have to be at the expense of the work situation and market advantages that are available in a market economy. The appeal of planning to the working class has always been rather different: removing the threat of redundancy, lay-offs and short-time, and enabling resources to be distributed in accordance with merit and need. By the end of the twenti-eth century both classes had good reasons to conclude that the inevitable compromises made planning no more attractive than the market.

The new middle class is certainly not anti-collectivist. Many of them work in the public sector; they use, and obtain good value from, state services such as health and education; and the new middle class are 'joiners'. These are the so-called chattering classes who ensure that their voices are heard, and they are well-represented. They have professional associations, and they are now more likely than manual employees to be members of trade unions. Forty-seven per cent of workers in the management and profes-sional grades compared with 42 per cent of skilled workers and 37 per cent of the unskilled were trade union members in 1992 (Gallie *et al.*, 1998). The middle class has marched into trade unions as its job security has been undermined, and as career opportunities have narrowed (see Redman *et al.*, 1997), and because so many work for the employer where trade union mem-bership is most common – the government. In terms of who is most likely to be represented by it, the working class has lost the trade union movement.

The middle class supplies most of the members, and certainly most of the activists, in all types of non-profit, voluntary organisations – those that work for charitable causes, and those that exist for the members' interests whether these lie in sport, the arts, maintaining the character of a neigh-bourhood, or reducing crime. Nowadays the middle class also supplies most of the activists, and even moreso the elected representatives, in all the main political parties. In this sense the Labour Party has been taken from the working class. Politicians in all parties now have very similar backgrounds – university, then employment in management or the pro-fessions. Politics has become another middle-class career, often a long-term career, and sometimes the individuals' only career. The activists may not be middle-class representatives in either a technical or a subjective sense, but middle-class dominance means that middle-class issues and preoccupations, and definitions of problems have good chances of reach-ing government agendas.

The advantages that collectivism offered to the working class have been sidelined. For the working class, collective organisation has been a safe-guard against individual victimisation. Collective agreements have ensured that everyone's rewards, and the contributions required, have been agreed or at least understood by all. Middle-class collectivism is rather different. It is a means of pursuing specific causes, often of creating or maintaining opportunities for personal enterprise and socioeconomic advance, and another source of career opportunities.

The working class has traditionally favoured state guarantees to meet everyone's basic needs, meaning, in practice, income maintenance during retirement, unemployment and sickness, plus assistance with onerous life events – basically births, child-care and death. Adequate housing has been another part of this agenda. Then, the working class has favoured other services, specifically health and education, being removed from the market and managed in response to need and/or merit. None of this clashes with middle-class aspirations. The middle class will endorse the entire agenda, but their motives are more likely to be altruistic than self-interested. They are unlikely to envisage that they themselves will ever depend wholly on the state retirement pension, for example. And members of the middle class are likely to take it for granted that those who want to do so will be able to top-up or opt-out of the 'basic' state provisions, thereby defeating the original working-class objective of having educational and health care resources used according to need or merit, nothing else, and state social security guaranteeing a standard of living close to other citizens.

There is also the question of how state services are to be financed. In recent years there has been cross-party and, apparently, cross-class agreement that income taxes must not be raised and, if possible, should be lowered. This consensus did not always exist. Until the 1950s people on below-average earnings did not pay income tax. They had everything to gain and nothing to lose when demanding state services funded through taxes on incomes. Subsequently, as incomes rose, virtually all employees were drawn into the income tax-paying bracket, and all tax-payers have shared a concern over the standard rate of income tax. Those with the highest incomes have the most to gain from tax reductions, or avoiding increased taxes on earnings, but this latter option has come to be regarded as above and contrary to all class interests. In is also noteworthy that the possibility of raising tax thresholds so that below-average earners are once again excluded, and making taxation on higher incomes much more steeply progressive, has left everyone's political agenda.

Everyone seems to want better state services and lower taxes, and there are votes to be won by offering both. Hence the advent of what Sylvia Walby (1999) describes as the 'regulatory state', a form of government that has been pioneered by the European Union. Here the state does not provide, but requires businesses and citizens to do so. For example, businesses can be required to pay a minimum wage. This costs governments nothing. Citizens could be obliged to save towards their retirement in private (non-state) funds. They could also be required to insure their housing costs (mortgage repayments) against the risks of unemployment and chronic illness. The principle could be extended to health care and education. Collectivism is thereby subtly recast in line with middle-class interests.

During the last 30 years the new middle class has taken up a raft of new radical issues which had no place on the old working-class radical agenda. The new issues have nothing to do (ostensibly at any rate) with specifically middle-class interests. They are about peace, race equality, sex equality, gay rights, fair treatment for asylum seekers, animal welfare and the environment, for example. Support for all these causes is much broader-based, but nearly all the activists in these 'new social movements' are middle class. As explained earlier, they tend to be from a particular section of the middle class: the highly educated, in arts or social sciences. They are usually from middle-class families rather than upwardly mobile and their parents often held or hold similar radical views. The activists are most likely to work in the public sector, in welfare, or in intellectual professions. Of course, not everyone with some or even all of these characteristics becomes a radical activist. There usually has to be a trigger; an 'event' or personally significant experience (Searle-Chatterjee, 1999). However, the same social profile has been discovered again and again no matter which radical movements have been examined (Cotgrove, 1982; Mattausch, 1989a,b; Parkin, 1968; Ridig et al., 1991). There has been intense, and so far unresolved, debate as to how this radicalism is to be explained. Does it indicate the spread of post-materialist values in post-scarcity societies? (Inglehart, 1977, 1997). Or are the causes expressing the class interests of a middle-class faction that works neither in the market economy nor in science or technology? (Cotgrove and Duff, 1980, 1981). Or are the activists radical despite, rather than because of, their class situations? (Heath and Savage, 1995). Do those concerned choose their education and occupations on the basis of their radical values rather than develop the values through their educational and occupational experience? (Bagguley, 1995). To what extent is it all just the intelligentsia playing its traditional role of supplying agendas for all social and political movements? (Bagguley, 1992).

The points that can be made unequivocally are as follows. First, it is easy to understand why quite substantial sections of the middle class (the social radicals) were turned off rather than attracted to the Conservative Party by Thatcherism in the 1980s (Savage et al., 1992). Second, there is nothing in the middle class's radicalism, collectivism, support for the welfare state, support for meritocracy or socioeconomic planning that requires any sacrifice of its own interests vis-à-vis the working class. To put this another way, there is little or nothing on offer for the workers. It can be argued that the working class benefits from sex and race equality, peace, environmental improvement and so on, but these have never been working-class priorities. Third, there is nothing to challenge the economic system and the position of the upper class within it. Alleging that we are now a classless society can be a way of side-stepping these matters. Fourth, it is middle-class preoccupations and causes that now shape the agendas of all the main political parties and the governments that they form.

Summary

We have seen that the new middle class has expanded strongly since the mid-twentieth century. During this growth, it has become more diverse in ethnic and gender composition, and is equally mixed in terms of its members' social class origins. During the twenty-first century the middle class is likely to remain just as mixed, if not more mixed, in terms of gender and ethnicity, but it will definitely become increasingly self-recruiting. It is only at this stage that any characteristic forms of consciousness and politics are likely to solidify. Perhaps the most important point to grasp about the new middle class is that it is still in formation.

The expansion of middle-class career opportunities has exacerbated rather than eased the pressures on the middle classes at work. There is now more competition to get in, then to get on. Middle-class payrolls have become more expensive to employers whether public or private sector, so the middle class has been deeply affected by cost-cutting and delayering. Promotions now have to be earned; linear career tracks have snapped. Yet, despite all this, chances of career success have not diminished and, if anything, the rewards today are better than ever.

We have seen that there are divisions within the middle class – by levels, between managers and professionals, those in the public and private sectors, and by lifestyle. But we have also seen that these divisions often pale into insignificance when set against the split between the entire middle class on the one hand and the working class on the other. Divisions within the middle class will affect, but will not necessarily impede the development of, a characteristic consciousness and political proclivities.

It is already possible to identify typical middle-class preoccupations – to maintain a 'service' relationship with their employers and opportunities for career progress, and that merit (signalled, above all else, by qualifications) should be properly rewarded. Middle-class preoccupations are not diametrically opposed to, but they are different from, working-class values. The contemporary middle class is not particularly conservative, in fact some sections are extremely radical. What characterises all sections is their ability to make their voices heard; middle-class causes, and personnel, have been obliterating other voices. While the working class has shrunk and become disorganised, the trends in the middle class are exactly the reverse.

7

The Upper Class

Introduction

This chapter is not primarily about the aristocracy. They feature because they are part of the present-day upper class, and their importance extends far beyond attracting tourists and offering quaint reminders of olde England. Yet the aristocracy is not the core of the present-day upper class; wealth is at the core – serious wealth that can be put to productive use and which can expand itself.

The first section deals with the creation of Britain's present-day upper class which occurred through a fusion between the aristocratic land-owners and the nineteenth century's nouveaux riches – the leading industrialists, traders and bankers. The next section analyses how ownership and control have subsequently been depersonalised during the growth of large, limited-liability companies, and the development of city (of London) intermediaries between private investors and the ultimate destinations of their investments. The following two sections deal with arguments which assert either that a separate upper class no longer exists because wealth has been democratised, or that the owners of wealth have been rendered innocuous by a separation of ownership and control. Both arguments are shown to be incredibly naive.

The final two sections outline some distinctive features of Britain's upper class: the inclusion of aristocrats; the class's integration within a single national business network, cemented by its use of elite educational institutions, inter-marriage, and a set of exclusive social practices; the upper class's confidence and assertiveness; the extraordinary economic power and political influence that the upper class exercises; and why, although essential in a capitalist economy, the existence of an upper class is inherently and never-endingly controversial.

The Old and New Upper Classes

This is another class that has been thoroughly reconstituted. In this case the crucial change occurred ages ago, while the older middle class, with

169

businessmen and independent professionals at its core, was still being formed.

The Aristocracy and the Present-day Upper Class

The aristocracy was the core of the old, pre-industrial upper class. Aristocrats owned land which gave them economic power; they were the economically dominant class in the era when agriculture was the mainstay of the economy; and they also had titles which gave them seats in parliament, in the House of Lords, which gave them political power. Everyone knew who was in the aristocracy, and also their precise ranks: the monarch was at the head, followed by dukes, marquesses, earls, viscounts, barons, baronets and knights (whose orders were ranked). The boundary beneath this old upper class was never crystal clear. The gentry and 'society' families were either lesser landowners or people who could claim kinship, sometimes close, sometimes distant, with someone who was definitely 'in'. Such links always ended within the aristocracy. Connections were absolutely crucial to many families' status, but they always needed to be complemented by a genteel way of life in which 'sordid' occupations, as in trade and manufacturing, played no direct part.

By the nineteenth century Britain had industrialists, merchants and bankers whose combined wealth exceeded the aristocracy's, and industry and trade had become the cornerstones of the economy. Britain was not alone in this respect, as throughout Europe the old upper classes were having to yield power. The British way, though, was rather special; aristocrats were not guillotined, they were not even stripped of their wealth or their titles or their seats in parliament. Rather, they became merged with the leading members of the new business classes. Industrialists bought land and were awarded titles; land-owners dug coal-mines, invested in industry, and especially in 'the city' – the financial institutions which were, and still are, based in the City of London. Old and new money sent its sons to public (independent) schools. It is amazing how little has changed since then. Thus the present-day upper class has retained the status and many of the privileges of its predecessor. Hereditary lords retained their right to sit and vote in parliament (in the House of Lords) until the very end of the twentieth century; and Britain still has its traditional honours system. Throughout the nineteenth century and, indeed, up to this present day, there have been people for whom the big social class issue is whether people who are just very wealthy, the nouveaux riches, should defer to members of old titled families. This question is unlikely to go away completely even if the monarchy is abolished. It can still take generations for families to establish themselves in upper-class networks; there are, for example, few members of Britain's ethnic minorities in the upper class. Discrimination apart, to be accepted socially people need to have been to the right schools and universities, to have close connections with other upper-class families, and to share their lifestyle. Caution over admission to its inner circles has been one of the upper class's strategies for survival. However, the distinction between old and new money is the really burning class issue at the present time only for the minute proportion of the population that is either titled or very wealthy.

The modern upper class, like any other modern class, is defined by its work and market situations. These are very distinctive. The distinctive work situation is employing other people, usually not directly and personally nowadays, but indirectly and impersonally. The distinctive market situation is having one's life-chances depend not on the sale of one's labour power and associated skills and knowledge, but the returns on one's capital investments. One would expect such distinctive work and market situations to give rise to equally distinctive forms of consciousness and political proclivities.

Identifying the Upper Class

It is pointless to try to identify members of the upper class routinely in survey research. They do not all have noble titles. So there is no point in including an upper class in class schemes that are intended for use in this type of investigation. 'How much are you worth?' is not a useful survey question; many people do not know. Another problem is that the assets of the very wealthy are often held in trusts, so even an honest answer to the above question could result in mis-classification. It is possible to conduct surveys which do establish how much individuals are worth, but this takes pages of questions. It is not as straightforward as, 'What is your occupation?'

People can be asked whether they own the businesses where they work, and how large the businesses are, but most 'capitalists' thereby identified are either managers with significant shareholdings (though very small as proportions of the companies' total worth) or proprietors of small to medium-sized enterprises (Marshall *et al.*, 1988). The very wealthy, the real upper class, are submerged. Even with huge samples, the numbers of very wealthy respondents would be too small to analyse even if they could be easily identified. The upper class needs to be studied in other ways. Inheritance and other tax data, and share registers, are useful sources of information. Published information about company directors, supplemented by whatever can be learnt about their backgrounds from *Who's Who* and similar publications, and from interviews and questionnaires, are also useful (see Scott, 1997; Scott and Griff, 1984). We do in fact know a great deal about Britain's upper class, albeit from investigations using rather different research methods than those routinely employed in studying other classes.

Most of the active members of the upper class (those who sit on company boards, and in the House of Lords) are males. This is a male-dominated class even though there are more or less just as many very wealthy women as very wealthy men. Traditional gender divisions are more entrenched within the upper class than in any other section of the population. Ownership of wealth is usually spread around within families, partly as a way of reducing tax liabilities, but families still pool their wealth when converting it into power, and the family 'representatives' are nearly all men. Titles still pass to the eldest son. Females may be wealthy individuals in their own right, but convention dictates that males control the wealth. The upper class is skilled at marginalising women from their own property, but, needless to say, women play important roles within and for the upper class. They sit on the boards of charities, and on other local and national committees. They orchestrate the upper class's social occasions. But it is quite rare, even today, for women to chair the boards of companies in which their families' wealth is invested, or to seek seats in parliament.

The upper class has an unrivalled record of intergenerational stability, and many families have retained their positions since pre-industrial times (Scott, 1982). Considering its small size (less than 1 per cent of the population) the upper class has a remarkable level of intergenerational continuity. Roughly a third of Britain's 300 wealthiest individuals have titles (Rojek, 2000). It is still the case that inheritance is by far the most common way in which individuals become wealthy, and the wealthiest individuals are worth thousands of millions of £s. There is no way in which such sums can be saved, even from top managers' salaries.

The upper class is, in fact, Britain's best example of a well-formed class, both as a demographic entity, and in terms of its level of internal social organisation which enables the class to act effectively in accordance with its interests. However, the upper class is not, and never has been, a closed group. It has recruited new blood constantly. Some people become seriously wealthy by developing what started off as micro-enterprises. Others acquire such wealth as a result of (very) successful middle-class careers. Nowadays there are others who become extremely wealthy by lottery (literally).

Empowerment

The position and power of the modern upper class derive ultimately from its ownership and control over productive resources. The members of the upper class set their own, and, directly or indirectly, everyone else's terms and conditions of employment. They decide which businesses will expand and which will close, and whose jobs will remain and whose will end. Yet the upper class are not reviled people. This is because their own hands usually stay clean: their power is exercised through intermediaries – the middle class of managers and professional people.

The power of the upper class is consolidated and enhanced through its ability to act as a class, through its members' relationships with one another which arise basically from the structure of their ownership and control of productive resources. There is no official or unofficial class governing body, but there are several bodies that operate in lieu (see below). And in recent times the upper class has been able to tilt the balance of power in its favour to an even greater extent than formerly.

The upper class has been able to control how new technology has been developed and used. This technology enhances owners' ability to exercise surveillance over their organisations, their direct employees, and other people who are contracted to act on their behalf. The owners of capital have also driven globalisation. Capital moves more easily across national boundaries than any other resource; there are institutions and procedures which can transfer capital almost instantly and effortlessly; and there are agents of the upper class, multinational companies, that are able to act transnationally. Globalisation is not so obviously in the interests of any other class.

All present-day governments need to listen to the requirements of capital. The upper classes have guaranteed access to influential politicians in virtually all countries. They can sponsor political parties and politicians who they favour, just as they can choose to invest in countries where their property is secure and will work productively for them. In Britain the upper class retains its connections with, and the prestige that is still attached to, the aristocracy. The upper class can command the attention and attendance of other celebrities, as can the upper classes in other countries, but the British upper class has additional, traditional cultural resources at its disposal. These relationships, with the very wealthy at their core, comprise what is sometimes called 'the establishment' or 'the old-boy network'. The relationships protect and consolidate the upper class. This class is not in decline; it has never been as confident and as powerful as it is today.

The Depersonalisation of Ownership and Control

Members of the upper class are rarely seen in public acting out their roles as owners and controllers of wealth. This slice of business life is usually publicised only in the financial pages of newspapers, and the reporting usually attributes actions and events to institutions and markets rather than individuals or a class of real people. Names are sometimes named, but the upper class's high-profile appearances on the public stage are typically at celebrity events, and when meeting government ministers, possibly to discuss investment plans. The upper class often appears to be doing the rest of us a favour, sometimes by its members' mere presence. John Scott (1997) has argued that the ownership and control of productive assets have been thoroughly depersonalised, which is the principal reason why many people today doubt the existence of a powerful upper class.

In detail, how industry is owned and controlled and the manner in which ownership rights are exercised and how these have changed over time are complex tales, but the main features and trends are very simple.

Personal Ownership and Control

In the early days of industrial capitalism most enterprises were small. This applied to metal factories, cotton mills, shipping companies and banks, though there were exceptions such as the merchant companies which were chartered by the crown and were granted rights not just to trade, but also, in effect, to rule the expanding British Empire. However, in most British-based companies there was a personal owner, a Mr Gradgrind, who everyone in the firm knew because Mr Gradgrind was at the works every day. He ran everything. Workers knew who the boss was. He hired, supervised and fired them. Workers also knew what was happening to the profits from their work. They could see how the Gradgrind family lived.

Managers

Once successful companies grew beyond a certain size it became impossible for a single owner to run everything. In addition to office staff who helped with the book-keeping, it became necessary to employ professionals and managers to supervise the technology, to develop and maintain appropriate accounting systems, and to actually run the works. This is the private sector origin of the new middle class that now accounts for around a third of the workforce. Everyone still knew that the factory belonged to Mr Gradgrind, but the boss who hired, supervised and sacked them would usually be a salaried manager. He was one of 'them', and often the target for all the workers' ill-feelings. Most of Mr Gradgrind's own public appearances could be as a benefactor – opening a civic park on land that he had donated, maybe a civic theatre, and hosting the works' christmas party, for instance. As his daily presence was no longer necessary, Mr Gradgrind could live further away, maybe in a mock stately home built in the surrounding countryside.

Joint-Stock Companies

For companies to grow beyond another certain size, there needed to be more than one investor. Even persons with sufficient wealth to own a giant company would probably prefer to spread their risks. Joint-stock, limited-liability companies make this possible. Here ownership is split between numerous stockholders – dozens, hundreds or even thousands. Each risks no more than his or her personal investment. So no-one need risk their entire fortune in just one business. People may purchase shares in dozens, even hundreds of enterprises. Once this happens, owners become faceless. Workers may not, probably do not, know precisely who they are working for. The owners become a depersonalised body of shareholders.

Intermediaries

Since the Second World War matters have become much more complicated. We have entered an ongoing era of mergers, takeovers and demergers, and few joint-stock companies have been unaffected. Sometimes a stronger business absorbs a weaker firm. Sometimes two strong firms merge for mutual advantage. An acquiring company may absorb its acquisition. Or the acquired firm may be left intact, with the purchasing company acting as the corporate owner. Some acquisitions may be within the same industry, or a company may decide to diversify, in which case it becomes a conglomerate. A subsidiary firm itself may acquire a third company. It may purchase the entire business or just a proportion of the shares. Others shares may be held by yet another company. Large firms are constantly acquiring bits of others and selling parts of themselves.

The largest companies often operate internationally, with sites in more than one country; they may buy existing companies located in different countries to where the parents are based. Some giant multinationals have turnovers in excess of the governments' budgets in some of the world's smaller states, and this can give the companies extraordinary power. They can switch production to countries with the cheapest or most compliant labour; they can switch their profits to the countries with the lowest taxes on such earnings; and it can be difficult to identify exactly who is commanding, and benefiting from, this power.

Another type of indirect ownership is via financial intermediaries – the city (of London) firms that handle investments for banks, countries, pension funds, companies and individuals. Most of the shares quoted on the London Stock Exchange are now held by financial institutions, usually on behalf of clients. Using the city in this way makes sense. The people who work there specialise in making investments to obtain the required returns. Why do it yourself when expert (and very well-rewarded) professional help is available?

The upshot of all this is that many people today have no idea who they work for. Woolworth's staff may know that their chain-store is owned by Kingfisher, but who owns Kingfisher? Exactly whose money is a merchant bank investing? Consumers rarely know who owns the firms from which they purchase goods and services. It was different in the past; everyone knew that the clogs were made at Mr Gradgrind's factory.

Some people do know exactly who owns what. City personnel and financial journalists need to know, certainly within the business sectors in which they specialise. It is their job to know who owns what, who is buying and who is selling. This applies even more so to the active members of the upper class. The information is not secret, but it has become a specialist body of knowledge, a bit like nuclear physics. People work for, and consumers buy from, impersonal firms; decisions on investment which create and abolish jobs are taken (so it appears) by impersonal organisations, or even blind market forces.

For present purposes there is no need to name names, but the crucial point is that at the end of the chains of subsidiaries and parent companies, merchant banks and investment funds, there are always private individuals who own the wealth. Some adopt high profiles. Everyone has heard of Rupert Murdoch and Richard Branson. Personal ownership and control are not entirely things of the past, but most wealthy individuals do not expose themselves in this way. Decisions appear to be taken by, and in the interests of, impersonal businesses.

Business can appear to be in everyone's interest. Government assistance to business can appear to benefit all concerned, so it does not appear to be extremely wealthy individuals who request governments, and tax-payers, to subsidise their investments. There was a time when no-one would have thought it possible that workers could be persuaded to pay for their jobs.

All Capitalists Now?

The above passages have referred to an upper class comprising less than 1 per cent of the population – extremely wealthy individuals, some titled, some politically active, a larger number well-known in business networks, but many living as rich but otherwise obscure private citizens – who share an ability to live comfortably on their investments, and whose life-chances hinge primarily on how they deploy their wealth. We need to consider an alternative view: that the idea of wealth and power being so concentrated is hopelessly outdated. For example:

> It is simply not possible today to draw a clear distinction between a class of 'capitalists' who own all the country's productive resources, and a class of 'workers' who own nothing, for most workers have a direct or indirect financial stake in capitalist enterprises, and most companies are owned directly or indirectly by millions of workers. (Saunders and Harris, 1994, p. 1)

Saunders and Harris notwithstanding, there are few British sociologists who dispute the existence of a separate upper class, but, outside sociology, most people either deny that one exists or have grossly mistaken ideas about its character. Political leaders rarely argue in class terms. The media (mostly in upper-class ownership) are inoffensive. We have been told for decade after decade that wealth and power have been democratised. Everyone knows that there are some extremely wealthy individuals, but we are told that we should be grateful to them for generating such wealth and keeping it in Britain. The preservation of noble titles is presented as rather quaint and rather useful since the aristocracy and their stately homes attract tourists who are good for the economy, and therefore for all of us.

Over the years a number of serious arguments have in fact been put forward denying the existence of a separate powerful and wealthy upper class. The arguments seem plausible only while the opposition is kept silent. We can start with Saunders and Harris's claim that all, or most of us, are capitalists now.

The Spread of Wealth

It is certainly true that in Britain wealth is now spread around much more widely than a century ago, and that far more than 1 per cent of the population own shares in companies. Personal share-owning rose substantially in the 1980s and 1990s when a series of nationalised industries were privatised, and shares were offered for sale to their employees and the general public. Roughly a fifth of the adult population bought shares. When building societies converted themselves into banks, shares were issued to most of their existing members, the savers and borrowers, millions of people in total. Of course, some immediately sold their shares and took a pure windfall or a quick capital gain, but many held on. The government-authorised PEPs (personal equity plans) and their successor the ISA (individual savings account) have also encouraged more widespread share-ownership. The net effect was that at the end of the 1990s 17 per cent of all adults held shares.

Other forms of wealth are even more widespread. As the population has become more prosperous, more people have saved regularly. Sometimes their savings are in banks and building societies, but it has become increasingly common for savings to be placed in 'unit trusts' where purchasers buy units in trust funds that are invested in many companies thereby enabling small investors to spread their risks.

However, a more significant development from the point of view of democratising wealth is that roughly a half of all employees are now in occupational pension schemes. A smaller number have personal pension funds. The sums accumulated in these ways can be considerable. For example, a person with lifetime earnings averaging £20,000 a year (roughly average male earnings in the mid-1990s), whose personal and employer contributions to a pension fund amounted to 15 per cent of his or her income, would have £120,000 invested over a 40-year working life, by the end of which there would have been considerable capital appreciation because most of the funds would be invested in company shares. Obviously, the sums vary depending on the levels of individuals' earnings and contributions, but roughly a half of the population invest substantial sums in pension funds, or have such sums invested on their behalf, and their financial circumstances in retirement, which can last for many years nowadays, depend on the performance of these investments.

The types of assets that are in fact held most widely are goods with a market value, mainly houses and motor cars, though some people also own art and antiques, and the furniture in people's homes has some value.

When all forms of wealth are taken into account, we see that, over time, wealth has indeed become distributed much more widely and equally throughout the population. So in 1911 the most wealthy 1 per cent of the population held 69 per cent of all personally-held wealth, whereas by 1993 it was just 17 per cent – a truly massive drop. Some of the redistribution has been within the top end of the wealth scale. So the proportion of personally-held assets held by the top 10 per cent decreased less steeply, from 92 per cent in 1911 to 48 per cent in 1993 (Futcher and Scott, 1999). Clearly, there is some truth in the view that wealth has been spread around and is no longer confined to a small capitalist class, though even in 1993 10 per cent of the population still commanded nearly a half of all personally-held wealth. Even after all the redistribution – the spread of home and car ownership, PEPs, ISAs, privatisations and building society conversions – wealth is still heavily concentrated. We are certainly not all capitalists now. In 1993 the least wealthy half of the population owned just 7 per cent of all personally-held wealth; around 30 per cent of adults do not own the dwellings in which they live; a half of all employees do not have significant occupational pensions. In fact a half of the population has near-zero assets, and many are in debt when account is taken of outstanding mortgages, bank overdrafts, hire-purchase commitments, loans on credit cards, store cards and all the rest. It is only roughly a half of the population that has any significant share in the country's wealth.

Wealth, Investments and Life-chances

Fifty per cent or thereabouts of the population with investments in productive assets, either directly or on their behalf, supports the Saunders and Harris view that capitalists are no longer a tiny class. But the fact that many workers have some assets, and that many capitalists also work (see below), does not necessarily prove that there is no longer a glaring class division between them.

First, we need to separate assets that people acquire for their own use (houses and cars, for example), and assets that are held primarily to make a gain on, or to derive income from, the investments. Works of art and antiques, and vintage or just 'classic' cars, may be purchased as investments, but this is not how most people regard their home furnishings and motor vehicles. Home owners can make capital gains, but this is not their main reason for buying their dwellings. We should note, however (see below), that the attractions of home-ownership include the acquisition of an asset which may, eventually, become wealth that cascades down the generations. Most cars depreciate, whereas most houses at least retain their original real value.

Second, there is a difference between, on the one hand, savings which transfer spending power from the time when the money was earned to some later point in life, like retirement, and, on the other hand, assets whose primary use is capital accumulation and/or the generation of a flow of income that need never be exhausted. People who become quite wealthy in terms of the sums invested on their behalf in pension funds do not expect, and cannot realistically hope, to keep most of this wealth intact throughout their retirements. It is only the extremely wealthy who can expect to die without having liquidated most of their capital. We must note, however (again, see below), that the size of the pensions that roughly a half of the working population will receive, depends primarily on the performance of stock-exchange investments. It is not only the very wealthy who now have a vested interest in growth rates, and rates of return on, productive assets.

Third, and perhaps most crucially, the crunch question in respect of class membership is what a person's life-chances depend upon. For most people, the types of housing that they can afford, and the amounts that they are able to save towards retirement, depend on their incomes from employment. We should note that as more and more wealth cascades down the generations, more and more people's types of housing and the sums that they can afford to keep as investments will depend on how much they inherit as well as how much they earn. This will widen rather than narrow class differences, and strengthen intergenerational continuity within classes, though it may well blur the class division between the very wealthy and the rest.

Similarly, whether people have been able to benefit from the privatisations, building society conversions, PEPs and ISAs has depended primarily on their earned incomes. In most cases these investments have not become principal determinants of their life-chances: the investors continue to depend basically on how much they are able to earn.

The proportion of the population with sufficient wealth to make it unnecessary for them to work for someone else, or for themselves in the conventional sense, and who are able to allow their capital to grow rather than deplete it during their lifetimes, is still less than 1 per cent. This tiny section of the population's life-chances depend on their ability to employ others to work for them. Other people's (the vast majority's) life-chances depend on the kinds of employment that they can obtain. Despite the spread of wealth, this remains a clear class relationship and division. It is, in fact, the clearest of all class divisions, and it still splits the population into a tiny minority on the one side, and the great mass of the people on the other.

Consciousness and Politics

The spread of wealth may not have turned even 50 per cent of the population into capitalists, but it may still affect their consciousness and politics. Their stock-exchange investments may not be the main factor in the life-chances of most of the 17 per cent of the population who are direct share owners, but these investments could make a disproportionate impression on the consciousness of many of those concerned. A half of the middle class has such investments, and they account for most of the 17 per cent. The privatisations and building society conversions have not bred a generation of working-class Sids but they have given the middle class another ground for perceiving their own interests as basically similar to those of people above. Owning shares, however small the investment, may encourage people to read share prices regularly, and to pay attention to the standard stock-exchange item on the broadcast news. A rising stock-market possibly makes them feel good, just like rising house prices (provided people have already bought their dwellings).

Saunders and Harris (1994) have speculated that the extent to which share-owning had been widened may have won the 1992 general election for the Conservatives. Their argument is plausible. Labour was threatening to restore many of the privatised businesses into some form of public ownership or control. The Saunders and Harris argument is that share owners may have voted Conservative in order to protect their investments, while few people would have voted Labour through a desire to renationalise. The 1992 election was closely fought, and it is just possible that this particular issue made the crucial difference. It is unlikely that any party that is perceived as anti-business will poll well among people who are direct share owners.

While it is true that home-ownership does not make those concerned into capitalists, it may well affect their perceptions of their positions in society. The renovations and customising, which make it clear which properties on council estates have been privatised, must be saying something about the occupants' feelings. We know that the transition from being a tenant to being a home owner rarely changes people's class identities or politics in the short term. Occupational class tends to determine types of housing, social consciousness and politics, but housing is rarely the crucial independent variable (see Forrest and Murie, 1987; Forrest *et al.*, 1990; Saunders, 1990; Wait, 1996). But this will not prevent home-ownership making some long-term difference to how the residents view themselves *vis-à-vis* others. Dwellings are different from most other assets; they are bought for use but are like substantial stock-exchange portfolios in that people have realistic chances of leaving these assets to their descendants. This does not always happen. People may need to sell their dwellings in order to provide income during retirement, especially if they need residential care. No wealth automatically cascades down, and increases in value, from generation to generation. However, the risk that assets might be dissipated may make those concerned all the keener to hold on, and to support policies and politicians who seek to assist people to retain their possessions. Members of other classes have been given, or have given themselves, sound material reasons for supporting policies which also enable the upper class to hang on to its assets.

Ownership and Control

The Managerial Revolution

As an alternative to contending that a wealthy class no longer exists because wealth is now spread around more equally than in the past, it has been claimed that the wealthy can no longer harm anyone because private wealth no longer confers power. This is a very long-standing argument. It is partly about politics – the widening of the franchise beyond the propertied classes – but it is mainly about who runs privately-owned businesses. Here the argument dates back to the time when joint-stock, limited-liability status was becoming the norm for large enterprises. Researchers counted the number of companies where the share of the largest stock-holder dipped beneath 50 per cent. These companies, which quickly became the majority, were deemed to have fallen into management control (Berle and Means, 1932).

The argument is straightforward. It observes that in most joint-stock companies the share owners are too numerous and too dispersed for them to act as a governing cabal. Also, most owners spread their risks by investing in numerous companies, and it would not be possible for them to take the time and trouble to try to become experts in the affairs of them all. Rational investors, it is argued, will leave the management of the companies that they own in the hands of the real experts – professionals with specialist expertise and managers who really know the nuts and bolts of the businesses.

The second part of the argument alleges that salaried managers will not run businesses in exactly the same way as the owners. To be sure, investors have to be given satisfactory returns on their investments – sufficient to persuade them to leave their money in the businesses. Beyond this, however, the managers have no need to worry, or so it is said. They do not need to generate the highest possible returns on capital; they are likely to be as concerned to satisfy other 'stakeholders', like the workforces whose cooperation they require. And, of course, the managers will want to enhance their own terms and conditions of employment. In addition to all other considerations, it is argued that professional managers will operate companies within the requirements of the law, and will be responsive to the wishes and policies of the government of the day, unlike owners, such as the petit bourgeoisie (see Chapter 5), who characteristically complain and do everything possible to sidestep bureaucracy.

In the 1930s managerialism was an exciting development. James Burnham's *The Managerial Revolution* was first published in 1941, but all his major predictions proved wrong. Burnham believed that managers would become a new ruling class, politically dominant, that they would eventually relieve share owners of their assets, and that fascist Germany and the Soviet Union were prototype manager-run societies. Fortunately for Burnham's reputation, he is best remembered, and became famous, for the phrase in his book's title.

The separation of ownership and control thesis was a sociological orthodoxy by the 1950s. Ralf Dahrendorf (1959) argued that functionalism (then the most influential sociological theory, especially in North America) understated the amount of class conflict, but that the main class division was no longer between owners and workers, as Marx had suggested, but between those in authority and those in subordinate positions. Managers were believed to have taken-over as the dominant class.

The Labour Party was profoundly influenced by the managerial philosophy. The vehicle that it adopted for taking the means of production into common ownership was the nationalised industry run by a board of management. Alternatives such as workers' and local community control were rejected. The nationalised industries were to be shining examples of efficiency, run by professional managers appointed for their competence rather than their connections, and unencumbered by the need to pay dividends to share owners.

By the 1950s a revisionist wing in the Labour Party had decided that ownership had become irrelevant (Crosland, 1956). This idea was less controversial in the social democratic parties of continental Europe than in the British Labour Party at that time. The aim of the so-called 'social market economies' is to use private enterprise to generate the wealth to fund public services, and to pursue whatever other social and economic objectives might be agreed by the 'social partners' – employers and trade unions, acting in collaboration with government. Britain never really embraced the social market, or corporatism as it was being called in Britain by the 1970s. And by then the original idea that the rise of managers had disempowered owners was in tatters.

Owner-power Rediscovered

Since the 1970s researchers have been studying exactly who runs joint-stock companies. One result of these studies is that the proportion of a company's shares that needs to be in a single set of hands in order to act as a controlling interest has been revised downwards radically. It has been discovered that a major shareholder with less than 10 per cent of a company's stock can occupy a dominant position if, as is typically the case, most of the smaller shareholders 'sleep' while the others vote in different ways or accept the advice of the leading shareholder on controversial issues.

It has also been discovered that in most companies there is in fact a controlling interest. Sometimes the controlling stock belongs to just one individual; sometimes it belongs to members of the same family; sometimes it belongs to a corporate investor or financial institution; or sometimes a 'constellation of interests' act in unison thereby establishing a dominant position (Scott, 1997).

It has also been discovered that some shareholders are highly active. It is true that the majority neither attend company meetings nor submit postal votes, but some are active, always including the dominant interest. Those who are active act in the interests of shareholders in general, which is why so many are prepared to 'sleep'. Owners, or their representatives, usually occupy key positions on company boards, such as chairperson (Francis, 1980; Scott, 1997).

Studies of business decision-making have shown that who takes decisions can be irrelevant. Salaried mangers may decide which new machines to instal, which products to develop and which staff to hire and fire, but they do so in a context where they know that they will be judged by the implications for profitability and the market value of a company's shares. In this sense, decisions are already 'made' before managers settle the technical details and put them into effect. Boards of directors, on which owners invariably play a dominant role or have someone else play such a role on their behalf, fix the parameters within which salaried managers operate (Herman, 1981). Company law in Britain requires boards of directors to act in share-owners' interests, and no-one else's. Managers are rewarded if their performances produce dividends (literally) and they are penalised for failure. An American study found that company profitability (or rather the lack of this) was the best predictor of management dismissals (James and Soref, 1981).

Company boards usually ensure that top managers' interests are aligned with those of the shareholders. A commonly-used device is the stock option: the right to purchase a given number of shares up to a specified date at a pre-fixed price. This gives managers a powerful incentive to run a business so as to ensure that the market price of the shares advances well-beyond what their own purchases will cost. Their salaries, bonuses and stock options can make top managers into extremely wealthy individuals. The costs to existing shareholders are minute; the total value of a company's shares is hardly diluted, and the astronomical salaries and bonuses paid to a few key managers are a minor cost when set against total turnover and profits. Owners would be foolish not to ensure that any managers with real power did not know whose side they are on.

When one company owns another, the managers of the parent company usually act as if they were personal owners, and the evidence suggests that they enjoy this role-play. Pressure on the subsidiaries' managers to deliver are magnified (Windolf, 1998). All the managers stand to gain, but the group that benefits most is the shareholders.

Management buy-outs are rarely what the phrase suggests. Most of the capital to purchase a company is invariably from outside investors. The managers who are part of the buy-out consortium will be required to invest substantial savings of their own, and may well be given additional stock options. It is a splendid vehicle for ensuring that a business is run in the interests of its (mostly absentee) owners (Campbell *et al.*, 1992).

Owners and Managers in the Class Structure

Managers have not been revolutionaries; they run businesses more effectively on the owners' behalf than would the latter if left to themselves. The relationship between the upper class and the middle class is crucial in the contemporary class structure. The upper class needs managers and professionals; large modern corporations could not be run without them. The businesses need expertise that the owners themselves could rarely supply. The owners also need managers and professionals to control other classes of employees.

Up to now the middle class has offered more than enough willing accomplices. They want to be committed to their organisations and professions. They want careers, and a condition for long-range ascent is accepting a service relationship with the upper class, though few may see their roles in exactly these terms. The rewards for managers and professionals can be considerable: they range up to assimilation into the ranks of the seriously wealthy. There is no fence across the division between the upper class and the middle class. Yet there is considerable discontent within the present-day middle class. If this was ever transformed into economic radicalism, the class structure really would be threatened.

British Capitalism

Every capitalist country has an upper class within which privately-owned wealth is concentrated. There are other similarities, including the access to political elites which active members of the upper classes invariably enjoy. However, there are inter-country differences even in this era of globalisation, and some specifics of the British upper class are noteworthy.

Aristocrats Included

We have already noted that Britain's modern upper class was formed by a nineteenth-century merger of the old upper class, the aristocracy, and the emergent business-based upper class. One result has been that the modern upper class has retained much of the status that was attached to the aristocracy. Another is that Britain never experienced an industrial cultural revolution, and a gentlemanly ethic was maintained in the higher echelons of businesses which, according to one school of thought, has been a persistent millstone for the British economy (see Weiner, 1981).

In some ways the aristocracy is an irrelevance, a distraction. They are not the core, and they are not essential to the maintenance of a modern upper class. To repeat, the base of the present-day upper class is not its titles and tradition but its privately-owned wealth that can be put to productive use. However, aristocratic connections add some 'real class' to Britain's uppers, and they give the entire upper class a circuit of social events where they can all meet people who they need to know. Its visible lifestyle gives the upper class a benign public image while setting them in a world apart. It is a world in which the start of grouse, partridge and pheasant shooting, and stag and fox hunting are significant dates, and likewise the Derby, the Grand National, Royal Ascot, the Cheltenham Gold Cup, Wimbledon, Hurlingham, Henley, Cowes, the Eton–Harrow cricket match, the Oxford–Cambridge boat race, Chelsea Flower Show, Queen Charlotte's and the rest of the London and county balls. Now it is true that it is unnecessary to be either rich or titled to attend some of these events, but invitations are required to be in the right places, like the royal enclosures. There are other events and places where the seriously wealthy can meet each other without intrusion – conferences of the Institute of Directors, the Confederation of British Industry, London clubs, the Lord Mayor's Banquet and city lunches to which top politicians are invited (and they attend). There are some leisure activities which exclude all but the very rich – those who can afford to buy ocean-racing vessels and racing horses, fly first class, stay in five-star hotels, and spend vacations at exclusive reports and maybe on privately-owned islands. The aristocratic circuit adds to the number, and adds gloss to the calendar.

At this point it is necessary to avoid creating an impression that the present-day uppers are a spendthrift leisure class. There are some men, and rather more upper-class women, whose lives evolve around social occasions, but the core members of today's upper class have work as their central life interest. Nowadays they do not abstain from labour; rather, they have embraced the work ethic. They have full diaries which may include business breakfasts in addition to lunches and dinners. They are not idle rich. Indeed, a typical lifestyle problem is 'finding the time'; they do not attend most of the events in the upper-class social calendar. It is more a matter of being able to attend if and when they wish, or, more likely, when doing so will be good for business (see Rojek, 2000).

Most wealthy individuals are inconspicuous. You may not have heard of Robson Walton, Paul Allen or Johanna Quandt, but they are all among the world's top-10 billionaires. Would you know them in the street? Richard Branson is one of the few seriously rich Britons with a high public profile, but in reality his life is basically work-centred (see Rojek, 2000). He is said to need eight hours sleep but works for virtually all the rest. Sometimes he may snatch naps during the day when en route between meetings. He is well-known for dressing casually and has no expensive gastronomic tastes: £15 is the most that he will pay for a bottle of wine in the restaurant on the Caribbean island that his company owns. For Branson, and in this he appears typical of the modern upper class, work is his main source of fun and excitement. He enjoys the excitement of potentially rewarding but risky ventures, as in air and rail transport. Branson also indulges in intense bursts of leisure activity. Here, once again, he appears to be typical of the present-day upper class. Most of Branson's leisure is not high-profile. He has the Caribbean island and a mansion in Oxfordshire as well as a home in London, but without doubt he is best-known for his attempts on trans-Atlantic water-borne records and long-distance hot-air ballooning. These are extremely expensive, and therefore exclusive, leisure activities. For Branson, they are brief interruptions in his normal way of life, just like Cowes and suchlike are for most of the seriously rich who attend.

Putting Wealth to Work

Other distinctive features of Britain's upper class are linked to the central economic role, some would say dominant role, of 'the city'. Britain has a single national business network, meaning that specific sources of capital are not tied to any particular regions, industries or firms. Capital markets, and therefore the business class, are not segmented. All the major financial institutions are based in the same 'city' through which capital flows to wherever will yield the most favourable returns.

Around 60 per cent of all shares in London stock exchange-quoted companies are held by financial institutions, acting on clients' behalf. The financial institutions are used for their expertise in securing returns on capital. The prized skill is being able to beat the market; to secure better returns than would have accrued to a random selection of investments. City traders who can achieve this earn spectacular bonuses. These are earned not by identifying firms with good prospects for long-term growth and profitability, but by anticipating short-term movements in share prices. This creates a high volume of stock-exchange transactions, most of which are purely speculative. Most purchases and sales of shares are not new investment and disinvestment, but movements of funds in pursuit of short-term gains. All markets in which such transactions predominate (foreign exchange markets are another) produce wide fluctuations in prices which usually bear only a slender relationship to the underlying strengths and weaknesses of the assets that are being traded. Funds are moved in anticipation of, and the movements themselves can help to create, short-term swings in share prices.

British-based capital will flow into any firms and business sectors that are judged likely to yield short-term gains. London is a world-class centre, arguably the world leader, in this operation; but the funds will flow out of the country if there appear to be better prospects elsewhere. Some analysts claim that this endemic short-termism is the really crucial weakness in the British economy (see Hutton, 1995).

A Well-Integrated Upper Class

Investments by very wealthy individuals criss-cross as they move through the city and into various companies. So directorships also criss-cross. Multiple directorships are the norm among active members of the upper class and their representatives from financial institutions. Most joint-stock companies appear to be related to most others, either directly or indirectly, through this interlocking system of directorships (Whitley, 1973; Scott, 1997). This lays the foundation for an unusually well-integrated British upper class. John Scott (1991) estimates that there are just 43,500 active members of the British upper class, and that they comprise only 0.1 per cent of the population. Such a small number of people can be well-integrated. Everybody may not know everyone else, but everyone's networks inter-lock, so that the entire class is bound in an exclusive system of interpersonal relationships. They are a well-integrated network, and powerful. They have strategic control over the economy. All businesses compete, including finance houses, but competition itself can be a source of bonds; and mergers and demergers mean that one can never be certain who one's partners and competitors will be tomorrow.

The social integration of the upper class is cemented through its use of Britain's elite system of public (independent) schools such as Harrow, Eton and Winchester, and these schools' links with Oxford and Cambridge universities. Independent schools educate 7 per cent of secondary age pupils but provide about a half of all Oxbridge undergraduates. During an elite education young people are introduced to the social events that help to integrate the upper class. They rub shoulders with one another and also with individuals who will become senior civil servants, judges and army officers. The upper class has personal relationships with key members of key professions, and with politicians, many of whom (in all the main parties) have Oxbridge backgrounds. These relationships are further strengthened by the upper class's tendency to inter-marry, and by the class's distinctive lifestyle (see above) which is possible only if one is rich and properly connected. The British upper class is certainly not disorganised. It is extremely well-organised; by itself, rather than by the state. An effect is to create a body of opinion that is known to, and which can be absorbed by, all insiders. So when members of the upper class deal with government personnel, they are most likely to be speaking for their entire class. This is 'the establishment' to which outsiders can find it so difficult to gain admission, especially if they are not male, white and from the right sort of background.

Assertiveness

Britain's upper class has rarely hesitated before making its views known, and making it clear that it expects its views to be heeded, and in the closing decades of the twentieth century this assertiveness strengthened.

This characteristic of Britain's upper class will owe something to the confidence that accrues after centuries of unbroken privilege. It is also a consequence of Britain having been the first industrial nation whose original mercantile and industrial creeds were *laissez-faire*. This has made free markets, in which property owners alone decide how to deploy their assets, appear to be an almost natural order of things. Assertiveness is also a product of Britain having developed only a weak version of social democracy. Even organised labour, at the zenith of its power, subscribed to much of the *laissez-faire* creed (free collective bargaining, for example). Then came Thatcherism which declared an end to consensus, and accelerated the disorganisation of the working class as a result of the sheer pace of economic restructuring, plus the industrial relations legislation of the 1980s and the denial of a government ear to leaders of organised labour, thus reducing their credibility within and further weakening the labour movement. On top of all this there is the international context created by the collapse of communism which prompted Fukuyama's (1992) non-joyous proclamation of 'the end of history'. At present there is no visible and viable alternative to capitalism.

The confidence of the upper class is also rooted in the closed world that its members inhabit, insulated from challenges to their opinions. They are schooled, work and spend their leisure separately. They have very little contact with the working class, even the workers who they (indirectly) employ, their customers, or even small shareholders. It is only occasionally that small shareholders self-organise and force themselves to the attention of the press and company boards, as in the case of 'Cedric the pig', the chair of British Gas in the mid-1990s, who was berated at an annual meeting for his astronomic compensation package before winning the vote (with the support of institutional shareholders). The media are mostly in upper-class ownership, and the owners are accustomed to seeing their views in print (though usually without their names attached). They may not dictate to, but they do not expect to be contradicted by, their editors. Politicians usually listen respectfully to actual or potential investors. The higher-rank members of the middle class can be relied on to be compliant and trustworthy. Members of the upper class can exercise extraordinary power within the businesses in which they are major investors. Closed worlds tend to breed closed minds; hence the apparent arrogance of the upper class when, as occasionally happens, they are exposed to a wider body of contrary opinion.

This is the context in which the British upper class, usually describing itself as 'business', has abandoned caution when making its views known to one and all. It is able to rely on most listeners assuming that whatever is good for business must be good for Britain. Clashes between governments and business are believed to be bad for the reputations of the governments rather than business. Even Labour Party politicians believe that their popularity will be jeopardised if they appear closer to organised labour than to business. So business expects its wishes to be decisive whether the issue is joining the Euro, setting statutory minimum pay, a ceiling on working hours, parental leave or trade union rights.

Occasionally the upper class experiences (usually tepid) scolding. Gordon Brown, the Chancellor of the Exchequer in the 1997 Labour government, distanced himself from the city by refusing to wear evening dress at its functions. Then during 2000 he went on a rant about the admissions practices of the top universities, provoked when Oxford turned down a state school applicant with A-grades who subsequently accepted a Harvard scholarship. During the 1980s and 1990s company directors were repeatedly invited by government ministers to exercise salary restraint, to set a good example, but they continued to add huge increases to their already huge salaries. Most hereditaries have now been expelled from the House of Lords but the upper class can be confident that it will be adequately represented in a reformed second chamber. None of the above attack the base of the upper class, its wealth, and its ability to deploy this wealth in its own interests. Tough government targets the working class – the unemployed, petty offenders, and single parents who draw state benefits and live in council houses: groups who are unable to bite back.

It has become acceptable for members of the upper class to sponsor/fund/bribe politicians and their parties. It is no secret that the funders expect access and business-friendly policies. If it's business, then, so it appears, it must be OK. The very wealthy expect political and public acquiescence when they keep their personal fortunes in offshore bases, or in trusts, or in other places where they avoid European levels of taxation. How can they expect to get away with it? Well, there's this assumption that if it is good for them, it must be good for business, on which we all depend.

Class Struggle Continues

The upper class's problem is that its mere naming makes it vulnerable. The upper class prefers to be described as business, and would prefer class itself to be regarded as a thing of the past, a hark-back to the days when the upper class had the aristocracy at its core.

Merely demonstrating the continued existence of an upper class, which is really quite simple, is easily mistaken for critique. So let's be clear – capitalism requires a capitalist (upper) class; 'Everyone a capitalist' is not a viable option. Markets work in the ways that they are supposed to do, and businesses become innovatory and enterprising only when there is a separate class of owners. We know from experience during the transition from communism that giving vouchers (shares) to all workers or all citizens changes virtually nothing. It is plausible to argue that capitalism has proved to be the best of all known economic systems for all classes of people in terms of the standards of living that it delivers, and the quality of life measured by that most sensitive of all indicators – how long people live (Saunders, 1995b). To vote for capitalism is to vote for the maintenance of an upper class.

Yet the position of the upper class can never be fully secure. Its very existence clashes with core values that have always been nurtured within the working classes (and the middle classes) that the system produces. The existence of an upper class offends both working and middle-class notions of meritocracy. The key issue here is not hereditary titles but privately-held wealth – the asset that is most easily passed from generation to generation. The upper class's ways of doing things also offend the working class's preference for matters to be subject to collective agreement, its yearning for the security of a planned economy, and the desire to limit the scope of the market by guaranteeing certain basic social rights, and gearing certain services – health and education – entirely to need or merit. Any open-class system harbours discontents. There is inevitably a gap between the aspirations that are nurtured and the opportunities that can be offered. This is the root cause, and an unavoidable cause, of the middle class's discontents. These may be channelled into unfulfilled ambition, and may even become 'functional' for the system, but the discontents themselves can never be removed.

This is why, although at present there may be no alternative in sight, people will constantly search for an alternative economic system, and will be tempted by the prospect of redistributing the wealth and power of the upper class. This has been, and still is, a basis of politics in capitalist societies. Politics expresses and helps to shape class conflicts. Politics expresses but can at least tilt the balance of class forces one way or another. Class is not dead. This is still, above all else, what British politics is all about.

Summary

Britain's upper class has demonstrated a remarkable capacity to survive and thrive. This chapter has explained how Britain's modern upper class was formed in the nineteenth century through a fusion between the aristocracy and new money. The mixture has worked. We have seen that privately-owned wealth and the accompanying power remain heavily concentrated, and that the position of the upper class has been strengthened and its wealth has increased during the transition from personal to impersonal ownership and control of major businesses. While some forms of wealth have indeed become more widely distributed than in the past, the class whose life-chances depend essentially on deploying its wealth effectively still amounts to no more than 1 per cent of the population, and these owners continue to exercise strategic control over the businesses in which their wealth is invested.

We have also seen that Britain's upper class has some distinctive features, apart from its close links with the aristocracy. It well-integrated into a single national business network, strengthened by its use of elite schools and universities, inter-marriage, an exclusive social circuit, and the ease with which private wealth can be transmitted down the generations. The upper class controls most of the media and is able to command the respectful attention of leading politicians. Despite its mere existence negating values nurtured in all other social classes, the upper class in this new millennium appears able to convince all who matter that they have no better alternative than cooperation on terms acceptable to the uppers.

8

Social Mobility

Introduction

A great deal of evidence about social mobility has been introduced in previous chapters. In examining each of the main classes we have noted the members' typical origins, and the likelihood of people born into the class ending up somewhere else. Here we draw together all the social mobility evidence. But there are dangers in doing this: the statistics cascade, so it is important to keep an eye on the main questions that we are trying to answer.

The first section of this chapter explains why mobility is an important topic in class analysis. We are all interested in whether we live in a fair society, commonly understood to mean a 'meritocratic' society where individuals' achievements depend on their own talents and efforts rather than their social origins. Second, and equally important for sociology, we are interested in whether the classes into which we divide the population are demographic entities, meaning whether they have characteristic life-chances, that is, chances of ending up in different positions that distinguish them from other classes.

The next section deals with absolute mobility flows: for example, the chances of people born into the working class reaching the middle class, and vice-versa. Exactly how much mobility is there and have the rates changed over time? We shall see that there is more upward than downward mobility in present-day Britain, and that the trend over time is for upward mobility to increase while downward mobility diminishes. These trends are due entirely to the changing shape of the class structure, and there are major implications for the composition of all the main social classes.

The following sections deal with gender and ethnic divisions. Do gender and ethnicity have independent effects on people's life-chances? We shall see that the answers are more complex than the questions. It is only among individuals born into the middle class that males are clearly the advantaged sex in terms of life-chances. As regards ethnicity, there are variations between, and gender differences within, all ethnic groups, but amidst the complexities two findings deserve highlighting: the 'ethnic penalty' which we have already encountered (see Chapter 3), and Afro-Caribbeans remaining clustered towards the base of the class structure while other ethnic minorities experience collective upward mobility.

The final main section of the chapter deals with relative rates of mobility. Here we are trying to measure the openness or fluidity of the class structure, trends over time, and differences between countries. The startling finding from the mass of evidence is how little variation there has been over time, and how similar the rates of fluidity are in different modern societies. We consider the possible explanations of this – inherited ability, reproduction theory, and rational action theory – and we see that, at present, none of the theories is able to marshall evidence to make itself wholly convincing.

Why Study Mobility?

A Fair Society?

Everyone is interested in social mobility. Within and outside sociology, people's initial interest is most likely to be in whether we are an equal opportunity society. Meritocratic values are powerful and widespread; early in its history, the Labour Party abandoned egalitarianism in favour of meritocratic ambitions (Parkin, 1971), and there is no difference between Old and New Labour, or the present-day Conservatives, in this respect. Inequalities are deemed justifiable only when they reflect merit, though both parties appear to forget the upper class when proclaiming their belief in meritocracy. Sociologists have generally shared the more prevalent belief that inequalities should be merited by the individuals concerned. Showing that people's achievements are often due to their social origins rather than their own merits is commonly regarded as sufficient proof that we live in an unjust world. If inequalities are not based on individual merit, then more or less everyone seems to believe that they cannot be justified. Of course, this begs the question (which we shall return to later) as to how merit is to be measured. However, it is not difficult to demonstrate that people who are born into different social classes have very different, very unequal, life-chances. The inequalities are so huge that people are often amazed when they first see the data. Within sociology a prevalent feeling has always been, and remains, that life-chance inequalities are so wide that they cannot possibly reflect neither more nor less than merit.

It is very easy to demonstrate that the children of middle-class parents are more likely – roughly four times more likely in fact – to remain in the middle class than those born into the working class are to reach a middle-class destination. Social mobility tables which describe the destinations of groups born into different social classes are easy to construct, to read and to understand.

Matters become complicated only when we ask questions such as whether life-chances have become more or less equal over time. Here it becomes necessary somehow to take into account changes in the proportions of occupations in different classes, and maybe differential class fertility rates and changes in these. Similar complications arise when trying to compare social mobility in different societies. We can never compare like with like. If a society changes very quickly – if the farm population contracts, or the middle class expands rapidly, for example – there is more or less bound to be more movement than in a more stable society. There are ways of subtracting mobility that is inevitable because of structural changes (in the proportions of occupations in different classes) and differential fertility rates, and being left with a measure of social fluidity. It is possible to make calculations comparing the fluidity of a society at different points in time, and the rates in different countries. These figures are important, but it is always equally important to bear in mind that such statistics have little relevance to the experiential worlds in which most people live. The simple figures describing the proportion of working-class children who are upwardly mobile, for example, bear a closer resemblance to the worlds that lay people inhabit.

Classes as Demographic Entities

It is also important, in sociology at any rate, to realise that establishing how far from, or how close we are to, an equal opportunity society is not the only reason why class analysis needs to engage with social mobility. Another reason is to establish the extent to which occupation-based classes are demographic entities. The assumption here is that the members of a class are especially likely to associate with one another rather than outsiders, and to develop a characteristic form of consciousness and political proclivities, when most members stay within the same class for their entire lives, from birth until death.

Everyone knows from personal experience or acquaintances that we are not a caste society where everyone remains within the groups into which they are born. But neither are we anywhere near to the other extreme, ideal-typical case of a society where everyone spends a part, and the same proportion, of his or her life in each of the different classes. We are somewhere between these extremes and we need to establish exactly where we are located, bearing in mind that some classes are always likely to be more stable than others.

We should note here that although demographically stable classes may be especially likely to develop distinctive class cultures, social mobility is not necessarily incompatible with this development. Specific mobility experiences may be characteristic among people who are born into a class, or who reach a particular class destination, in which case the experience is likely to become part of the characteristic consciousness of the group in question. Hence the importance of identifying major mobility flows and channels. The crucial test of whether a class is a demographic entity is not whether those who are born into it tend to remain, but whether they have characteristic life-chances, that is, chances of mobility and immobility that set them apart from other classes. It is very, very simple to demonstrate that people with working and middle-class origins do indeed have very different life-chances.

Actually, it is much easier to demonstrate this for men than for women because, as we shall find repeatedly in the following passages, there has been far more research into male than into female social mobility. Until fairly recently, nearly all social mobility research assumed (sometimes tacitly and sometimes explicitly) that, in studying class structures and processes, female employment could be safely ignored (see Chapter 2, p . 42).

Absolute Mobility

As good a starting point as any in examining social mobility in present-day Britain is the findings from John Goldthorpe's 1972 survey, one of the enquiries that studied just men. The Goldthorpe findings are not recently off the press and bang up to date; they are from a sample of approximately 10,000 men who had been born before, during or shortly after the Second World War. The survey also gathered information about the sample's fathers' occupations (when the respondents were aged 14), so it enables us to look backwards in time at the shape of the class structure and mobility flows several generations ago. We can then examine more up to date figures which show how things have changed since 1972, or remained much the same as before. The more recent data used in the following passages are from the life histories of a sample of people who were born in 1958 (the NCDS – the National Child Development Study) who have been followed up ever since. They were surveyed in 1991 when they were aged 33, and are roughly a generation on from Goldthorpe's 1972 sample of adult males. Setting the findings from these different studies alongside each other enables us to identify long-term trends. This is valuable because it shows that most recent and current trends are in fact very long-running.

The 1972 survey was the first occasion when the Goldthorpe class scheme was used, and Tables 8.1 and 8.2 present, in summary form, some of the pertinent findings. Tables 8.3 and 8.4 present comparable information from the NCDS. The tables are very easy to understand, and anyone who wishes to grasp the realities of class in Britain today needs to know these figures, or at least the approximate values, and how these have been changing over time.

Some information from these surveys was presented in Chapter 3 (see Table 3.3, p. 69). Comparing the respondents' occupations in Goldthorpe's 1972 survey with their fathers' occupations, and adding the NCDS findings

Table 8.1   Class outflows

Sons	Fathers			
	Service (%)	*Intermediate (%)*	*Working (%)*	*Total (%)*
Service	59	30	16	27
Intermediate	25	36	27	30
Working	15	34	57	44

Source: Adapted from Goldthorpe *et al.* (1980).

Table 8.2   Class inflows

Fathers	Sons			
	Service (%)	*Intermediate (%)*	*Working (%)*	*Total (%)*
Service	32	12	5	14
Intermediate	35	37	24	31
Working	33	50	71	55

Source: Adapted from Goldthorpe *et al.* (1980).

Table 8.3   Class outflows, males

Sons	Fathers			
	Service (%)	*Intermediate (%)*	*Working (%)*	*Total (%)*
Service	61	40	26	36
Intermediate	20	26	19	21
Working	18	34	55	43

Source: Adapted from Savage and Egerton (1997).

Table 8.4   Class inflows, males

Fathers	Sons			
	Service (%)	Intermediate (%)	Working (%)	Total (%)
Service	32	18	8	19
Intermediate	28	32	20	26
Working	40	50	72	56

Source: Adapted from Savage and Egerton (1997).

from the 1990s, portrays the main long-term trends in the shape of the class structure: the contraction of the working class and the expansion of the middle class. Fourteen per cent of the Goldthorpe fathers had middle-class jobs compared with 27 per cent of the sons; over just one generation the middle class had doubled in size. Then in the 1991 NCDS survey 36 per cent of the males held middle-class jobs. Conversely, the working class shrank from 55 per cent to 44 per cent of the male population between the Goldthorpe generations. Thereafter, the middle class continued to grow whereas the male working class was much the same size in the 1990s as in 1972 – 43 per cent of the NCDS sample. The main drop between the 1970s and the 1990s was in the intermediate ranks – from 30 per cent to 21 per cent of all male jobs. Rather than accelerating, according to this evidence the long-term numerical decline of the male working class may be ending.

Tables 8.1 and 8.3 are class outflow tables. They take individuals who were born into the middle class, the intermediate groups, then the working class, and describe their destinations. Tables 8.2 and 8.4 use exactly the same data but calculate the percentages differently. These are class inflow tables. They group the respondents according to their own occupations, and describe their origins.

In discussing social mobility it is customary to distinguish between intergenerational and intragenerational movements. At present we are dealing with intergenerational mobility, that is, between fathers and sons. Ideally the comparisons should be between fathers and sons when they were the same ages. People's occupations and their class positions can change during their working lives, which is what is meant by intragenerational mobility. It is unsafe to assume that a 25-year-old son who is in a lower class to his father's peak career achievement has been downwardly mobile and will not recover. However, we can work only with the data that is actually available. Similarly, we would ideally like comparable information about mothers and daughters, but, as explained earlier, much of the mobility research has studied males only.

As well as distinguishing between intra- and intergenerational move-ments, it is also customary nowadays to distinguish between absolute and relative mobility rates. Absolute mobility rates are the chances (percent-ages) of individuals from specific origins reaching specified destinations. So 16 per cent of the working-class sons in the Goldthorpe study had risen into the middle class by 1972, and 15 per cent of the middle-class sons had descended into the working class. In the early 1990s, the NCDS sweep had both figures somewhat higher: 26 per cent of the working-class males had made the middle class, and 18 per cent of middle-class sons had made the reverse trip. These are absolute mobility figures. Here is another: 32 percent of the males who were in the middle class in 1972, and exactly the same percentage in the 1990s, had started life in the working class (see Tables 8.2 and 8.4).

Relative rates are the relative chances of people with different origins reaching a specific destination. So 16 per cent of the Goldthorpe respon-dents who were born into the working class had reached the middle class by 1972, whereas, of those from middle-class families 59 per cent had remained there. In other words, the latter group had been nearly four times as likely as the former to become middle-class adults. Fifty-seven per cent of the Goldthorpe sample who were born into the working class had remained there whereas only 15 per cent of those who had begun life in the middle class had descended that far. Once again, the differential is roughly 4:1, and this is a relative mobility rate.

Absolute and relative mobility rates are both important. It is the relative rates that we need to consult in deciding how far we are from being an equal life-chance society. The answer is that we are a long way from this ideal-type. People are often surprised when they first encounter these fig-ures because we are being told constantly that nowadays everyone has the same opportunities. So the next point that has to be made is that very few people outside sociology consult social mobility tables and calculate rela-tive mobility rates. These rates describe a real world, but not a world that most people outside sociology ever experience. Very few if any people live in neighbourhoods which are microcosms of the national class structure. Very few children attend schools where children from different social class backgrounds are present in the same proportions as in the national popu-lation. The classes tend to live, and to have their children educated, sepa-rately, not necessarily consciously and deliberately, but because primary schools in particular tend to have local catchment areas, certainly in towns and cities. People are better able to compare, and are more likely to be con-scious of, the difference between how they themselves have fared in life and the achievements of others from the same neighbourhoods and schools, than how their entire classes' achievements compare with those of other classes.

Good Chances of Ascent

It can be seen in Tables 8.1 and 8.3 that children who started life in the working class in mid- and late-twentieth century Britain enjoyed reasonably good chances of ascent. It is true that majorities in both tables, 57 per cent and 55 per cent respectively, remained in the working class, but this means that over 4 out of every 10 rose, at least into the intermediate grades, and 16 per cent in 1972 and 26 per cent in the 1990s had reached the middle class proper. OK, those upwardly mobile into the middle class were clear minorities in both cases, greatly outnumbered by those who remained working-class, but 26 per cent and even 16 per cent making it into the middle class are not negligible proportions. Twenty-six per cent represents 7 or 8 children from a primary school class of 30 composed wholly of working-class pupils. It means that roughly a half of all working-class families (assuming a norm of 2-plus children per family – but note that all this evidence is from sons only) must have had a child who 'got on'. Most working-class adults who became parents in the second half of the twentieth century would have seen one of their children ascend at least into the intermediate classes. So despite the very wide inequalities in life-chances as seen in the relative mobility rates for people starting life in the working class, upward mobility has been a quite common experience, nothing exceptional. Those who have remained immobile will have seen others getting ahead: people who they knew at school, in their neighbourhoods, and sometimes from their own families. Cross-class family links and friendships will mitigate against any tendency for people to see other classes as enemies.

Some plain facts about mobility realities and possibilities are often misunderstood even within sociology. Among the respondents in Goldthorpe's 1972 survey, 27 per cent were in middle-class occupations. So if there had been equal life-chances for individuals with all social origins, 27 per cent from every starting point would have reached, or remained in, the middle class. In practice, 59 per cent of those who started life in the middle class remained there, against just 16 per cent of those from working-class backgrounds who reached this destination. If there had been equal life-chances, another 11 per cent of working-class children would have ascended. It is often not appreciated, even within sociology, how small a proportion of the working class stands to gain from equalising life-chances. Most would remain excluded from the middle class even in an equal life-chance society because there is simply insufficient room at the top. In a sense, among the generation that Goldthorpe studied in 1972, the middle class stood to lose more than the working class stood to gain from equalising opportunities. Most of the men with middle-class origins who had maintained their positions (59 per cent) would have descended in an equal life-chance society (in which just 27 per cent would have remained in the middle class). The same applied within the NCDS cohort. In both cohorts, higher proportions from the middle class gained, than the proportions from the working class who lost, as a result of the prevailing inequalities in life-chances. From this evidence, we should expect stronger opposition from those who stand to lose, than support from those who stand to gain, towards measures that would equalise life-chances.

Risks of Demotion

Those who start at the bottom can only rise. For the working class, social mobility will appear attractive. Start at the top and the only possible move is down; at this level social mobility is a threat. We have seen that there are wide inequalities in life-chances in Britain, but, despite this, working-class parents have reasonably good chances of seeing their children ascend. These statements are not contradictory, though they may appear so at first. One is based on relative, and the other on absolute mobility rates. Both statements are true. Likewise the facts that, on the one hand, risks of demotion for those who start at the top are much lower than they would be in an equal life-chance society, but still sufficient to give the middle class realistic grounds for worry.

Among the respondents in Goldthorpe's 1972 survey and within the NCDS birth cohort, 59 per cent and 61 per cent respectively of those who began life in the middle class had remained there; far more than the 27 and 36 per cent who would have done so in the ideal-typical equal life-chance situation. But another way of looking at these same figures is to say that roughly 40 per cent had not maintained their positions, and 15 per cent and 18 per cent in the respective studies had dropped right down into the working class. These statistics mean that it was odds-on, during the second half of the twentieth century, and probably in the first half as well, that the typical middle-class family with two children (or two sons, at any rate) would see at least one of them descend. From a primary-school class of 30 composed wholly of middle-class pupils, around 12 would not maintain their positions. People who start life in the middle class know full well that not everyone holds on, just as those who start in the working class know from personal experience that not everyone remains.

Social mobility looks most attractive, indeed it *only* looks attractive, when we contemplate the upward variety. Most working-class parents are keen for their children to get on, if at all possible. Downward mobility is entirely different. Does anyone aspire towards or hope for it? When it happens in objective terms, people often go to great lengths to convince themselves and others that they have not really slipped. They will regard their current positions as temporary, or use class markers (type of housing or who your friends are rather than occupation) that make it appear that they have maintained rank (Roberts *et al.*, 1977). Or they will focus on how they have maintained or even improved upon their parents' standards of living (not usually difficult in a society in which living standards have been improving over time). But, of course, some people achieve such outstanding success in business or the professions that it is near-impossible for their children to equal, let alone exceed, their achievements. It can be a mixed blessing to be the child of highly advantaged parents.

Downward mobility from the middle class is sufficiently common to be perceived as a very real threat. Hence the concern of middle-class parents to reduce the risks – to do almost anything that might achieve this (see Walkerdine *et al.*, 2001). Middle-class parents are keen for their children to attend schools with good academic records, and at any sign of failure they are likely to provide private coaching or opt for full private education. The children are under enormous pressure to succeed. Middle-class parents constantly seek assurances that their own children are doing well. Entering higher education used to give such assurance. At one time passing the 11-plus did likewise. Nowadays the parents expect their children to be in the higher streams or sets in their secondary and primary schools, and to achieve high scores in the national tests at ages 7, 11 and 14.

Internal and External Recruitment

The larger a class, the more likely are those born into it to remain, and the higher the proportion of its adult members who will be inbred. These statements do not require evidence, they are simply mathematical truisms. If a class accounted for 75 per cent of the population, then, in an ideal-typical situation of equal life-chances, and if the society remained stable over time, 75 per cent of those born into the class would remain, and 75 per cent from all other classes would reach this destination. Continuing with the same example, 75 per cent of the adult members of the 75 per cent class would be immobile, internal recruits, and 25 per cent would be drawn-in from elsewhere. If the class contracted to just 40 per cent of the population, and stabilised at that level, then only 40 per cent of those born into the class would remain, and 40 per cent would reach the destination from all other origins. Just 40 per cent of the class's adult members would be life-long, and 60 per cent would be intergenerationally mobile, all assuming, once again, equal life-chances.

The decline from around 75 per cent to around 40 per cent is what in fact happened to Britain's male working class in the course of the twentieth century. Britain was not a country of equal life-chances, as amply demonstrated in mobility tables, but at any constant rate of social fluidity the point holds that the smaller a class becomes, the less likely are those born into it to remain. Throughout the twentieth century the working class was usually the life-long position of people born into the class, not due mainly to unequal life-chances, but simply because for most of the century the working class accounted for most of the population.

Now the working class was contracting throughout most of the twentieth century and by its end the class comprised just 40 per cent or thereabouts of the male workforce, and a somewhat smaller proportion of women (see below). The effect of the long-term contraction of the working class was that each successive cohort of working-class children had better chances of ascending than its predecessor. This was not due to any equalisation of life-chances: it was due simply to the changing shape of the class structure. In Goldthorpe's 1972 sample, 43 per cent of the males with working-class origins had moved upwards, at least into the intermediate classes. Within the 1958 birth cohort, by 1991 when they were aged 33, a slightly higher proportion of working-class sons, 45 per cent, had been upwardly mobile. In the first half of the twentieth century the comparable figures must have been much lower simply because the working class was then much larger. Working-class parents who have told their children that the latter have better opportunities to get on than their parents enjoyed have not been deluding themselves or anyone else; they have been reflecting accurately their own experience. Upward mobility has become increasingly common, nowadays a very widespread experience, for those born into the working class. The sheer volume makes it increasingly difficult for the immobile to explain this in terms of the absence of opportunities; they will have seen too many of their childhood acquaintances succeed to be comfortable with this explanation. Throughout the twentieth century it will have made increasing sense for working-class parents who wanted their children to experience better lives than their own to concentrate upon assisting the children to become upwardly mobile rather than engaging in political struggles to gain a better deal for the working class in its entirety.

There are other implications of the rise in the absolute rate of upward mobility from the working class. The present-day equivalents of earlier generations of working-class trade union and Labour Party leaders are not leaving school at age 16 and joining the manual workforce but are continuing in education then entering middle-class jobs. The diminishing working class will have been progressively stripped of its more talented and/or more ambitious members. Trends in absolute rates of social mobility that are consequences of the working class's contraction will have contributed to its disorganisation. Economic trends and government policies (especially policies towards trade unions in the 1980s) were undoubtedly the main factors in the disorganisation of the working class towards the close of the twentieth century (see Chapter 4), but longer-term trends in the shape of the class structure, with their implications for absolute rates of mobility, will have contributed. Higher proportions of working-class children have been moving upwards, and the immobile will have found it more difficult to blame society rather than themselves for their lack of ascent (they will have seen so many childhood acquaintances getting ahead). More of those remaining in the working class will have family links with other classes. The upwardly mobile may well be the very persons who, had they remained working-class, would have played leadership roles in working-class organisations. Moreover, as the middle class grows in size, the downwardly mobile comprise a growing proportion of working-class adults (see Noble, 2000).

A class that is large but in numerical decline will normally be overwhelmingly self-recruiting. It has no need of new blood. So just over 70 per cent of Goldthorpe's working-class respondents in 1972 had working-class origins. The figure was much the same in the 1958 birth cohort. Throughout the twentieth century the working class was demographically well-formed and will remain so well into the twenty-first century, though at some future point it may stabilise at a somewhat smaller size than today, and, if and when this happens, just as occurs with all smaller classes, all other things remaining equal, a higher proportion of its members will be recruited from outside. All told, the prospects for working-class reorganisation look bleak.

The middle class is entirely different. Throughout the second half of the twentieth century, and probably before then, most of its members had been upwardly mobile – 68 per cent of the middle-class respondents in Goldthorpe's 1972 survey, and exactly the same proportion in the 1958 birth cohort. This is what happens when an initially small class grows consistently from decade to decade as the middle class has in Britain, accounting for 14 per cent of the fathers in Goldthorpe's 1972 study, 27 per cent of their sons, and 36 per cent of the male members of the 1958 cohort.

When members of Britain's present-day middle class look at each other they do not see a group with uniformly, or even mainly, privileged origins. This is despite most middle-class sons remaining middle-class, and very wide inequalities of life-chances that operate in the middle class's favour. If the middle class regards the class structure as open, and if they believe that they live in a society where anyone from any background can get on if they have the ability and make the effort, this is not solely because they find these ideas comforting: they accord with the middle class's own experiences. Most of them have been upwardly mobile. It is true that if we take people at the peak of prestigious professions – high court judges and the civil service elite, for example – we find fewer individuals with working-class origins than in the middle class as a whole. Even so, the fact remains that what is now a broad band of middle-class occupations in Britain is populated by people with varied origins.

This will change slowly in the twenty-first century, assuming, as seems likely, that the growth of the middle class continues but at a slower rate. The larger the middle class becomes, the larger will be the proportion of these positions filled by people born into the class. All discussions about the contemporary middle class must allow for the fact that it is still being formed. The manner in which its demography will change in the twenty-first century (we can predict confidently because the developments are 'in the pipeline') will favour the formation of a distinctive lifestyle, consciousness and politics. Remember, however, that the larger the middle class becomes, the larger will be the proportion of working-class children who will reach middle-class destinations: 16 per cent of the working-class respondents in Goldthorpe's 1972 survey, but 36 per cent of all the males from working-class homes in the 1958 birth cohort. It may seem paradoxical at first, but it really can be true that the chances of working-class children ascending can rise, while the upwardly mobile comprise a declining proportion of all middle-class adults, and while risks of demotion from the middle class subside. This is not just a hypothetical possibility: it is what is actually happening in Britain.

Gender

Social Class Profiles

Chapter 3 explained, first, that the proportion of adult women in the workforce, and the proportion of the workforce that is female, have both risen over time. Second, it explained that despite equal pay and opportunity laws there is still a strong tendency for men and women to enter different occupations, and overall women's jobs are inferior to men's, most visibly in their pay being lower per hour and in total. Here we can look more closely at these differences using the (admittedly limited) available evidence that permits systematic comparison of men's and women's experiences of social mobility and immobility. What difference, if any, does gender make?

Chapter 2 explained that how women should be located in the class structure (in sociological analysis) is hotly contested, and there is some dispute as to whether the Goldthorpe class scheme (and all other class schemes for that matter) are suitable for classifying women's jobs. There are also uncertainties about how part-time employees and housewives should be treated. We also noted in Chapter 2 that at present there seems to be no single answer to these questions that is right for all cases. Here it will be best to place these controversies to one side, to continue to use the class scheme that has been adopted, to place women on the basis of their own jobs ignoring the part-time/full-time split and periods spent out of the labour market, and to examine where women from the same starting points end up compared with men.

All work on female social mobility up to now has used their fathers' occupations to indicate the women's starting points. If women are to be classed by their own occupations, it might appear more reasonable to use their mothers' occupations, or at least to take these into account in identifying females' social origins. However, all the available data use fathers' occupations as the baseline, so here we have no real option but to follow suit.

We can compare the occupations of the men and women in the NCDS study in 1991 when they were age 33 (see Table 8.5). The main gender differences are clear. There were far more women (40 per cent as opposed to 21 per cent of men) in the intermediate grades (mainly in low-level office jobs), and far more men (43 per cent against 29 per cent of women) in the working class. Men were also more likely to be in middle-class jobs but here the gender gap was narrower (36 per cent against 30 per cent).

There are further differences, which have been mentioned in previous chapters, namely, in the occupations typically held by men and women within all social classes. Within the middle class, men are the more likely to be on the upper rungs and women lower down. Within the working class, the men are the more likely to be in skilled occupations, and the women in non-skilled jobs. In the intermediate classes, men are the more likely to be self-employed, and when doing office jobs the men are the more likely to have administrative tasks that place them on career ladders while the women are more likely to be in secretarial pools from which there are few chances of ascent into the middle class.

Who is Disadvantaged?

From the above it may appear all too obvious that women are the disadvantaged sex. Maybe, but as we shall now see, not equally so in all social

Table 8.5   Male and female class distributions

Class	Males (%)	Females (%)
Service	36	30
Intermediate	21	40
Working	43	29

Source: Savage and Egerton (1997).

Table 8.6 Class outflows, males and females

| | Fathers | | | | | | | |
| | Service (%) | | Intermediate (%) | | Working (%) | | Total (%) | |
	Males	Females	Males	Females	Males	Females	Males	Females
Service	61	45	40	35	26	24	36	30
Intermediate	20	40	26	43	19	39	21	40
Working	18	16	34	22	55	37	43	29

Source: Adapted from Savage and Egerton (1997).

classes. Table 8.6 compares the destinations of the NCDS sample broken down by sex and social origins. Among those from middle-class families, the males had clearly been the more successful in the labour market. By the 1990s they were more likely to have entered middle-class jobs (61 per cent compared with 45 per cent of the women), while the women were the more likely to be in intermediate jobs (40 per cent against 20 per cent). Well-qualified men tend to achieve better labour-market returns on their credentials than equally qualified women. Females have needed to be better than men in terms of qualifications in order to obtain the same jobs. Looking at this from another angle, women in all occupational grades tend to be better qualified than male co-workers. Viewed from within the middle class, it seems crystal clear that women are the disadvantaged sex.

This is not so obviously the case among the groups from working-class and intermediate-class backgrounds. The main gender difference within both of these groups is that women are more likely to obtain intermediate-level jobs, and men are more likely to enter or remain in the working class. Among those from working-class homes in the NCDS sample, 55 per cent of the males but only 37 per cent of the females had manual occupations, while 39 per cent of the women against 19 per cent of the men were in intermediate-level jobs. Among people with below-average qualifications, women have tended to achieve better labour-market returns than men in terms of their types of occupations, though not necessarily in terms of pay (see Marshall *et al.*, 1988). Here we have an example of an interactive effect; the implications of being male or female differ from class to class.

Intragenerational Mobility

We study intergenerational mobility by comparing parents and their children (as above). Intragenerational mobility can occur between any two points in the same person's life, but in practice the period focused on is usually the person's working life. An individual who is upwardly or downwardly mobile intergenerationally may make the entire rise or descent in childhood and youth, while in education. Alternatively, part or all of the movement may be after the individual's working life has started. A person who is immobile intergenerationally may hold the same type of job throughout his or her working life, or recover after initially starting employment at a lower level than his or her parents.

There is a great deal of intra-career movement, and no decline over time in the volume. In his 1972 survey John Goldthorpe tested the 'counterbalance' or 'tightening bond' thesis which suggests that, when it occurs, nowadays mobility is more likely than in the past to happen as a result of, and while the subject is still in, education. This thesis is plausible. We now spend much longer in education than a century ago. It seems likely that those destined to rise and fall will be more likely to do so on the basis of their educational performances rather than their achievements, or the lack of them, when in the labour market. In practice, however, there appears to be just a much intra-career mobility as ever, usually short-range, and along a limited number of main routes.

People who start their working lives as apprentices become skilled workers. Others who are not formally trained may become informally recognised as skilled. Some manual workers are promoted to supervisory and even management posts. Some make this step on the basis of qualifications earned through part-time study, or after a return to full-time education (the number of mature higher-education students has risen). Another common career move is from lower-level office and sales jobs into the middle class proper. Another is from the lower to the higher grades within the middle class. A further type of movement is from all other kinds of occupations into self-employment.

Intragenerational mobility is being discussed here (in the section of this chapter which deals with gender) because, up to now at any rate, all these career movements have been most common among men. Women's working lives have followed a rather different typical career pattern. While men have normally built continuous, full-time, labour-market careers lasting from full-time education until their retirement, women have normally taken career breaks following child-birth. Women returners have often opted for part-time hours and, overall, their career breaks have been followed by occupational demotion (Martin and Roberts, 1984). On returning to their office jobs or to their professions, women have often been relocated outside the main career streams. Many have stepped downwards, in effect starting again. There have been many cases of quite substantial demotion – from office jobs to supermarket check-outs, cleaning and suchlike.

However, in recent times there has been some convergence in men's and women's typical career patterns. More women are now pursuing continuous full-time careers, a trend which is discussed further, below. Meanwhile, more men's careers have been terminated prematurely. This is a consequence of post-Fordist flexibility and the rise in levels of unemployment. Company downsizing and site closures, and technological change, have seen people who once believed that they were in stable jobs and career grades, become surplus to requirements. Sometimes all their skills and experience have become redundant, and spells of unemployment have become more common since the 1970s. What was once the female career pattern – a discontinuous working life with risks of demotion at each break – has spread among men. Men over age 50 often settle for retired status, and some manage to qualify for incapacity benefit, rather than remain in the labour market where they know that the only jobs that they are likely to be offered will be inferior to their earlier positions. As seen in Chapter 3, some supermarket chains have realised that it is now possible to hire quality staff from the pool of unemployed over-50s.

Gender Convergence, Class Divergence

Men's career preferences (though not their actual opportunities) seem much as ever, whereas women themselves have changed. Recent school-leaving cohorts have been the first waves of young women in modern times whose mothers worked for the greater part of their own adult lives, and during their daughters' (and sons') childhoods. These mothers (and the fathers) have encouraged their daughters to aim for decent jobs – not to be left in the typing pools or at the supermarket check-outs. The girls' teachers (a mainly female occupation) have encouraged female pupils to be ambitious. Recent cohorts of female teenage school-leavers have regarded their own future occupational careers as just as important as boys regard theirs (Roberts and Chadwick, 1991).

Girls nowadays are certainly doing better at school than their predecessors. There have been some remarkable improvements – in their GCSE performances, the numbers taking and passing three or more A-levels and the grades they obtain, and in the numbers going to university (more females than males nowadays, unlike in the 1960s when two-thirds of university students were men). Girls now out-perform boys at all levels in education. Boys' performances have not deteriorated: in fact they have improved. Both boys and girls today are doing better than formerly. There are more grounds for applauding girls' achievements than deploring male underachievement. Qualified female school-leavers now aim for career jobs, though, just like boys, many have to accept jobs that do not match their preferences. More well-qualified female recruits have been studying towards, and obtaining, post-entry professional and other vocational qualifications (Crompton and Sanderson, 1986). Provided they remain childless, young women's career prospects remain more or less in line with males', at least until their mid-20s (Bynner *et al.*, 1997). What happens then? Well, women have been postponing marriage and parenthood. When they become parents, more and more women have been taking maternity leave rather than terminating their employment. More of these women have been returning to work on a full-time basis and remaining in the career streams, hence the forecast that the future will be female with more and more women shattering former glass ceilings. The numbers of women MPs, and members of the government, rose sharply following the 1997 general election.

If women really are to experience more career success this can only be at the expense of men, so there will be more and more pressure on males' career prospects. In the 1950s the leading banks could assure male recruits that one in two of them would become managers (I know because I was one of them). How was this possible? Because none of the female employees, the majority of recruits at that time, would reach management. Times really have changed, but not equally so, or in exactly the same way, for men and women in all social classes.

More women with children aged under five are working full-time, but most of these women are highly-qualified and are in middle-class occupations. They are 30 times more likely to work full-time than mothers whose former or current occupations are non-skilled (Kay, 1996). The middle-class women tend to have partners in similar occupations; they are in households with two middle-class salaries which enable them to pay for quality child-care. Needless to say, some of the women become single parents (usually a temporary situation) but the fathers of the children are usually able, and obliged, to make worthwhile contributions to their upkeep. Other mothers (particularly working-class mothers) are still returning to work on a part-time basis and accepting the occupational downgrading that can be involved. Working-class women's child-care arrangements are most likely to involve family and neighbours. These women's male partners are more vulnerable than formerly to occupational change, and there has been a serious decline in the number of effective male breadwinners in the working class. It is not the men themselves who have changed so much as their opportunities. Fathers who go absent may be simply unable to remain reliable supporters of their children. Many of the women prefer to be independent of men whose own earning capacities are vulnerable.

Gender convergence at the top of the class structure has been accompanied by wider class inequalities within both sexes, though it is important to bear in mind here that the most common jobs that women enter are still in the intermediate grades. Many male professionals and managers on the one hand, and manual workers on the other, have female partners in intermediate jobs. Polarisation is the wrong label for the trends; there is more distance in lifestyle and living standards between the top and the bottom, but as much blurring as ever in the middle.

Ethnic Differences

The main differences in the mobility experiences of Britain's ethnic minorities *vis-à-vis* the majority population can be restated briefly here (see Chapter 3, p. 78). First, and very important, so well worth repeating, all the non-white minorities experience an ethnic penalty. Their occupational achievements are lower, and their risks of unemployment are higher (except among Indians), than those of whites with equal qualifications (see Heath and McMahon, 1997; Jones, 1993). This is not an immigration effect – most members of Britain's minorities are now British-born and bred – it is a race relations effect.

Thereafter much the same mobility patterns and processes occur as within the majority population. The children of middle-class ethnic-minority parents are more likely to remain middle-class than are individuals from working-class families in the same ethnic groups to reach the middle class. The minorities have been affected in much the same way as the majority by long-term changes in the shape of the class structure.

Gender differences vary from minority to minority just as greatly as from class to class within the majority population. Females in some Asian minorities experience family and other community pressures to prioritise the domestic role, although many of the women who have been born and educated in Britain resist these pressures. Afro-Caribbean girls were out-performing their male peers at school long before white females followed suite (see Fuller, 1980), and Afro-Caribbean women are more likely to work full-time than females in any other ethnic group. Black women often expect to be main family breadwinners. Their risks and rates of single parenthood are considerably higher than throughout the UK population in general.

Perhaps the ethnic difference that has the most significant implications for the class structure in general is that while most minority groups are slowly being dispersed, the Afro-Caribbeans are tending to stick at the bottom. Despite the ethnic penalty, most of the ethnic-minority groups are becoming scattered throughout the class structure, and residentially. The initial settlers tended to enter the British class structure at the base. The main exceptions were the minorities within all the minorities who had skills and qualifications that could be transferred into employment in Britain. Health workers are an example. Other groups have slowly improved their overall class positions. Indeed, some Asian groups seem likely to become overrepresented in the middle class during the twenty-first century, which, needless to say, will not necessarily be accompanied by their full assimilation, integration or acceptance. The Afro-Caribbean minority is proving the stark exception; its children underperform in education compared with the majority population and most other ethnic minority groups. Add to this the 'normal' ethnic penalty in the labour market, and the entire group remains trapped at the bottom (see Connolly *et al.*, 1991).

We need not delve in detail into the reasons for this here: these are extraneous to class theory. Genetic explanations are sometimes offered, but cultural explanations look more plausible. Asian immigrants brought strong presenting cultures with them into Britain – cultures which had been developed and preserved over centuries. These may not have aided their absorption directly, but they seem to have acted as a kind of springboard for engaging with the wider society. The traditional cultures of the Afro-Caribbean groups were shattered by colonialism and slavery, thereby, as immigrant minorities, setting them in weak positions.

However, the point of wider relevance to the shape of the class structure is that here we have a minority (and there may be other non-ethnic minorities) that is stuck at the bottom, liable, especially in times of high unemployment, to become part of any emergent underclass (see Chapter 4).

Relative Mobility

We now turn to the more complicated issues mentioned at the beginning of this chapter: those that involve measuring relative mobility and fluidity, and making comparisons across time and place.

The Constant Flux

We have the mathematics and computer power to take account of structurally induced mobility – the volume that is inevitable as a result of changes over time in the shape of a class structure, and class differentials in fertility rates – and similarly to take account of differences in the shapes of the class structures in different countries. We are then left with measurements of social fluidity which can be used to compare the openness of different societies, or the same society at different points in time. These comparisons require nationally representative samples from all the times and places to be compared, and the relevant information has to be coded using the same class scheme. All this has in fact been done, by several groups of researchers using the Goldthorpe, and other, class schemes. The statistics are best left to the experts but their conclusions are straightforward.

It appears that there are no major differences among the modern industrial societies in their rates of social fluidity (Marshall *et al.*, 1997). There are big differences in absolute rates because of differences in the shapes of the class structures, and the particular times, ways and the pace at which these have changed. There are in fact some differences in fluidity – the rates are not totally identical – but the differences are fairly minor and rather difficult to explain. The overall impression is summarised aptly in the title of Erikson and Goldthorpe's (1992) book on the subject, *The Constant Flux*.

Constant fluidity is not a completely solid and unanimously agreed conclusion; some social-mobility researchers do not regard the issue as completely settled. They point out that nearly all the evidence is about male mobility; that there may have been changes over time and inter-country differences in female mobility, especially in view of the trend towards women spending more time in the labour market. They also argue that the measurements of fluidity are rather blunt, and typically involve grouping together individuals born over periods of 30 or even more years, which will conceal shorter-term fluctuations in mobility rates. Researchers who have looked in detail at the history of social mobility in Britain and Ireland (Payne, 1999; Prandy and Bottero, 2000) have concluded that fluidity did increase (temporarily) in the last three decades of the nineteenth century when the examination system was being introduced, and large private businesses, with new middle-class jobs, were being formed (see Chapter 6). Payne also detects an increase in fluidity, especially among women, since the 1970s. Prandy and Bottero's research, using a version of the Cambridge class scheme (see Chapter 2) adapted to the historical circumstances, traces mobility rates since the end of the eighteenth century, and finds that there was less change during the nineteenth century than had previously been assumed: that pre-industrial Britain was more fluid, and the industrial revolution did less to increase openness, than virtually everyone had previously supposed. This latter finding, if correct, extends the 'constant flux' historically, and it has to be said that the variations in fluidity that these studies have detected amount to no more than ripples. All the evidence points to impressive similarities in rates of social fluidity in all present-day modern societies, and since (and maybe preceding) the development of modern industries.

This finding (little variation in fluidity) really is an amazing discovery. Critics of sociology have a habit of complaining that the discipline discovers, and wraps in jargon, what people already knew. In this case most people would surely have believed that rates of social fluidity do vary. If sociology had discovered that although there are still wide inequalities in life-chances, these had narrowed since the beginning of the twentieth century, we could have been fairly accused of simply confirming common-sense.

After all, everyone knows that a series of educational reforms that lasted throughout the twentieth century aimed to equalise opportunities. It does seem amazing that all the reforms should have made absolutely no difference. This evidence is contrary to the liberal hypothesis that industrial societies become progressively more open. It is also contrary to predictions of class structures becoming more rigid and closed.

It is equally amazing that there are no major differences in the rates of fluidity between different modern societies. Britain is not particularly class-ridden. America is no more open than Europe. The communist countries were neither more open nor closed than Western market economies. The social democratic governments of the Scandinavian countries, despite decades of meritocratic policies, appear to have made virtually no impact on the fluidity of their class structures. For once sociology seems to have discovered a surprising but hard social fact.

Comparative mobility research has become infamous for exploding what appeared to be reasonable assumptions. Whatever changes or differences are alleged, the evidence proves the contrary. This applies to the counterbalance/tightening bond thesis (between education and occupational attainments). It also applies to an alleged buffer-zone between the manual and other classes across which mobility – either upwards, downwards or both – was supposed to be more difficult and rarer than between, for example, the skilled and non-skilled manual groups, and between the intermediate classes and those above. Another suggestion has been that mobility rates will be especially low at the apex of the class structure, but this has also been disproved. We should bear in mind here that surveys never capture sufficient numbers from, and usually do not try to distinguish, an upper class, so we do not know exactly how rates of movement into and out of this class compare with those elsewhere. The evidence about the upper class that we do possess (see Chapter 7) indicates an unusually high rate of intergenerational continuity. Similarly, the petit bourgeoisie (see Chapter 5) retains a higher proportion of its sons (despite its small size) than the other intermediate class (lower non-manuals). Property appears to be the asset that is most easily passed-down the generations. However, if the propertied classes are set aside, all the measurements that have been made indicate no major differences in rates of fluidity at different levels in the class structure.

Many mobility researchers would have liked the evidence to be different. It is not the case that the class boundaries identified in Goldthorpe's, or any other, class scheme prove especially difficult to penetrate. This evidence, it must be admitted, is grist to the mill of supporters of gradational class schemes. It would have strengthened the case for boxes if the class boundaries had been shown to act as barriers to mobility, but this is simply not the case.

The constant flux – constant across time and place, and at different levels of the class structure – is a sociological fact that cries out for explanation. The easy part is to explain how it has been possible for all the educational reforms to make no difference.

The Limitations of Educational Reform

Educational reform has widened the opportunities of working-class children and boosted their educational attainments. It has created and sustained one of the great illusions of modern times – of society becoming progressively fairer while consistently failing to deliver a more open society. How has this been possible?

First, the expansion of educational opportunities has accompanied the change in the shape of the class structure that has already been described and discussed at length – the long-term upgrading. So, to an extent, the enlarged opportunities for able working-class children to qualify for good jobs have simply enabled the additional room at the top to be filled by suitably qualified people (Halsey *et al.*, 1980).

Second, the middle class has managed to take at least equal advantage of every expansion of educational opportunities. Changes have been introduced under the slogan of a fairer deal for the less privileged, and the privileged have instantly seized them. So when publicly-funded scholarship places were created in secondary schools and universities at the beginning of the twentieth century, these were not restricted to poor children. Those with parents who would otherwise have paid for secondary and higher education were able to, and did, compete. One of the consequences of the 1944 Education Act was that middle-class children who would formerly have received a paid-for grammar school education subsequently qualified for free places. More working-class children did enter the grammar schools after 1944, but so did more middle-class children (see Halsey *et al.*, 1980). The effect of the abolition of fees, and the introduction of mandatory (means-tested) maintenance grants for university students in 1949, was not a new influx of working-class entrants, but more state support for the existing students. When former Colleges of Advanced Technology were upgraded to Polytechnics in the 1960s it was not the former, largely working-class, students who experienced educational upgrading. Rather, the composition of the student bodies changed to resemble the profiles in the existing universities (Whitburn *et al.*, 1976). We should expect similar results from the upgrading of the Polytechnics to universities that occurred in 1992.

Figure 8.1 describes how the proportions of young people from different social classes entering higher education (whether in old or new universities, or other institutions) changed during the early 1990s. The graphs show that there were all-round increases in participation, while the class gap remained virtually unchanged. The middle class benefited as much as the working class from the expansion of higher education in the 1990s, just as the middle class had taken full advantage of all earlier educational reforms. Figure 8.1 also reveals the size of the class gap in educational achievement – huge. Nowadays around 80 per cent of middle-class children make it into higher education compared with less than 15 per cent in the unskilled working class.

It is not only in education where this class trick has been played. A consequence of the creation of the National Health Service in 1948 was that middle-class patients who formerly paid, subsequently accepted free state medicine. In more recent times, sports centres have been opened throughout the land, often with the declared aim of catering for the disadvantaged, and have then been booked by middle-class users.

Figure 8.1 Class participation rates in higher education, Great Britain, 1991/2–1995/6

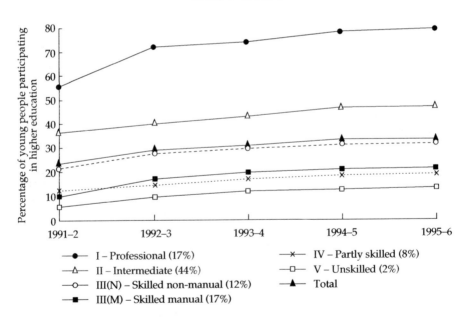

Notes: This figure uses the Registrar General's class categories. Students were assigned to classes according to admissions data. The distribution of the population by classes was taken from the 1991 Census.
Numbers in brackets indicate the proportion of participants falling into that particular social class.

Source: National Committee of Enquiry into Higher Education (1997; p. 23), from Fulcher and Scott (1999).

Third, the expansion of educational opportunities has accompanied, but pushed well-ahead of occupational upgrading; hence the all-round devaluation of qualifications. It is necessary nowadays to achieve higher standards in education than in the past in order to qualify for any type of job. Careers such as the law and banking which were once open to 16-year-olds were first re-targeted at those with A-levels, and more recently at higher education graduates. So as more working-class children have reached given levels they have found the achievements counting for less. It was once a labour-market advantage to have simply attended a secondary school. This changed when secondary education became universal, and subsequently it has been the qualifications earned in the schools that have counted. The same has now happened in higher education. Attending university is insufficient; employers want to know your class of degree. As all-round enrolments and attainments at any level have risen, the class gap at that level has necessarily narrowed, but the attainments have counted for less and the old differentials have resurfaced at subsequent educational levels (Heath and Clifford, 1996).

Fourth, it is not only education and qualifications that determine the types of jobs that individuals obtain, and how their careers progress subsequently. At all levels of qualification, social class origins have always made a difference to immediate job prospects. And entrants from middle-class backgrounds have always been more likely to achieve promotions than those from the working class. Why should this be? The answers lie in social and cultural capital (see Box 8.1), which are evident in young people's ambitions. The higher their social origins, the more determined they are to gain full value from their qualifications. Connections are also useful – knowing people who will put in a word at the right time. Then there is the matter of having the right kind of accent, tastes and dress sense to be regarded as the right type of person.

In terms of the social mechanics of what happened during the successive waves of educational reform, we have no difficulty in explaining the constant flux. Unresolved controversies arise only when we seek higher-level explanations as to why things worked out this way. There are several higher-level explanations on offer; all have some plausible features, but insufficient to be wholly convincing.

Intelligence

This is an argument that never goes away because up to now it has been impossible to obtain the crucial evidence to either nail or prove it. Even so, it is one of those issues on which the protagonists are prepared to take firm stands. So it is important, first of all, to get the argument right. No-one

---

Box 8.1

Social and cultural capital

Economic capital can be passed-down the generations, drawn on when needed, and, when able to do so, individuals can add to their investments. Social and cultural capital are comparable in all these respects.

Social capital consists of social relationships. Kinship relationships are given, but others are made. One can invest by building up a circle of friends, and by offering them assistance when possible. People can draw on their social capital when they need to do so – for assistance in finding a job, for instance.

Cultural capital consists of the skills, knowledge, beliefs and values that we acquire in our particular social milieux. Some skills and knowledge are certificated, but others, like a particular accent, can also be useful. Cultural capital is built up gradually. We all have it. The crucial differences are not so much in the amounts, but the types, and how valuable they prove to be. The stocks that individuals acquire depend on their families, their schooling, the neighbourhoods where they live and who their friends are. When they start work individuals continue to add to their cultural capital. People can add deliberately to their cultural capital: for example, by enrolling in education or training.

How pupils fare at primary school (how easily they adapt to the classroom regime, and learn school subjects) depends partly on the cultural capital that they take into school with them. At all subsequent life stages, and in all spheres of life, the cultural capital that individuals bring to the situations affects their opportunities.

---

claims that innate (genetically determined) ability is the sole determinant of what people achieve in education, employment or anywhere else. Everyone accepts that abilities relevant to success in all spheres of life, including intelligence tests themselves, are influenced by nurture (the effects on our development of the environments in which we are reared and live), and that matters such as being in the right place at the right time, and connections, can be extremely important.

What has to be explained for present purposes is not exactly how each and every one of us obtains our particular jobs, but the constant flux – and innate ability is, in fact, as plausible an explanation as any. The argument is that, first, people with middle-class jobs are generally brighter than those with working-class jobs. Second, it is argued that there is a genetic base to all or most of the abilities that people develop (as with height and weight). So bright parents tend to have bright children but there is always a tendency for offspring to regress towards the mean, meaning that bright parents tend to have children who are rather less bright than themselves, and vice versa for the below-average. Of course there are extreme cases, as in everything else that is governed by genetics. So some parents with above-average ability produce extremely gifted children. Parents with below-average ability may also do this, but such cases will be even more exceptional. No-one claims that these are the only processes that determine people's life-chances. All that we are asked to accept is that innate ability is one of the factors, and its alleged role is in fact consistent with the constancy of the flux, the rates of fluidity, in modern societies.

Peter Saunders (1995) has shown that in Britain, and presumably in other modern societies since they are all so similar in their rates of fluidity, the volume of mobility and the distances that people typically move are almost exactly what one would predict from the distribution of measured intelligence (IQ scores) among children from different social class backgrounds. He has also shown, using evidence from the NCDS in which the sample's abilities were measured while they were at school, that this proves to be the best single predictor of their adult destinations. The second best predictor is a childhood measure of motivation (Bond and Saunders, 1999; Saunders, 1997). On the basis of this evidence, Saunders lambasts what he calls the SAD hypothesis which claims that it is primarily social advantages and disadvantages which determine who gets on.

This is an argument about which many people have feelings as well as opinions. Hackles are easily stirred. The objections are well-known (see Lampard, 1996; Marshall and Swift, 1996; Breen and Goldthorpe, 1999). First, and crucially, it is impossible to measure raw ability (though genetic measurement may one day solve this problem). Performances in intelligence tests, the construction of these tests, and what we mean by ability, are all socially contaminated. There are ideological and political dimensions to these arguments which stem from the firm and widespread hold of meritocratic values in modern societies. If achievements are due to individuals' abilities, then, one can appear to be arguing, the resultant inequalities are merited and therefore justifiable, though Gordon Marshall has queried why having inherited certain talents should be regarded as particularly meritorious (Marshall *et al.*, 1997). It must also be said that sociologists have a professional/ideological stake in rejecting explanations of anything which threaten to remove the topic from their own competence. Saunders is scathing towards sociologists, such as Goldthorpe, who simply refuse to take the ability/intelligence hypothesis seriously, and who conduct massive, expensive studies without even attempting to measure their subjects' abilities.

As we shall see, as an explanation of the constant flux, intelligence is in fact just as plausible, possibly more plausible, than any of the alternatives. It can account for rates of fluidity remaining more or less constant whatever the institutional arrangements in a society. However education is organised, and whatever the political and economic regime in a modern society, the same 'cream' seems to rise to the top while the dross sinks. Pareto, an early twentieth-century Italian social theorist who is rarely read nowadays, made the 'circulation of elites' a major feature of his theory. He argued that elites needed to replenish themselves regularly by recruiting talent from beneath, otherwise they would eventually face successful challenges. In other words, ability would eventually tell in some way or another. Inherent ability is a plausible explanation of the constant flux, but as we shall now see, how people interpret the relevant evidence depends largely on their predispositions. There are usually alternative ways in which all evidence can be read.

Reproduction Theory

This has its origins in the imaginative neo-Marxist theory-building that captured much of sociology in the 1970s. The core arguments are: different classes tend to develop their own cultures; politically and economically dominant classes have their cultures adopted in education; therefore their children are at an advantage, but the children's success appears to be due to their superior ability in a socially impartial contest; class inequalities are thereby legitimised and the class structure is reproduced in a double sense – class relationships themselves endure, and class positions are transmitted from parents to children (Bourdieu and Passeron, 1977). Everyone has always realised that the real world is not quite this simple. For a start, there is some mobility. This is explained in terms of structural changes which require some movement to be permitted, and concessions which are necessary to sustain an ideology of equal opportunity.

Savage and Egerton (1997) have used this theory to interpret the evidence from the NCDS – exactly the same evidence that Saunders uses to argue the importance of individual ability. Here we have a prime example of how investigators who approach the same evidence with different theoretical perspectives are able to reach entirely different conclusions. Egerton and Savage's predisposition is to treat the volume of mobility that occurs as a product of structural requirements, especially the expansion of the middle class. They prefer to treat individual ability as an explanation of exactly who rises, or remains, rather than an explanation of the volume of movement.

Their analysis of the NCDS certainly produces some interesting results. They show, of course, that it is not only ability (IQ) and educational qualifications that account for individuals' eventual destinations. People from working-class backgrounds have a greater need for raw ability and qualifications in order to reach the middle class than middle-class children need in order to stay there. The able working-class child may or may not get on, whereas the equally-able and qualified middle-class child rarely slips. Ability and qualifications are rather more important in determining girls' labour-market achievements than those of boys. Among boys, other kinds of social and cultural capital seem to carry rather more weight than among girls.

These findings are interesting, but they do not amount to a vindication of reproduction theory, the objections to which are as follows. First, there is the evidence from Saunders (and others) that individual ability and motivation, not background, are the best predictors of people's destinations. Second, reproduction theory postulates unrealistically wide differences between class cultures, and far too close a match between the culture of education (the subjects that are taught, for example) and the culture of middle-class pupils' homes. Third, there is simply too much mobility for the theory to handle. If the theory was true, why should there be any downward mobility? Related to this, there is far more upward mobility than is structurally required. Fourth, the theory seems inconsistent with the constant flux. If the theory was correct, then one would expect levels of social fluidity to change with the balance of class forces, and, for example, to be higher than elsewhere in countries where political parties with working-class bases, like the social democratic parties in Scandinavian countries, have enjoyed long periods in office. Reproduction theory may explain why there is a tendency towards inertia in the class structure (people sticking in the classes into which they are born), but, at present at any rate, it cannot explain just how powerful this tendency happens to be, or why it should be so constant across time and place.

Rational Action Theory

This is John Goldthorpe's (1996) preferred explanation of the constant flux; he discounts innate ability as a possible explanation. Goldthorpe has always taken the view that inequalities in life-chances are simply too wide for individual ability to be a credible explanation, though Saunders (1995) has now shown that this is not in fact the case. The rational action explanation does not require us to postulate entirely different class cultures. Indeed, it assumes that everyone will prefer a middle-class to a working-class position, and will want their own children to reach the former if possible. So if ability is not the answer, why do not more working-class children ascend? Goldthorpe's explanation is that mobility outcomes, and the constant flux, are the result of rational actors calculating the relative costs and benefits of trying to reach different destinations, and the crucial point here is that these relative costs and benefits will vary in value depending on the actors' starting points. A couple of illustrations will clarify the argument. Supporting a child through higher education will be a greater burden on a working-class family, relative to its resources, than for a middle-class family. A working-class child who achieves an intermediate-class position is likely to be regarded as successful, whereas a middle-class family will view this as failure and might well do everything possible to secure a better outcome.

The theory does not require us to imagine that all families use electronic calculators to estimate the costs and likely returns from investing in their children's education, any more than economic theory asks us to believe that all consumers make themselves aware of the price of a good at all the accessible outlets prior to every purchase. The assumption in economics is simply that there will be a tendency for consumers to choose the cheapest, all other things being equal, and the cheapest will therefore, eventually, become the market leader. Likewise, the rational action theory makes behaviour comprehensible at the individual level but it is explaining group norms and tendencies rather than attributing to everyone all the rational thought processes that are specified.

Is this theory the best explanation of the constant flux? There are surely too many problems, like ruling out the intelligence explanation by fiat. Also, in this instance, there are wider class cultural differences that are relevant to success and failure in education and the labour market than the theory takes into account – in speech patterns and styles of sociability, for example. Perhaps most crucially, the constant flux is hardly what the theory would lead us to expect. Free secondary education, and financial support, especially means-tested financial support, for students in higher education should have tilted the balance of costs and benefits and made the greatest difference to the poorest families, So why did fluidity not increase when these measures were introduced?

At present, sociology has a startling and agreed finding, the constant flux, give or take a few quibbles, but no explanation backed by the kind of evidence that sceptics would require.

What has Mobility Research Achieved?

The big achievement of mobility research has been to show how the volume and directions of absolute mobility depend on the shape of the class structure and how this changes over time. Another, still incomplete, success is the startling discovery of the constant flux (assuming that the finding is in fact correct) – how little variation there is over time and between modern societies in rates of social fluidity or relative mobility. This sociological success is incomplete because, at present, we cannot offer an agreed explanation.

There is a cop-out. One might argue that the overall volume of movement up and down a class structure will be a product of all the processes highlighted in the different explanations – the distribution of raw ability, the desire and efforts of advantaged parents to pass their advantages on to their children, and the ways in which both the rewards of success and the costs of its pursuit have different values for actors starting out from different positions. All the theories can probably help in explaining all the mobility that occurs, but adding them together does not explain the constancy of the flux. Only the intelligence hypothesis has a truly plausible (though not necessarily the correct) explanation for this constancy.

What cannot be explained cannot be changed – not deliberatively at any rate. Policy-makers do not seem to have got the message. Every modern society still has batteries of measures that are supposed to improve the life-chances of the disadvantaged; there has been a never-ending stream of such measures since the end of the nineteenth century and the stream shows no sign of drying up. The policy-makers do not seem to have heard: none of their attempts worked in the past and there are no grounds for expecting different results in the present and future. A rational response would be to stop trying, for the time being at any rate, but we know that in practice this is not going to happen. Reproduction theory may not explain the constant flux but it can explain why all countries try constantly to equalise life-chances, or at least appear to do so: those with privileges to protect need to be seen to be making all possible efforts to ensure that success is open to all the talents.

A harder puzzle is why so many sociologists continue to lend support to measures that are supposed to equalise opportunities. Sociologists should know that the best way to change mobility flows is to change the structure of opportunities itself. We are more likely to reduce unemployment rates among the least-qualified by reducing general unemployment than by providing the least-qualified with yet more education and training.

Summary

It is not a straightforward matter, but is has been possible for sociology to produce agreed answers to questions about the volume of mobility flows, and the extent to which our society is fluid or closed. Whether it is all fair and meritocratic proves an entirely different matter.

We have seen that there is a substantial and increasing volume of upward mobility from the working class, and a smaller and diminishing downward flow from the middle class. All this is due to the shape of the class structure, and changes therein over time. Current trends in mobility will be contributing to the disorganisation of the working class. The diverse origins of its members will have helped to keep the middle class disorganised during the twentieth century, but twenty-first century trends in mobility favour the development of characteristic middle-class lifestyles, forms of consciousness and political dispositions.

We know less about women's than about men's social mobility, but one crystal-clear finding is that while middle-class women have been the disadvantaged sex (up to now at any rate), matters are not so clear-cut in the working class. We have also seen that despite the 'ethnic penalty', Britain's ethnic minorities are gradually being dispersed, with one major exception, namely, the Afro-Caribbeans.

In this chapter we have encountered one of the most startling discoveries in the whole of sociology: the absence of major variations between modern societies, and over time within these societies, in their degrees of fluidity. There are explanations on offer – inherited ability, reproduction theory, and rational action theory – but up to now none have been able to marshall the evidence that would win all-round assent. It is equally startling that this finding, one of sociology's firmer conclusions, has been ignored by virtually all social policy-makers, and by many sociologists who continue to act as if they expect modest interventions in education or labour markets to bring about a significant redistribution of life-chances between the social classes.

9
Politics

Introduction

This chapter gets to the heart of claims that class is dead. It is argued, first, that to assess these claims we need to focus on persistent regularities and trends rather than 'events' such as Margaret Thatcher's ascendancy in the 1980s and the success of New Labour in the 1990s.

Post-1950s trends in British politics are unravelled. We see that the social class–party choice link has weakened (though it has not disappeared), and that this has occurred alongside other trends:

- A decline in Labour support (up to 1997).

- Contraction in both of the main parties' bedrocks of reliable support.

- 'Other' parties gaining a higher proportion of the vote.

- Politicians becoming a distinct (middle class) career group.

The chapter then considers possible alternatives to class as a basis for twenty-first century politics:

- Cleavages between public and private-sector workers and consumers.

- Issue voting.

- New social movements whose appeal criss-crosses class divisions.

The chapter, and the book, conclude that a complete separation of class from politics is a remote possibility while class divisions are so deep. We then consider alternative forms of class-based politics which could develop during the twenty-first century if an older type of class politics is indeed in terminal decline.

Issues

Politics is at the heart of current claims that class is dead. The death of class would be a consequence of jobs ceasing to be clustered into groups with characteristic work and market situations, and life-chances, but previous chapters have surely demonstrated that economic life has not become a mush of classless inequality. Alternatively, class would be killed if these common experiences of economic life ceased to make characteristic impressions on the consciousness of those concerned, or if any such consciousness ceased to have political consequences. Given that people spend so much time at work, or in and out of work in some cases today for the greater part of the life-course, the absence of any impression on their attitudes and perceptions of their positions in society and related interests is hardly plausible. Nevertheless, some believe that class politics is becoming a thing of the past. Their evidence is superficial and unconvincing.

It is true that, in the past, business (the upper class) funded the Conservative Party, while the Labour Party obtained most of its income from (working-class) trade unions. It is also true, again in the past, that most white-collar workers voted Conservative and most manual workers voted Labour. It is claimed that times have changed, and clearly they have in some ways. Business now supports New Labour as well as the Conservatives, and the relationship between class and voting has weakened (see below). Pakulski and Waters (1996) attach much significance to there being few references to class nowadays in the parties' policy statements and electioneering.

Some supporters of the 'class lives' school have tried to deny that there has been any significant weakening of the old class–politics relationship, but the contrary evidence (see below) is really too strong to be explained away; the evidence of change is all too stark. But the 'death of class' is not the only possible explanation of the relevant evidence. First, as regards political rhetoric, in the past it was usually other parties that were accused of being dependent upon, and seeking to serve, the interests of particular classes. The leaders of all the main parties have always attempted to appeal across class divisions. Second, the political parties' funds and members still tend to be drawn from specific classes rather than equally from all sections of the population. Increasingly, all parties look to business (the upper class) for funds, and their active members are middle-class. The class bases of the parties, in terms of members and sources of funds, especially the Labour Party's base, have certainly changed, but without becoming classless. Third, the relationship between class and voting may have weakened, but it was never a perfect relationship. There were always class deviants – more in the working class than in the middle class. Had this not been the case, then in the days when there was a working class majority the Labour

Party would have won every election. The class–vote link has weakened, but it has not disappeared, nor is it near to doing so, and it is still our best predictor of voting.

The recent changes in the politics–society relationship are in fact exactly what we should expect given the ways in which the class structure has changed. The most plausible explanations of the relevant political changes are in class terms. We now have a stronger upper class, an enlarged middle-class, and a disorganised working class. Characteristic forms of middle-class consciousness and politics are still in formation, and work-ing-class disorganisation may or may not persist indefinitely. The odds are on disorganisation persisting, but one can never be sure. Likewise as regards the strength of the upper class. The chances are that middle-class consciousness and politics will become more distinct as the middle class becomes a more stable, and larger, demographic entity. No-one can know for certain, but it is likely that during the twenty-first century the class–pol-itics link will once again firm-up, following its current transitional state, to reflect more clearly the current balance of class forces and any future changes that may occur in this balance.

What Sociology can Explain

Sociology is best at explaining what Emile Durkheim called social facts – persistent regularities and trends in social behaviour. It is futile to seek a class explanation, or any other sociological explanation, of political events where the most plausible explanations are simply political.

In the 1980s there were numerous attempts to explain the success of Thatcherism, and some sociologists were drawn into this game. Some said that Thatcherism was the outcome, which might have been predicted, of deep-seated changes in the economy and class structure (Jessop *et al.*, 1988). Others explained the success of Thatcherism in terms of the pro-ject's 'authoritarian populism' – its stances on law and order, immigration, nationalism, and intolerance of homosexuality. Thatcherism was said to harmonise with some deeply-rooted traits in working-class culture (Hall, 1988; Hall and Jacques, 1983). Maybe, but was this the prime reason for the Conservatives' four successive election victories?

Despite the huge parliamentary majorities, the Conservatives were actu-ally no more popular in the 1980s than on the occasions of their election victories in the 1950s and in 1970. Many of the Thatcher government's poli-cies were distinctly unpopular – its economic management, tolerance of high unemployment, and cutbacks in public services, for example. There was no upsurge of an enterprise culture. The policies that appealed to working-class voters were not all nationalist and socially authoritarian.

Tax-cutting was popular, and likewise the restrictions on trade unions' power, and the sale of council houses to sitting tenants. Even so, only a minority of voters could be described as Thatcherites. Fairly solid and enthusiastic support was confined to limited sections of the electorate, mainly the upper class and the petit bourgeoisie (see Edgell and Duke, 1991). Instead of trying to explain a non-existent popularity, Thatcherism's success really needed, and still needs, to be explained despite its unpopularity in many sections of the population (as recognised at the time by, for example, the contributors to Brown and Sparks, 1989).

The best explanations of the success of Thatcherism in the 1980s are basically political. There was the depth of unpopularity to which the Labour Party sank, and the divisions in its ranks which led to the break-away of the Social Democratic Party in 1982. A Labour government had presided over the 'winter of discontent' (strikes in the public services) in 1978–79; it is possible that Labour could have held onto office had it called the general election six months earlier (before the winter). It is possible that Labour would have won in 1979 if it had been able to maintain a parliamentary pact with the Liberals, or if the Scottish National Party had not been making inroads into the Labour vote in Scotland. It is also possible that Labour could have regained office in 1983 with more effective leadership; the image projected by Michael Foot, the new Labour leader elected following the 1979 defeat, was unattractive to many voters. His famous donkey jacket, and his long-standing links with CND and other left-wing causes, rallied traditional support within the Labour Party itself but invited much ridicule beyond, and played a role in provoking a split in the Labour Party when the 'gang of four' (all senior Labour MPs) formed the breakaway Social Democratic Party in 1982. Soon the SDP was syphoning-off additional MPs, party workers, and hundreds of thousands of former Labour voters. Later on the SDP formed an electoral alliance with the Liberals, and later on still the two parties merged and became the Liberal Democrats. To this day they have offered an alternative to Labour for anti-Tory voters at local and national levels. The crucial point here is that with more skilled leadership in the late-1970s and early-1980s, Labour might have been the main party of government during the latter decade.

We also need to pay due respect to the political skill of Margaret Thatcher herself. In 1979 the policies that became the hallmarks of Thatcherism would not have received majority support if placed before her cabinet or the parliamentary Conservative Party. In her early years in office it appeared quite likely that, before long, Thatcher would be ditched by her own party. As unemployment rose towards 3 million in 1980–81, the Conservative government's popularity nose-dived. It looked as though Margaret Thatcher would be a one-term prime minister. Then, in 1982, there was the Falklands War, the government's popularity soared, the 1983 election was won with an increased majority, and 'wets' were gradually relieved of key government posts. Had Argentina not invaded the Falklands, it is quite likely that we would never have heard of Thatcherism. It is pointless to seek the explanation of her success in deep-seated changes and tendencies in the wider society when there is a much simpler political explanation.

In the late-1990s pundits were seeking the deep-seated sources of the appeal of Blairism and New Labour. Once again, it is best to look first at the simple explanations. At the time, Tony Blair was an extremely popular party leader and prime minister. Even so, the share of the vote achieved by Labour in 1997 was lower than in the Labour victories between 1945 and 1966. Labour was assisted by the unpopularity of the Conservatives in the 1990s – the sleaze, the split over Europe, sterling being forced out of the European exchange rate mechanism and the aura of economic incompetence that this created. Also, we need to recognise that with a little more luck or astute election campaigning, Labour under Neil Kinnock might well have won the general election in 1992. John Smith, who replaced Neil Kinnock as Labour leader, might have lived to become prime minister. In either event there would have been no New Labour. Given these circumstances, it is futile to seek a correspondence between the New Labour project and fundamental shifts in the class structure or any other deeply-rooted features of Britain in the 1990s.

If class analysis can deliver, its achievements will not be in explaining political events, but longer-term trends and stabilities.

Trends

There have been important changes, alongside some impressive stabilities, in the relationships between politics and society in Britain since 1945, and it is on these that sociology is best-equipped to focus.

Labour Party Support

Table 6.1 (p. 164) presented the proportions of the total vote received by the two main political parties, Conservatives and Labour, in every general election from 1945 up to 1997. Although the electoral fortunes of Labour fluctuated, the fluctuations were around a long-term trend which was downwards up to 1997.

Now the most plausible explanation for the pre-1997 trend is sociological, and involves the changing shape of the class structure. Labour's electoral base was contracting – most of its support had always been from the working class, and the working class was becoming smaller from decade to decade. Furthermore, it was becoming rarer for manual workers to possess additional characteristics which increased their likelihood of voting Labour. Manual workers have been most likely to vote Labour if they have rented rather than owned their own homes, if they have been trade unionists, and if they have worked in the public sector. Owner-occupation has risen gradually since the 1950s, and in the 1980s (aided by the sale of council houses) it surged upwards in the class where it had been least common, namely, the working class. Since the 1970s trade union membership has declined, especially among manual workers. Thatcherism's denationalisation programme, and the contracting-out of non-core services from the remaining public sector, transferred swathes of manual jobs into private businesses. All these trends have been bad for Labour. The sole favourable long-term trend has been a rise in the number of people dependent on state benefits due to the increase in those of pensionable age, the rise in single parenthood, and higher unemployment than from the 1940s up to the 1970s. State welfare dependents are another group who have been particularly likely to vote Labour, and in the 1970s and 1980s this was creating a danger (for Labour's appeal in other sections of the electorate) of the party becoming too closely associated with welfare dependents.

In 1997 Labour bucked the trend. By then the Labour Party had reinvented itself; it had become New Labour with new policies, a new image and, perhaps most important of all, a new publicity machine. As yet this election, and the next as well, are best regarded as events. Despite its record majority in 1997, the share of the vote achieved by Labour was still beneath its victory levels of the 1940s, 1950s and 1960s. In 1997 Labour achieved a stronger swing against the government than any other opposition party in post-1945 history. This achievement was remarkable, but it is still just a political event, and not necessarily a historical shift. Labour may have become the new 'party of government'; but it is still too early to say. As already noted, in 1997 Labour was assisted by the Conservatives' dire unpopularity. It is also the case that the longer the political pendulum takes to swing, then the stronger a swing is likely to be. It is possible that Labour will retain the level of support that it achieved in 1997 through the first decades of the twenty-first century, but it is also possible, in the longer-term, that 1997 will stand out as an abberation.

Conservative Party Support

Since 1945 Conservative support has been remarkably stable. There have been trendless fluctuations – ups and downs from election to election but no long-term trend whatsoever.

As noted in Chapter 6, this is more remarkable than the decline of Labour, given the wider social trends which one might have expected to work in the Conservatives' favour, especially the expansion in the numbers of white-collar employees and home owners. Why did the Conservative Party fail to benefit electorally from these trends? This question was partly answered in Chapter 6. As it has grown, the middle class has become better-educated, and the types of middle-class voters who have increased in number are those least likely to be conservative either socially or politically. This has neutralised the effects of the change in the shape of the class structure which should otherwise have been to the Conservatives' electoral benefit.

Another crucial fact of this matter is that the rate of expansion in the middle class has placed many upwardly mobile, first-generation managers and professionals in the Conservative Party's major electoral base. Many will have retained class identities and political loyalties from their social origins, and the Conservative Party has needed to win these new middle-class voters. In its early years the Labour Party was unable to rely on the working-class vote; this vote needed to be won. The Conservatives were in a similar position *vis-à-vis* the expanding middle class in the second half of the twentieth century, and at the turn of the century it was far from clear that the Party would eventually be victorious.

The 1997 general election result was exceptional for the Conservatives as well as for Labour. The Conservative vote collapsed to its lowest level in the entire twentieth century. Maybe this will be the new normal level of Conservative support, but, again, it is still too early to say. The Conservatives could bounce back. In 1997 the Conservatives polled a higher share of the vote than Labour achieved in 1983, and look what happened to Labour 14 years later.

The Decline of Partisanship

Since the 1970s, voters' loyalties have been more fickle than in the 1940s, 1950s and 1960s, though, surprising to everyone at the time, stability returned in the 1990s when, after 1992, Labour remained consistently popular and the Conservatives unpopular until the end of the century. Pundits were confident that Labour's opinion poll lead in the mid-1990s would not survive a general election campaign. They were wrong. Even so, analysts have remained convinced that much of New Labour's support is 'soft'.

From the 1970s until the 1990s the parties' opinion-poll ratings swung sharply. Governments could plumb depths of unpopularity between elections, then achieve re-election, and opinion sometimes swung decisively during election campaigns. Unless the opinion polls were wrong (as many suspect), it appears that in 1992 some voters left home intending to vote Labour, changed their minds before entering the polling booths, then became Labour supporters again by the time that they had returned home.

Earlier-on, political scientists had developed theories of political socialisation (Butler and Stokes, 1974; Rose and McAllister, 1990). These emphasised how most people formed party loyalties during childhood, usually identifying with their parents' parties. These loyalties developed prior to young people acquiring any detailed knowledge about party policies. Often this knowledge was acquired later, and filtered through pre-formed loyalties. Some young people changed their loyalties during youth; which was especially likely if they were socially mobile. Thereafter, voters became attached to their preferred parties and were most likely to remain loyal supporters for the rest of their lives. So the main parties had solid bedrocks of reliable support. The parties' electioneering problem was to 'get the vote out'; their supporters could abstain, but there was usually no danger of them switching to the other side.

These solid bedrocks of support still exist, but in a shrunken state. The Economic and Social Research Council's 16–19 Initiative questioned representative samples (panels) of young people in four parts of Britain on three occasions between 1987 and 1989, and found that just 43 per cent (including the don't knows) gave the same replies on each occasion to the standard, 'How would you vote?' question. Only 28 per cent were firmly attached to either Labour or the Conservative Party (Banks *et al.*, 1992). This sample was aged 16–20 at the time of the research. The proportion with firm party loyalties could expand with age, or the majority could remain non-partisan. Recent cohorts of young people have been moving into adulthood and passing the age when they become eligible to vote without, in most cases, developing any firm party attachments.

There has been a corresponding decline in party memberships. In the 1950s the Conservatives had nearly 3 million individual members. By 1979 there were just 1.5 million, and a mere 300,000 in 1997 with an average age of 62. Most of Labour's members have always been affiliated via their trade unions. From the 1940s until the 1980s Labour could not match the Conservatives' figures for individual party members. The Labour Party had around a million individual members in the 1950s, and around 300,000, roughly the same as the Conservatives, in the mid-1990s. New Labour has launched repeated recruitment drives, using its party political broadcasts for this purpose. The party's problem has not been in persuading people to sign up so much as retaining them. The present-day recruit, it appears, is more likely to be a temporary paying supporter than a long-term active member. New Labour's aim of regaining a million members has remained just a distant aspiration.

Political party membership and activity appear to be like many other leisure pastimes; some people become involved when young, and remain involved through their life-stage transitions from education into employment, and into marriage and parenthood. If their leisure interests endure through these events, those concerned are most likely to remain active throughout the remainder of their adult lives. Those who drop out, or who never become involved when young, may be 'converted' or 'reclaimed' in adulthood, but their relapse rates are extremely high. In some respects, churches and exercise classes have much the same problem as political parties. Over the last 50 years, the main parties have become less successful in attracting and holding on to young activists.

Minor Parties

As party support has softened, the share of all votes attracted by the two main parties has declined. The Northern Ireland parties have severed their earlier connections with the Conservatives and Labour. Actually, Northern Ireland is the one part of the UK where there has been little political change. In every election there are on fact two contests: one for the unionist/protestant vote, and the other for the nationalist/catholic vote, with hardly anyone crossing this divide.

In Scotland, and to a lesser extent in Wales, nationalist parties have grown in strength – sufficiently so to gain a parliament for Scotland and an assembly for Wales, both of which opened in 1999. In England, the Liberal Party, the Social Democrats, then the alliance between the two, then the Liberal Democrats, have achieved a larger share of the vote since the 1970s than the Liberals achieved during the 30 previous years. Indeed, there have been periods in recent times when the Liberal Democrats have been England's second party of local government in terms of council seats held, and the number of council chambers where the party has been in sole or joint control.

The so-called centre-parties in England have suffered under the first-past-the-post, single-member constituency, electoral system, especially in national elections. This system has proved less disadvantageous for the regional/nationalist parties because their support is concentrated in a limited number of constituencies where they have been able to take seats in parliament reflecting their popularity in the regions where their support is based. Needless to say, support for 'other' parties has been just as fickle in recent times as Conservative and Labour support.

It is possible that all the above are features of a new politics, but it is also possible that politics in the UK is currently in a transitional state. There have been earlier historical periods when the main parties had only narrow bedrocks of reliable and dependable support, and when the combined vote for the two main parties was squeezed. This applied early in the twentieth century when Labour was replacing the Liberals as the main alternative to the Conservatives (see Figure 9.1). No-one can be sure, but it is possible that UK politics will firm-up once more at some point in the twenty-first century.

Class De-alignment

There is no dispute about the basic facts of this matter. There are different ways of calculating index scores of class voting, but they all combine the

Figure 9.1   Vote-share of the top two parties

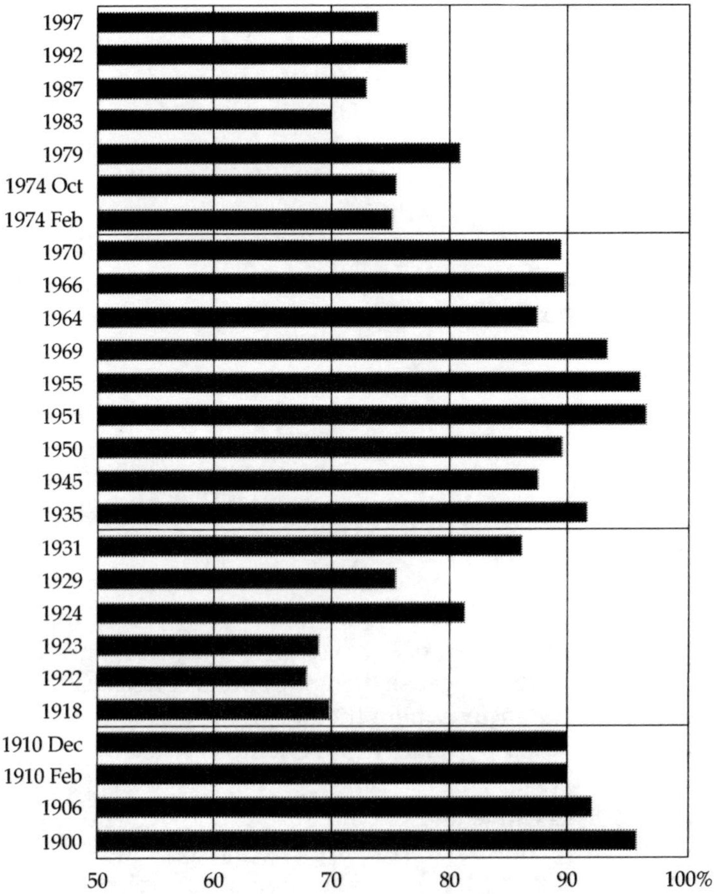

Source: Dunleavy (1999).

proportions of white-collar workers who vote Conservative, and of manual workers who vote Labour. Since the 1970s, these index scores, however calculated, have been well-beneath the levels of the 1940s, 1950s and 1960s. Anyone can see this from Table 9.1, which gives the proportions of non-manual and manual electors who voted Conservative and Labour in each election since 1964. Both figures were above 60 per cent in the two elections in the 1960s, whereas this has never happened since then. In 1997, in its landslide victory, Labour polled a lower share of the manual vote than in 1964 and 1966, while the Conservatives polled a lower share of the non-manual vote in 1983, 1987 and 1992 than in 1964, 1966 and 1970.

Ivor Crewe was among the first analysts to identify class de-alignment (Crewe, 1977, 1986; Sarlvik and Crewe, 1983), and nowadays most political scientists accept that this trend has in fact taken place (see Franklin, 1985). It is said that class alignment occurred when each party was identified with a particular class, when most people had definite class identities and voted for the parties that represented their classes. The de-alignment thesis claims that some, if not all, of these links have weakened.

Now it is possible to show that if votes for parties other than Labour and the Conservatives are taken out of the picture, and if we make allowances for the general decline in partisanship (party support becoming more fickle), and if we also take into account Labour's unpopularity in all sections of the electorate in the 1980s, and the Conservatives' unpopularity in the 1990s, we see that class alignment is as strong as ever: that there have

Table 9.1 Occupational class and vote, 1964–97

	Non-manual (%)	Man. (%)	Non-manual (%)	Man. (%)	Non-manual (%)	Man. (%)	Non-manual (%)	Man. (%)
	1964		*1966*		*1970*		*1974F*	
Conservation	62	28	60	25	64	33	53	24
Labour	22	64	26	69	25	58	22	57
	1974O		*1979*		*1983*		*1987*	
Conservation	51	24	60	35	55	35	54	35
Labour	25	57	23	50	17	42	20	45
	1992		*1997*					
Conservation	56	36	38	29				
Labour	24	51	40	58				

Source: Sanders (1997).

been fluctuations from election to election but no long-term trend (Evans, 1993; Heath *et al.*, 1985, 1991). This is all rather ingenious, but the manipulation of the evidence is not really convincing. These analysts are taking out of account the very features of voters' attitudes and behaviour that the de-alignment thesis seeks to explain.

We have seen that support for 'other' parties has been higher since the 1970s than during the previous 30 years. These other parties have drawn support from all social classes, and since these parties now account for a significant share of the vote in local, national and European elections, their presence really needs to be taken into account when measuring the strength of the class–vote link. After all, the LibDems have become a major force in local government in England, and it is not inconceivable that the Scottish National Party could gain control of its country's parliament. It is possible that after what turns-out to be a period of transitional politics, the main parties will regain their former dominance, but it is equally possible that the present so-called transitional state is in fact the new politics.

Even so, it is possible to insist that there remains a clear, albeit weakened, relationship between class and voting, and that class is still the best of all single predictors (Robertson, 1984; Weakliem, 1989, and see below). In 1997 manual workers were roughly one-and-a-half times as likely to vote Labour as non-manuals, and the latter were roughly one-and-a-half times as likely to vote Conservative. There was still a very clear class–vote relationship after 30 years of de-alignment. The relationships between age and voting, and sex and voting, are extremely weak when compared with the present-day class–vote relationship (see Table 9.2). In 1997 men and women hardly differed in their party choices. This was novel, because in previous elections women had been the more Conservative sex. In 1997 older voters were more Conservative than younger voters, and this has been the case ever since the relevant information began to be collected. We really do become more Conservative, on average, as we grow older. Note, however, that in 1997 the age relationship was weaker than the class–vote link, certainly as regards Labour support, just as it always has been. Nowadays all political parties are aware of the importance of the so-called 'grey vote'. There are more older voters, and they are more likely to actually vote than the under-25s. The grey vote is becoming heavier, and will be even more so in the future, because we are living longer, men have been retiring earlier, and the 'baby boomers' – the products of the swollen birth-rate after 1945 – are beginning to grey. However, no major party will want to be associated with grey issues to an extent that weakens its support in other age groups, and there are huge class and gender-related inequalities among the elderly. There are lots of good reasons why the age-vote link is unlikely to firm-up and replace class voting.

Table 9.2 Voting by class, gender and age: 1997 General Election

	Occupational class				Sex		Age				
	AB (%)	C1 (%)	C2 (%)	DE (%)	Men (%)	Women (%)	<25 (%)	25–34 (%)	35–44 (%)	45–64 (%)	>65 (%)
Conservative	37	32	29	25	31	32	24	27	28	31	38
Labour	31	41	52	52	44	44	52	46	49	40	40
Liberal Democrat	24	22	12	15	17	17	17	19	16	20	15
Other	8	5	7	8	8	7	7	8	7	9	7

Source: Sanders (1997).

Ethnicity is very strongly related to voting. Labour wins overwhelmingly in all the non-white ethnic minorities, and has done so ever since the 1960s. It is difficult to say whether it is the Conservatives' policies, people or rhetoric that repels the minorities; there are too few respondents from specific minority groups to draw conclusions from the normal opinion polls. It is necessary to amalgamate the responses from several polls, and to collapse the minorities into Asians and blacks. We then see that in 1996–97, Labour had 70 per cent of the Asian vote against the Conservatives' 25 per cent. Among blacks, Labour had 86 per cent and the Conservatives just 8 per cent. The LibDems had 4 per cent in both minority groups (Coxall and Robins, 1998). There are implications here for both politics and race relations. The ethnic vote has become crucial to Labour's success in constituencies where the minorities are concentrated, which could lead to Labour being highly responsive to minority concerns. Alternatively, Labour could take the minorities for granted on the basis that they had nowhere else to go. The Conservatives might well decide to concentrate on more friendly sections of the electorate. However, the crucial point here is that the minorities are not numerous enough, even in total, for ethnicity to become the main base of UK party politics.

Voters, Parties and Representatives

Another change over time has been in the types of people who become elected representatives, and how these correspond to both party memberships and the people who vote for the parties' candidates in elections. The most dramatic changes in recent years have been in the Labour Party. The Conservative Party changed earlier on, from the late-nineteenth century onwards, as aristocrats in parliament gave way to people from business and the professions. Nowadays the Conservative Party's elected representatives have a broadly similar class profile to the party's active rank and file, whereas lower-level white-collar employees and the working class are much better represented among Conservative voters. There is a much wider discrepancy nowadays between Labour voters and the types of people who they elect.

In the Labour Party the trend throughout the twentieth century was for elected representatives with personal experience in working-class jobs to give way to people from the professions and management. In 1906, 86 per cent of Labour MPs were from the working class. By 1945 this was down to 38 per cent, and by 1997 to just 13 per cent. There has been a similar exodus of working-class activists from many local Labour Parties and their replacement by people from the non-conservative middle class. Barry Hindess (1971) noted such a trend in Liverpool as early as the 1960s.

The higher up we look in both parties, the more elevated are the backgrounds of the personnel. A half of the 1945 Labour cabinet was from the working class compared with just 5 per cent (one person, John Prescott) in 1997. One might argue that the Labour Party has not really changed as dramatically as these figures suggest. The volume of upward mobility from the working class has increased, and many of the present-day Labour MPs whose own previous jobs were middle-class spent their childhoods in working-class homes. The kinds of people from working-class backgrounds who once left school before age 16, entered manual jobs, became active in trade unions and politics and eventually became elected politicians, are now staying in education beyond age 16 and becoming university graduates. However, the fact remains that personal experience of being an adult manual worker has become quite rare among Labour parliamentarians. The contrast with the typical Labour voter (still a manual worker) is glaring.

Another trend has been towards politics as a full-time, long-term career; it is now quite common for national politicians to spend almost their entire working lives in politics. This is not a completely new development. The head offices of the main parties always recruited some bright young graduates who went on to become MPs, but in the past there were very few such jobs. Over time, the party headquarters establishments have expanded. Also, elected representatives at national and European levels have acquired budgets with which they can appoint staff. When parties are in government, it is now normal for ministers to make political appointments to their state-paid staffs. Also, there are now numerous pressure and campaigning groups with paid staff in which starters can gain political experience. A consequence of all this is that politics has become another (middle-class) career: one which exhibits, in a very extreme form, many more widespread features of present-day middle-class careers – the insecurity and work pressure, for example. The European and Scottish parliaments, and the Welsh Assembly notwithstanding, there has been little change over time in the number of paid positions for elected politicians. There has been a greater increase in the number of unelected career politicians. Some stay backstage by choice, others because they are unable to gain elected office.

There has been a major shift in the relationship between paid politicians and the people. The political parties used to be composed of active members who were broadly representative, in socio-demographic terms, of the parties' voters. In this sense, the parties represented broad sections of society. Elected representatives gained their positions on the basis of their skill in saying, and putting into effect, what other members willed. But politics no longer works in this way; nowadays the young adults who remain active in politics for years and years tend at least to envisage paid careers as elected or unelected politicians. There are fewer active stalwarts who do not expect such careers, and the activists who become elected representatives in all the parties tend to be from much the same social backgrounds – university educated, with subsequent career experience either confined to politics, or in management or the professions.

Today's politicians are more of a distinct career group, but, even so, they are probably better-informed than ever before about the state of public opinion. All the parties pay for regular opinion surveys and run focus groups to ensure that they remain in touch. The leaders want to know, and they are in fact well-informed about what all classes of people are thinking. None want to ignore any substantial sections of the population. Party channels are considered less trustworthy. The party leaders often suspect, usually with good reason, that their party activists' opinions are unrepresentative of the electorate, and party conferences are always likely to pass embarrassing resolutions unless they are managed carefully. Election campaigns are now fought through the media. Active members are not as crucial as they once were. Parties that are represented in parliament are able to draw some funds from taxpayers. They continue to need, and to seek, contributions from individual members and supporters, but in practice they rely heavily on corporate sponsorship – from trade unions and business in the case of Labour, and from business alone in other parties. Needless to say, the manner in which grassroots party members are treated, often bypassed, by their party leaders, can only reduce the rank and file's incentives to engage in long-term political activity.

We should note that both Thatcherism and New Labour were initially the projects of small elites who gained the acquiescence first of parliamentary colleagues, then, on the basis of electoral success, their parties in the country. Europe is a similar elite project. As yet there can be few people outside Brussels who are excited and enthusiastic about a future United States of Europe.

Politicians worry not so much about whether they are in touch (they know what voters are thinking) as whether they are trusted. On this they have cause for concern. There is also periodic alarm at low voter turn-outs, especially in local and European elections, though in fact there has been no long-term decline in the proportion of electors who vote. There is constant discussion about possible constitutional reforms. Should there be proportional representation at Westminster and on local councils as well as in the Scottish parliament, the Welsh assembly, and all elected bodies in Northern Ireland? Should there be elected regional assemblies in England? What about having elected mayors in additional cities, as in London since 2000? It is doubtful whether any of these reforms will do the trick. Proportional representation can leave people feeling that, whoever they vote for, the same faces reappear and fix things among themselves. Moreover, all the above reforms would increase the party machines' control: over the individuals offered to the electorate on party lists for election to assemblies and parliament, and as candidates to become city bosses, for example.

Alternatives to Class

If politics is losing its class base, what are the new foundations? Several candidates have been proposed, but none have matured into really strong contenders. The situation here is comparable to the changes that are taking place in middle-class careers. It is easier to find evidence of the disintegration of old careers than confirmation of the birth of new models. Likewise, although the class–vote link has weakened, class has remained a fairly good predictor of voter behaviour, in general elections at any rate. It is possible that class de-alignment will continue until the relationship is non-existent; and some between-election opinion polls in the late 1990s found that the class–party link had all but disappeared. Fluke results? Another sign of voter volatility? Straws in the wind? It is impossible to say. Even long-term trends are not laws, and it is equally possible that the class–vote link will become tighter once more sometime during the early decades of the twenty-first century. We have seen that class de-alignment is not the only recent change to have taken place in the politics–society relationship. In combination, the changes suggest that politics is in transition. The old politics has been shaken by, and politics is currently adjusting to, changes in the class structure. As yet, all the alternatives to class, as bases for voters' choices, are simply not convincing.

New Social Cleavages

It has been suggested that other cleavages could replace 'producer classes' as the main base for partisanship. One such alternative base could be the sector – public or private – where people work, but we have already seen in Chapter 6 (p. 164) that although private-sector workers are the more likely to vote Conservative, and public-sector workers are the more likely to vote Labour, these relationships are much weaker, even after the recent class de-alignment, than between voting and conventional producer classes.

Consumption cleavages or classes are another possible base for a new politics, and some of the evidence here is quite persuasive. The basic consumption cleavage is said to separate people who depend for their incomes on state welfare from those who earn their livings, and, related to this, those who rely on state services for their pensions, housing, education and health care, and those who purchase these services privately. It has been argued that the population is in fact being divided into state dependents on the one hand, and, on the other, the growing numbers who are able to provide for themselves by paying for private services from their own incomes, and that the two main parties in recent decades have drawn their core support from one or the other of these groups (see Dunleavy, 1980, 1989).

In the late-1980s Edgell and Duke (1991) categorised their sample of voters according to whether they used private or public services, and the variation in party choices that was revealed was wider than when the respondents were divided into more conventional producer classes (see Figure 9.2). Indeed, if electors are divided simply into home owners and council/housing association tenants, the political cleavage is wider than between manuals and non-manuals (see Table 9.3).

However, there are serious problems with the claim that these consumption cleavages are replacing class as the foundation for politics. First, whether people depend on state services or are able to make private purchases depends primarily on the producer classes to which they belong. Consumption is not a truly independent variable; conventional class positions determine consumption rather than vice versa (see Sullivan, 1989; Wait, 1996). The extreme groups in the Edgell and Duke analysis, which were relying entirely on public and private services respectively, were, in practice, the most disadvantaged section of the working class (or an underclass) on the one hand, and the more privileged members of the middle class on the other.

Second, consumption behaviour does not divide the population as clearly as working and middle-class work and market situations. Most people use combinations of state and private provisions. Some parents use private secondary education having sent their children to state primary schools. Everyone who attends university nowadays needs to meet a significant proportion of the costs from private resources. The services that people use often change during the life-course. People may have private medical insurance while they are in employment, then rely on the

Figure 9.2   Percentages voting against Conservatives in 1987

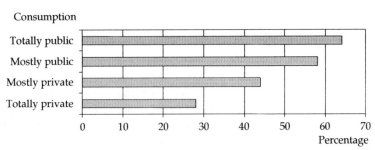

Source: Edgell and Duke (1991).

Table 9.3 Voting by class and housing: 1997 General Election

	Occupational class				Housing	
	AB (%)	C1 (%)	C2 (%)	DE (%)	Owner-occupier (%)	Council tenant (%)
Conservative	37	32	29	25	35	13
Labour	31	41	52	52	41	65
Liberal Democrat	24	22	12	15	17	15
Other	8	5	7	8	7	7

Source: Sanders (1997).

National Health Service after retirement. In other words, there is simply not the kind of clear division between sections of the population as would be required for political parties to appeal exclusively and successfully to groups with absolutely no interest in either private or public services.

Issue Voting

There is an alternative view of the future of politics to expecting class to be replaced by any other socio-demographic base. One argument is that as the electorate becomes better-educated, partisanship declines, and voters cease treating political parties like football teams. Voters are said to 'float', and to decide who to support at each election on the basis of the issues, and the parties' policies. There is said to be a trend towards voters deciding, first, which issues are important to them (the economy, immigration, Europe, education or whatever), then deciding which party attaches the highest priority to, and has the best policies on, the issues in question (Crewe, 1986; Sarlvik and Crewe, 1983).

This is a plausible theory whose only problem is the lack of evidence. In practice, the theory credits voters with levels of political interest and knowledge that the majority do not possess. Non-partisans – the floating voters whose support may be captured by any party – are the electors who are the least-informed about, and interested in, the parties' policies (see Rose and McAllister, 1990). The most knowledgeable and interested voters are in fact the most partisan – the most strongly attached to particular parties. The floaters who swing elections do not mirror the behaviour of the TV and radio panels that are sometimes used for edification and entertainment. Floaters are likely to be swayed by whether they generally 'feel good' or 'feel bad' about how things are going, by the impressions of competence, or the lack of it, that a government and opposition create, or simply whether the floaters are tired of the 'same old faces' and feel that it is 'time for a change'. Party leaders know that it is the images that they present to poorly-informed and scarcely-interested floating voters, rather than whether they satisfy their parties' active and generally highly interested and well-informed members, that settles their fate at the ballot box. Western democracy works differently in practice than in the classic treatises on political theory.

New Issues and New Social Movements

There have always been pressure groups which seek to influence public opinion and political parties rather than to replace them in government. So 'new' social movements have some familiar features. It is more the character of the campaigning groups, and the types of issues that they represent, that are novel. The new issues are said to arise from the interests of no particular classes, or any other specific sections of the population, and are said to actually create collective political actors.

New social movements campaign for peace, animal welfare, the quality of our food and other environmental causes, gay rights, women's rights, civil rights for all or for particularly vulnerable groups, the right to life, or to abortion. It is claimed that these movements are characteristic of, and are engaged in the most important struggles about the character of, late-industrial societies. The movements are not based on pre-existing socio-demographic groups, rather, the issues create the groups, which become movements. It is claimed that nowadays it is these movements rather than the older political parties that are addressing the basic faults in modern societies, mobilising the people and generating visions of alternative futures. In time, some believe, these movements will change the world. The growth of these movements has been likened to the earlier rise of the bourgeoisie, and subsequently the working class (see Galtung, 1986; Meier, 1988; Touraine *et al.*, 1983).

Most of the movements exist in more than one country. Britain has not been at the forefront, and British sociologists and political scientists have been somewhat less excited about new social movements than their continental counterparts. This is likely to be related to Britain having two of Europe's stronger political parties, which, in turn, is related to Britain's voting system for elections to the Westminster parliament. Proportional representation in Europe has enabled representatives of new social movements, notably the 'greens', to gain seats in most parliaments.

Memberships of the main political parties have shrunk, but, it is claimed, these figures have ceased to be good guides to the level of political activity among the population. Political scientists estimate that around a half of all adults participate in politics solely by voting in elections, that a quarter are (for practical purposes) completely inactive, and that the remaining quarter vote and do other things besides (Coxall and Robins, 1998). The extra activities include signing petitions, writing to MPs, and attending meetings and demonstrations. It is claimed that much of this activity is coordinated by new social movements, or related to these movements' issues. New social movements, it is said, raise issues that really capture people's interest, ignite their enthusiasm and mobilise them into political action.

The crucial issue for present purposes is not whether these movements really are destined to change the world, but the ways in which their development, and the extent to which they develop, affect the class–politics relationship. Now it is true that the new social movements do not explicitly appeal to any specific class interests; rather, all the movements claim to represent 'the people'. In this sense the movements are classless. There is no class rhetoric, except in so far as some activists believe that their opponents are the political-industrial-military-financial establishment. 'Except' is probably the wrong word here, because this type of thinking implies an awareness of, indeed an acute sensitivity to, the division between the upper class and the rest. In contrast, none of the movements see a major division of interest separating the working class and the middle class.

However, a fact of this matter is that the activists in all the new social movements are mainly from the non-conservative middle class. The activists are certainly not representative of 'the people' in general in terms of social backgrounds. Some activists are active in several new social movements; hence the 'rent-a-crowd' accusation. While the movements may not seek to promote explicitly middle-class interests, they are based on issues which, from the activists' profile, appear to be of greatest concern to the middle classes. The rise of these movements, and the insertion of their issues onto political agendas, are in fact political outcomes of the enlargement and the progressive organisation of middle-class opinion. Traditional working-class issues – economic management to secure regular work and income, linking rewards to merit (skills, effort and hours worked), settling issues by collective agreement, guarantees of social security for all, and the extraction of crucial services from the marketplace – are sidelined on new political agendas.

Restructuring Class and Politics

The 'class is dead' school can cite de-alignment. Class theory can more than match this. It can explain not just de-alignment but all the other long-term trends in the politics–society relationship: trends in support for Labour and the Conservatives, the general decline in partisanship, increased support for minor parties, and the rise of new social movements. All these developments are exactly what should be expected given the way in which the class structure has changed.

The Upper Class

For the upper class the late-twentieth century was a new dawn. With the collapse of communism, capitalism became a truly global system; capital was able to internationalise itself and harness new technology. Enterprises, their managers and workers, and even countries, have been placed in the position of needing to compete for capital, and the rich are now able to demand subsidies for their investments. In 1999 BMW was offered £152 million by the UK government to help re-equip its Longbridge (Birmingham) site. This subsidy amounted to roughly £4 per UK adult. Would BMW have received such generous treatment had its owners been obliged to plead personally to UK voters? Every job saved at BMW/Rover would have cost the UK taxpayer roughly £12,000: a bargain, maybe. It is true that the subsidy amounted to just 10 per cent of the sum that BMW was prepared to invest. In the event, the cash offered by the UK government proved insufficient: BMW pulled out. We can be sure that Ford, General Motors, Peugeot and Nissan/Renault will have got the message.

Capital is no longer throttled by regulation, burdened by taxation or threatened by trade unions. Representatives of the upper class advise one-and-all on how to become business-friendly. Ownership and control have been depersonalised. Investment appears a neutral force which rewards workers, firms and countries that are efficient and competitive. Business is willing to fund all business-friendly, and at least potentially powerful, political parties. The parties need this sponsorship in order to campaign; so they are all business-friendly. The upper class has no need to explain and justify itself in person to the middle and working classes: there are others who will do the job better. It used to be said that, despite their radical intentions, socialist politicians became servants of capitalism through the logic of operating in a capitalist economic system. This logic is now part of all the major parties' policies. The middle class is tempted with the prospect of extremely rewarding careers, for the successful. It is no surprise, therefore, that middle-class radicalism is no threat to the capitalist economy. It is truly remarkable how the upper class escapes censure. Site closures that create unemployment, human resource management that creates precarious jobs, huge hikes to already huge directors' salaries: it seems that everything is tolerable if only it is good for business.

The Middle Class

This class has grown in size, and has an expanding, intergenerationally stable core. It has taken-over the leadership positions, and comprises the majority of the activists in all the significant political parties. The threat of working-class power has receded. Small wonder then that the middle class today is less securely attached to any single party than in previous years. Up to now the main political division within the middle class has been between the socially radical and the rest. The latter have mostly voted Conservative, while the former have voted for other parties, and some have been active in new social movements. The Conservatives still benefit from being the traditionally middle-class party. Unless they have a particular reason to change, middle-class adults from middle-class Conservative families are most likely to continue to vote Conservative. However, there is no necessary reason why the Conservative Party should repel the socially radical, or why the latter should be attracted to Labour. Indeed, in the late-1990s New Labour was anxious to demonstrate that it was socially responsible, authoritarian when necessary (tough on crime and *vis-à-vis* asylum seekers), while the Conservatives under William Hague tried to appear open to all races and sexual orientations.

The middle class is now too large to be ignored by any political party with pretensions to office. So none threaten middle-class incomes with more progressive taxation. Indeed, all the parties seem to agree that the middle class must be provided with tax shelters. History may still tell the middle class that its interests lie with the Tories, but New Labour has been desperate to prove otherwise.

However, at present none of the parties have answers to characteristic middle-class discontents: basically the gripes of those whose career commitment is unrewarded, sometimes unwanted, whose career progress is blocked, or who are not given the opportunities that they feel their qualifications merit. Up to now the middle class's typical responses to its discontents have been non-political, though most who work in the public sector have become trade unionists, and likewise the lower and middling ranks in large, private-sector organisations. However, the standard middle-class responses to career discontents have been to try even harder, or to withdraw psychologically from work and engage in lifestyle politics, sometimes alongside involvement in new social movements. It is possible to switch to organic food without changing the entire economic system. Up to now there has been no significant middle-class challenge to the upper class, nor any widespread desire to ally with the working class. None of the main political parties are offensive to the middle class, but neither are any answering its discontents. In this context, individual non-partisanship and collective multi-partisanship are understandable political dispositions.

The Working Class

During the last third of the twentieth century the entire working class became, in a sense, an excluded group. Many workers' links with the labour force became precarious or non-existent. They lost the protection of trade unions, in some cases through loss of employment, in others through moving to non-unionised firms, and in others because the unions to which they continued to belong were unable to defend them.

There are remnants of the working classes that were shaped earlier-on. There is still an original working class of trade union members, living in rented accommodation, who remain in the Labour Party, and who would support Old Labour if that was still an option. The original working-class culture is not completely extinct. Then there are still examples of the new working class that was created in the postwar years – employees in large unionised firms, with well-paid jobs, who nowadays own their own homes and take regular overseas holidays. But the core of the new millennium working class is simply disorganised. At the end of the twentieth century, a fifth of all households which contained adults had no-one in employment, and a third of all children were being born into poverty. The core members of today's working class are unemployed or in precarious jobs. None of the political parties have much to offer to this new working class.

All sections of the present-day working class know that they have failed to 'get on' while others who were reared in similar circumstances have done better. They do not necessarily blame themselves, but they know that others believe that they are responsible for their own problems, or, at any rate, that they should devise solutions by making themselves employable. They can, of course, hope that their children or grandchildren will benefit from their enhanced opportunities to get on.

Politics, it must appear, has nothing more to offer. Even if it was possible to rebuild the old working-class coalition, this would represent but a minority of the population. There is not even an agenda around which the working class might be remobilised. Key elements of the old working-class agenda have ceased to inspire. Public ownership may have improved, but it did not transform, the status of workers. Public services are often poor quality, especially those on which the middle class has never depended. And workers find that they themselves need to pay for these services through taxation. There is no longer a vision of a better future. Hence the weakening of support for working-class parties. Tradition still works for Labour within the working-class, but these voters know that

Labour is no longer their party – its leaders are not people like themselves and are not even offering a better future.

The Future of Class and Politics

No-one can predict the future; this is one thing that we have learnt from nearly two centuries of sociology. The twenty-first century could be shattered by war. At the end of the nineteenth century, very few, if any, social theorists envisaged the new modern societies becoming more violent than their predecessors. Alternatively, the twenty-first century could be shaken by global economic collapse, eliminating everyone's savings and pushing life back to basics. There could be a nuclear, or a slower, ecological disaster. Even if we avoid all calamities, politics will not have to remain class-based in any particular way, or at any particular strength.

The international indications are that the most likely alternatives to class-based politics are politics based on national, ethnic, religious or regional populations and identities. Party choices may be guided by gender issues, but there is no democracy where the main cleavage among voters is between men and women, or between age groups, though everywhere, as in Britain, there are tendencies for older people to be relatively conservative (which in Eastern Europe means communist, at present), and for new issues and movements to make their strongest initial impressions among the young.

Nationality and its equivalents are rather different. These are the principal bases on which humanity is divided into political units. It can be argued that the fundamental political problem, always and everywhere, has been to decide which people should belong in a given political entity, or to align a political entity with people's actual identities, and then to settle their own polity's relationships with others. These matters have in fact now become major political issues in much of the UK – in Northern Ireland, Scotland and Wales, aided in the latter two cases by the 1979–97 experience of being governed by a party that had only minority support in the countries concerned, and since 1997 by the perception of New Labour as an English project. Europe may be the big divisive issue of the twenty-first century.

However, once nationality and related matters have been resolved, and even while they remain unresolved, peoples and their governments have to decide which other policies to pursue. At this point, in any class-divided society, it is hardly conceivable that politics could be completely classless. Classes can be defined (as in this book) as groups with similar life-chances arising from their distinctive market and work situations. Life-chances can be identified objectively, as when we study mobility flows and chances, but life-chances are also the lived experiences of class members. As such they give rise to characteristic preoccupations, priorities and values. A political party can gear its policies towards such class interests and thereby try to maximise its support within the class in question, and only one major party need act (successfully) in this way for the entire party system to acquire a particular kind of class base. British politics was patterned in this way for most of the twentieth century, but since the 1960s this 'traditional' type of class politics has weakened. There are still clear remnants, but these might slowly disappear. They could be resuscitated, but there are alternative ways in which politics can be class-related. One is for all the main parties to be led by people from the same social classes, which has been the direction of change in UK politics in recent years. Such parties may or may not be more or less equally successful in seeking support in all classes of the electorate.

The USA is a good example of this type of politics. America is as class-ridden as Britain in terms of the contrasts between different groups' work and market situations, and their attitudes towards employment-related issues, but politics has been relatively insulated from all this (see Gerteis and Savage, 1998). Or maybe American politics has simply appeared more class-insulated than is really the case. The main American political parties do not maintain the same characters across states and regions therein, and class structuration, including class–politics links, are more easily discerned at local rather than national level (Grusky and Sorensen, 1998).

Real cases are never as pure as ideal-types, but it is possible that UK party politics will become based upon two, three, four or more main parties, all acceptable to and therefore funded by the upper class, run mainly by middle-class activists, and with very few elected representatives from any other class. Such parties could compete, possibly with more or less equal success, for the votes of the intermediate and working classes. This in fact is the way in which British politics has been developing since the 1960s. It will take a long time, generations rather than decades, for the historical legacy of class voting (middle class–Conservative, working class–Labour) to be expunged entirely, but this is the current direction of change.

It is misleading to call this kind of politics classless. It is a blatant mistake to infer from such politics that class divisions themselves must have disappeared. The parties simply ignore class issues and try to appeal on issues that matter to all classes like keeping the economy growing and thereby making most people better-off, maybe toughness on crime and immigration, ensuring that education, health care and the transport system improve rather than deteriorate, and that major ecological damage and war are avoided. Unless nationality (or its equivalent) is included in these issues, party support is likely to be 'soft'. Voters will be volatile.

Turnout at elections will be low, Voters will complain that all politicians and parties are 'just the same'. Public life will atrophy. People will invest their efforts in devising private solutions to their problems.

What is to stop this development? If there are no disasters and if nationalism is contained, the most likely disturbances will be through the mobilisation of one or both of the two main classes, and one or more of the parties (probably in an effort to avert decline) deciding that it needs to prioritise its traditional 'heartland' vote, or that it can enlarge its vote by appealing to a particular class. A remobilisation of the working class would send the middle class scurrying back to a party that was prepared to put middle-class interests first, and up to now most people have looked to the working class as the most likely source of a return to the mid-twentieth century brand of class politics. But the working class is no longer the mass of the people; it is disorganised and becoming more so. Its characteristic preoccupations and associated values may well be as always, but the means to their realisation (nationalisation and the development of state services) that once ignited enthusiasm have been tarnished. All the current conditions are wrong for the rebirth of a modernised, but basically old-style, working-class politics.

In the twenty-first century it is more likely that the middle class will take the initiative, using its collective organisations – professional bodies and trade unions. Remember, the middle class is now more likely to be in trade unions than manual employees. There are widespread, often keenly felt, specifically middle-class frustrations and aspirations which could be politicised. Working-class politics might then be revived as a defensive response.

This is not a prediction. It is just one of several possible future scenarios. The crucial point is that all of the more likely political scenarios are class-linked in some way or another. Class analysis has been, and still is, the key to understanding the links between the economy, politics and society, how these have changed in the past, and the alternative ways in which they might change in the future.

Bibliography

Abercrombie, N. and Turner, B.S. (1978) 'The Dominant Ideology Thesis', *British Journal of Sociology*, **29**, 149–70.

Abercrombie, N. and Warde, A. (2000) *Contemporary British Society*, 3rd edn (Cambridge: Polity Press).

Abbott, P. (1987) 'Women's Social Class Identification: Does Husband's Occupation make a Difference?', *Sociology*, **21**, 91–103.

Abrams, M., Rose, R. and Hinden, M. (1960) *Must Labour Lose?* (Harmondsworth: Penguin).

Allatt, P. and Yeandle, S.M. (1991) *Youth Unemployment and the Family: Voices of Disordered Times* (London: Routledge).

Arthur, M.B., Inkson, K. and Pringle, J.K. (1999) *The New Careers: Individual Action and Economic Change* (London: Sage).

Bagguley, P. (1992) 'Social Change, the New Middle Class and the Emergence of New Social Movements: A Critical Analysis', *Sociological Review*, **40**, 26–48.

Bagguley, P. (1995) 'Middle Class Radicalism Revisited', in T. Butler and M. Savage (eds), *Social Change and the Middle Classes* (London: UCL Press).

Bagguley, P. and Mann, K. (1992) 'Idle Thieving Bastards? Scholarly Representations of the Underclass', *Work, Employment and Society*, **6**, 113–26.

Bain, G.S. (1970) *The Growth of White-Collar Trade Unionism* (Oxford: Clarendon Press).

Bain, A.N.J. (1972) *Pilots and Management* (London: Allen & Unwin).

Banks, M., Bates, I., Breakwell, G., Bynner, J., Emler, N., Jamieson, L. and Roberts, K. (1992) *Careers and Identities* (Milton Keynes: Open University Press).

Bechofer, F. and Elliott, B. (eds) (1981) *The Petit Bourgeoisie: Studies of the Uneasy Stratum* (London: Macmillan – now Palgrave).

Berle, A.A. and Means, G.C. (1932) *The Modern Corporation and Private Property* (London: Macmillan – now Palgrave).

Beynon, H. (1973) *Working for Ford* (Harmondsworth: Penguin).

Blackburn, R.M. (1967) *Union Character and Social Class* (London: Batsford).

Blackburn, R.M. (1998) 'A New System of Classes: But What Are They and Do We Need Them?', *Work, Employment and Society*, **12**, 735–41.

Blackburn, R.M. and Mann, M. (1979) *The Working Class in the Labour Market* (London: Macmillan – now Palgrave).

Blanchflower, D.G., Deeks, A.J., Garrett, M.D. and Oswald, A.J. (1987) *Entrepreneurship and Self-Employment in Britain*, Department of Economics, University of Surrey, and Centre for Labour Economics, London School of Economics.

BMRB International Limited. (1997) *Prince's Youth Business Trust. (PYBT 1 Scheme)* Research Report 5, Department for Education and Employment, Sheffield.

Bogenhold, D. and Stabler, U. (1991) 'The Decline and Rise of Self-employment', *Work, Employment and Society*, **5**, 223–39.

Bond, R. and Saunders, P. (1999) 'Routes of Success: Influences on the Occupational Attainments of British Males', *British Journal of Sociology*, **50**, 217–49.

Bottomley, D., McKay, S. and Walker, R. (1997) *Unemployment and Jobseeking*, Department for Education and Employment, Sheffield.

Bourdieu, P. and Passeron, J.D. (1977) *Reproduction in Education, Society and Culture* (London: Sage).

Braverman, H. (1974) *Labour and Monopoly Capital* (New York: Monthly Review Press).

Breen, R. and Goldthorpe, J.H. (1999) 'Class Inequality and Meritocracy: A Critique of Saunders and an Alternative Analysis', *British Journal of Sociology*, **50**, 1–27.

Breen, R. and Whelan C.T. (1995) 'Gender and Class Mobility: Evidence from the Republic of Ireland', *Sociology*, **29**, 1–22.

Bridges, W. (1995) *Job Shift*, (London: Allen & Unwin).

Britten, N. and Heath, A. (1983) 'Women, Men and Class Analysis', in E. Garmarnikow, D. Morgan, J. Purvis and D. Taylorson, *Gender, Class and Work* (London: Heinemann).

Brown, P. and Scase (1994) *Higher Education and Corporate Realities* (London: UCL Press).

Brown, P. and Sparks, R. (eds) (1989) *Beyond Thatcherism: Social Policy, Politics and Society* (Milton Keynes: Open University Press).

Brown, R.K. and Brannen, P. (1970) 'Social Relations and Social Perspectives Amongst Shipbuilding Workers: A Preliminary Statement', *Sociology*, **4**, 71–84, 197–211.

Buckingham, A. (1999) 'Is there an underclass in Britain?', *British Journal of Sociology*, **50**, 49–75.

Burchell, B.L., Day, D., Hudson, M., Lapido, D., Mankelow, R., Nolan, J.P., Reed, H., Wichert, I.C. and Wilkinson, F. (1999) *Job Insecurity and Work Intensification* (York: Joseph Rowntree Foundation).

Burnham, J. (1941) *The Managerial Revolution* (New York: John Day).

Butler, D. and Stokes, D. (1974) *Political Change in Britain* (London: Macmillan – now Palgrave).

Butler, T. and Savage, M. (eds) (1995) *Social Change and the Middle Classes* (London: UCL Press).

Bynner, J., Ferri, E. and Shepherd, P. (eds) (1997) *Twenty-Something in the 1990s* (Aldershot: Ashgate).

Byrne, D. (1995) 'Deindustrialisation and Dispossession: An Examination of Social Division in the Industrial City', *Sociology*, **29**, 95–115.

Campbell, N. (1999) *The Decline of Employment Among Older People in Britain*, CASE Paper 19, London School of Economics, London.

Campbell, S., Bechoffer, F. and McCrone, D. (1992) 'Who Pays the Piper? Ownership and Control in Scottish Based Management Buyouts', *Sociology*, **26**, 59–79.

Cannon, I.C. (1967) 'Ideology and Occupational Community: A Study of Compositors', *Sociology*, **1**, 165–85.

Carter, R. (1985) *Capitalism, Class Conflict and the New Middle Class* (London: Routledge).

Charles, N. (1990) 'Women and Class: A Problematic Relationship', *Sociological Review*, **38**, 43–89.

Cloke, P., Phillips, M. and Thrift, N. (1995) 'The New Middle Class and Social Constructs of Rural Living', in T. Butler and M. Savage (eds), *Social Change and the Middle Classes* (London: UCL Press).

Coffield, F., Borrill, C. and Marshall, S. (1986) *Growing Up at the Margins* (Milton Keynes: Open University Press).

Connolly, M., Roberts, K., Ben-Tovim, G. and Torkington, P. (1991) *Black Youth in Liverpool* (Culemborg: Giordano Bruno).

Cotgrove, S. (1982) *Catastrophe or Cornucopia?* (Chichester: Wiley).

Cotgrove, S. and Duff, A. (1980) 'Environmentalism, Middle Class Radicalism, and Politics', *Sociological Review*, **28**, 333–51.

Cotgrove, S. and Duff, A. (1981) 'Environmentalism, Values and Social Change', *British Journal of Sociology*, **32**, 92–110.

Coxall, B. and Robins, L. (1998) *Contemporary British Politics* (Basingstoke: Macmillan – now Palgrave).

Craine, S. and Coles, B. (1995) 'Youth Transitions and Young People's Involvement in Crime', *Youth and Policy*, **48**, 6–26.

Creighton, C. (1996) 'The Family Wage as a Class-Rational Strategy', *Sociological Review*, **44**, 204–24.

Crewe, I. (1977) 'Political Dealignment in Britain, 1964–1974', *British Journal of Political Science*, **7**, 129–90.

Crewe, I. (1986) 'On the Death and Resurrection of Class Voting: Some Comments on How Britain Votes', *Political Studies*, **34**, 620–38.

Crompton, R. (1996a) 'The Fragmentation of Class Analysis', *British Journal of Sociology*, **47**, 56–67.

Crompton, R. (1996b) 'Gender and Class Analysis', In D.J. Lee and B.S. Turner (eds), *Conflicts About Class*, (London: Longman) 115–26.

Crompton, R. and Jones, G. (1984) *White-Collar Proletariat* (London: Macmillan – now Palgrave).

Crompton, R. and Sanderson, K. (1986) 'Credentials and Careers', Sociology, 20, 25–42.

Crosland, A. (1956) The Future of Socialism, (London: Cape).

Crossick, G. (ed.) (1977) The Lower Middle Class in Britain, 1870–1914 (London: Croom Helm).

Dahrendorf, R. (1959) Class and Class Conflict in an Industrial Society (London: Routledge).

Dale, A., Gilbert, G.N. and Arber, S. (1985) 'Integrating Women into Class Theory', Sociology, 19, 384–409.

Dale, J.R. (1962) The Clerk in Industry, Liverpool University Press.

Daniel, W.W. (1990) The Unemployed Flow (London: Policy Studies Institute).

Davidson, J.O. (1990) 'The Road to Functional Flexibility: White-Collar Work and Employment Relations in a Privatised Public Utility', Sociological Review, 38, 689–711.

Davidson, J.O. (1990) 'The Commercialisation of Employment Relations: The Case of the Water Industry', Work, Employment and Society, 4, 531–49.

Davis, N.J. and Robinson R.V. (1988) 'Class Identifications of Men and Women in the 1970s and 1980s', American Sociological Review, 53, 103–12.

Dennis, N., Henriques, F. and Slaughter, C. (1956) Coal is Our Life (London: Eyre and Spottiswoode).

Denny, C. (1999) 'You're Only as Insecure as You Feel', Guardian, 2 November, 27.

Devine, F. (1992) Affluent Workers Revisited? Privatism and the Working Class, Edinburgh University Press.

Dunleavy, P. (1989) 'The End of Class Politics?' in A. Cochrane and J. Anderson (eds), Politics in Transition (London: Sage).

Dunleavy, P. (1999) 'Electoral Representation and Accountability: The Legacy of Empire', in I. Holliday, A. Gamble and G. Parry, (eds), Fundamentals in British Politics (Basingstoke: Macmillan – now Palgrave).

Ebbinghaus, B. and Visser, J. (1999) 'When Institutions Matter: Union Growth and Decline in Western Europe, 1950–95', European Sociological Review, 15, 135–58.

Edgell, S. and Duke, V. (1991) A Measure of Thatcherism (London: Harper-Collins).

Egerton, M. and Savage, M. (2000) 'Age Stratification and Class Formation: A Longitudinal Study of the Social Mobility of Young Men and Women, 1971–91', Work, Employment and Society, 14, 23–49.

Erikson, R. and Goldthorpe, J.H. (1988) 'Women at Class Crossroads: a Critical Note', Sociology, 22, 545–53.

Erikson, R. and Goldthorpe, J.H. (1992) The Constant Flux: A Study of Class Mobility in Industrial Societies (Oxford: Clarendon Press).

European Commission (1998) Job Opportunities in the Information Society (Luxembourg: European Commission).

European Commission, Directorate-General for Employment, Industrial Relations and Social Affairs (1999) Employment in Europe 1998, Office for Publications of the European Communities, Luxembourg.

Evans, G. (1993) 'The Decline of Class Divisions in Britain?' British Journal of Sociology, 44, 449–71.

Evans, G. (1996) 'Putting Men and Women into Classes?' Sociology, 30, 209–34.

Evans, G. (1998) 'On Tests of Validity and Social Class: Why Prandy and Blackburn are Wrong', Sociology, 32, 189–202.

Evans, G. and Mills, C. (1998) 'Identifying Class Structure: A Latent Class Analysis of the Criterion-Related and Construct Validity of the Goldthorpe Class Scheme', European Sociological Review, 14, 87–106.

Field, F. (1989) Losing Out: The Emergence of Britain's Underclass (London: Blackwell).

Fieldhouse, E. and Hollywood, E. (1999) 'Life After Mining: Hidden Unemployment and Changing Patterns of Economic Activity Amongst Miners in England and Wales, 1981–91', Work, Employment and Society, 13, 483–502.

Fielding, T. (1995) 'Migration and Middle Class Formation in England and Wales, 1981–91', in T. Butler and M. Savage (eds), Social Change and the Middle Classes (London: UCL Press).

Forrest, R. and Murie, A. (1987) 'The Affluent Home Owner: Labour Market Position and the Shaping of Housing Histories', Sociological Review, 35, 370–403.

Forrest, R., Murie, A. and Williams, P. (1990) Home Ownership, Differentiation and Fragmentation (London: Unwin Hyman).

Francis, A. (1980) 'Families, Firms and Finance Capital', *Sociology*, **14**, 1–27.

Franklin, (1985) *The Decline of Class Voting in Britain* (Oxford: Oxford University Press).

Fukuyama, F. (1992) *The End of History and the Last Man* (London: Penguin).

Fulcher, J. and Scott, J. (1999) *Sociology* (Oxford: Oxford University Press).

Fuller, M. (1980) 'Black Girls in a London Comprehensive School', in R. Deem (ed.), *Schooling for Women's Work* (London: Routledge).

Gallie, D. (1994) 'Are the Unemployed an Underclass?' *Sociology*, **28**, 737–57.

Gallie, D. (1996) 'New Technology and the Class Structure: The Blue-Collar/White-Collar Divide Revisited', *British Journal of Sociology*, **47**, 447–73.

Gallie, D., Marsh, C. and Vogler, C. (eds), (1994) *Social Change and the Experience of Unemployment* (Oxford: Oxford University Press).

Gallie, D. and White, M. (1993) *Employee Commitment and the Skills Revolution* (London: Policy Studies Institute).

Gallie, D., White, M., Cheng, Y. and Tomlinson, M. (1998) *Restructuring the Employment Relationship* (Oxford: Clarendon Press).

Galtung, J. (1986) 'The Green Movement', *International Sociology*, **1**, 75–90.

Genov, N. (1999) 'Risks of Unemployment: Global, Regional, National', in N. Genov, (ed.), *Unemployment: Risks and Reactions* (Paris-Sofia: MOST/Friedrich Ebert Stiftung).

Gerteis, J. and Savage, M. (1998) 'The Salience of Class in Britain and America: A Comparative Analysis', *British Journal of Sociology*, **49**, 252–74.

Giddens, A. (1973) *The Class Structure of the Advanced Societies* (London: Hutchinson).

Goldthorpe, J.H. (1969) 'Social Inequality and Social Integration in Modern Britain', *Advancement of Science*, **26**, 190–202.

Goldthorpe, J.H. (1979) 'The Current Inflation: Towards a Sociological Account', in F. Hirsch and J.H. Goldthorpe (eds), *The Political Economy of Inflation* (London: Martin Robertson).

Goldthorpe, J.H. (1983) 'Women and Class Analysis', *Sociology*, **17**, 465–88.

Goldthorpe, J.H. (1996) 'Class Analysis and the Re-Orientation of Class Theory: The Case of Persisting Differentials in Educational Attainment', *British Journal of Sociology*, **47**, 481–505.

Goldthorpe, J.H., Llewellyn, C. and Payne, C. (1987) *Social Mobility and Class Structure in Modern Britain* (Oxford: Clarendon Press).

Goldthorpe, J.H., Lockwood, D., Bechoffer, F. and Platt, J. (1969) *The Affluent Worker in the Class Structure* (London: Cambridge University Press).

Goldthorpe, J.H. and Payne, C. (1986) 'Trends in Intergenerational Class Mobility in England and Wales, 1972–1983', *Sociology*, **20**, 1–24.

Gregson, N. and Lowe, M. (1994) *Servicing the Middle Classes* (London: Routledge).

Grusky, D.B. and Sorensen, J.B. (1998) 'Can Class Analysis be Salvaged?' *American Journal of Sociology*, **103**, 1187–234.

Gubbay, J. (1997) 'A Marxist Critique of Weberian Class Analyses', *Sociology*, **31**, 73–89.

Hakim, C. (1996) *Key Issues in Women's Work* (London: Athlone Press).

Halford, S. and Savage, M. (1995a) 'The Bureaucratic Career: Demise or Adaptation?' in Butler T and M. Savage, (eds), *Social Change and the Middle Classes* (London: UCL Press).

Halford, S. and Savage, M. (1995b) 'Restructuring Organisations, Changing People: Gender and Restructuring in Banking and Local Government', *Work, Employment and Society*, **9**, 97–122.

Hall, S. (1988) *The Hard Road to Renewal* (London: Verso).

Hall, S. and Jacques, M. (eds) (1983) *The Politics of Thatcherism* (London: Lawrence & Wishart).

Halsey, A.H., Heath, A.F. and Ridge, J.M. (1980) *Origins and Destinations* (Oxford: Clarendon Press).

Hanlon, G. (1998) 'Professionalism as Enterprise: Service Class Politics and the Redefinition of Professionalism', *Sociology*, **32**, 43–63.

Hayes, B.C. and Jones, F.L. (1992a) 'Marriage and Political Partisanship in Australia', *Sociology*, **26**, 81–101.

Hayes, B.C. and Jones, F.L. (1992b) 'Class Identification among Australian Couples', *British Journal of Sociology*, **43**, 463–83.

Hayes, B.C. and Miller, R.L. (1993) 'The Silenced Voice: Female Social Mobility with Particular Reference to the British Isles', *British Journal of Sociology*, **44**, 653–72.

Heath, A. and Clifford, P. (1996) 'Class Inequalities and Educational Reform in Twentieth Century Britain', in D.J. Lee and B. S. Turner (eds), *Conflicts About Class* (London: Longman).

Heath, A., Evans, G., Field, J. and Witherspoon, S. (1991) *Understanding Political Change: The British Voter, 1964–87* (Oxford: Pergamon Press).

Heath, A., Jowell, R. and Curtice, J. (1985) *How Britain Votes* (Oxford: Pergamon Press).

Heath, A. and McMahon, D. (1997) 'Education and Occupational Attainments: The Impact of Ethnic Origins', in A. H. Halsey, H. Lauder, P. Brown and A. S. Wells, (eds), *Education, Culture, Economy, Society* (Oxford: Oxford University Press).

Heath, A. and Savage, M. (1995) 'Political Alignments Within the Middle Classes, 1972–89', in T. Butler and M. Savage, (eds), *Social Change and the Middle Classes* (London: UCL Press).

Herman, E.S. (1981) *Corporate Control, Corporate Power* (New York: Cambridge University Press).

Hindess, B. (1971) *The Decline of Working Class Politics* (London: MacGibbon & Kee).

Hoggart, R. (1957) *The Uses of Literacy* (London: Chatto & Windus).

Hutton, W. (1995) *The State We're In* (London: Jonathan Cape).

Inglehart, R. (1977) *The Silent Revolution* (New Jersey: Princeton University Press).

Inglehart, R. (1997) *Modernization and Postmodernization: Cultural, Economic and Political Change in 43 Societies* (New Jersey: Princeton University Press).

Inkson, K. and Coe, T. (1993) *Are Career Ladders Disappearing?* (London: Institute of Management).

James, D.R. and Soref M. (1981) 'Profit Constraints on Managerial Autonomy', *American Sociological Review*, **46**, 1–18.

Jessop, B., Bonnett, K., Bromley, S. and Ling, T. (1988) *Thatcherism: A Tale of Two Nations* (Cambridge: Polity Press).

Jones, T. (1993) *Britain's Ethnic Minorities* (London: Policy Studies Institute).

Jordan, B. and Redley, M. (1994) 'Polarisation, Underclass and the Welfare State', *Work, Employment and Society*, **8**, 153–76.

Kay, T. (1996) 'Women's Work and Women's Worth: Implications of Women's Changing Employment Patterns', *Leisure Studies*, **15**, 49–64.

Kellard, K. and Middleton, S. (1998) *Helping Unemployed People into Self-Employment*, Research Report no. 46, Department for Education and Employment, Sheffield.

King, R. and Nugent, N. (eds) (1979) *Respectable Rebels*, Hodder and Stoughton, London.

Lampard, R. (1995) 'Parents' Occupations and their Children's Occupational Attainments', *Sociology*, **29**, 715–28.

Lampard, R. (1996) 'Might Britain be a Meritocracy?', *Sociology*, **30**, 387–93.

Lash, S. and Urry, J. (1987) *The End of Organised Capitalism* (Oxford: Polity Press).

Lee, D.J. and Turner, B.S. (eds) (1996) *Conflicts About Class* (London: Longman).

Leiulfsrud, H. and Woodward, A. (1987) 'Women at Class Crossroads: Repudiating Conventional Theories of Family Class', *Sociology*, **21**, 393–412.

Lewis, R. and Maude, A.U.E. (1949) *The English Middle Classes* (London: Phoenix House).

Lockwood, D. (1958) *The Blackcoated Worker* (London: Allen & Unwin).

Lockwood, D. (1966) 'Sources of Variation in Working Class Images of Society', *Sociological Review*, **14**, 249–67.

MacDonald, R. (1994) 'Fiddly Jobs, Undeclared Working and the Something for Nothing Society', *Work, Employment and Society*, **8**, 507–30.

MacDonald, R. (1996) 'Welfare Dependency, The Enterprise Culture and Self-Employed Survival', *Work, Employment and Society*, **10**, 431–47.

MacDonald, R. and Coffield, F. (1991) *Risky Business? Youth and the Enterprise Culture* (Lewes: Falmer).

McGovern, P., Hope-Bailey, V. and Stiles, P. (1998) 'The Managerial Career After Downsizing: Case Studies from the Leading Edge', *Work, Employment and Society*, **12**, 457–77.

Mann, K. (1991) *The Making of an English Underclass* (Milton Keynes: Open University Press).

Mann, M. (1970) 'The Social Cohesion of Liberal Democracy', *American Sociological Review*, **35**, 423–39.

Mann, M. (1973) *Consciousness and Action in the Western Working Class* (London: Macmillan – now Palgrave).

Marsden, D. (1982) *Workless* (London: Croom Helm).

Marsh, C. (1988) 'Unemployment in Britain', in D. Gallie (ed.), *Employment in Britain* (Oxford: Basil Blackwell).

Marshall, G., Rose, D., Newby, H. and Vogler, C. (1988) *Social Class in Modern Britain* (London: Hutchinson).

Marshall, G. and Swift, A. (1996) 'Merit and Mobility', *Sociology*, **30**, 375–86.

Marshall, G., Swift, A. and Roberts, S. (1997) *Against the Odds?* (Oxford: Clarendon Press).

Marshall, T. H. (1950) *Citizenship and Social Class and Other Essays* (Cambridge: Cambridge University Press).

Martin, B. (1998) 'Knowledge, Identity and the Middle Class: From Collective to Individualized Class Formation', *Sociological Review*, **46**, 653–86.

Martin, J. and Roberts, C. (1984) *Women and Employment: A Lifetime Perspective* (London: HMSO).

Mattausch, J. (1989) 'The Peace Movement', *International Sociology*, **4**, 217–25.

Mattausch, J. (1989) *A Commitment to Campaign*, Manchester University Press.

Meager, N. (1992) 'The Fall and Rise of Self-Employment (again): A Comment on Bogenhold and Stabler', *Work, Employment and Society*, **6**, 127–34.

Meier, A. (1988) 'The Peace Movement – Some Questions Concerning its Social Nature and Structure', *International Sociology*, **3**, 77–87.

Metcalf, H. (1998) *Self-Employment for the Unemployed: The Role of Public Policy*, Research Report no. 47, Department for Education and Employment, Sheffield.

Mills, C. (1994) 'Who Dominates Whom? Social Class, Conjugal Households and Political Identification', *Sociological Review*, **42**, 639–63.

Mills, C. (1995) 'Managerial and Professional Work Histories', in T. Butler and M. Savage (eds), *Social Change and the Middle Classes* (London: UCL Press).

Milner, A. (1999) *Class* (London: Sage).

Moorhouse, H.F. (1976) 'Attitudes to Class and Class Relationships in Britain', *Sociology*, **10**, 469–96.

Morris, L. (1992) 'The Social Segregation of the Long-Term Unemployed in Hartlepool', *Sociological Review*, **40**, 344–69.

Morris, L. and Irwin, S. (1992) 'Employment Histories and the Concept of the Underclass', *Sociology*, **26**, 401–20.

Mulholland, K. (1998) 'Survivors Versus Movers and Shakers: The Reconstitution of Management and Careers in the Privatised Utilities', in P. Thompson and C. Warhurst (eds), *Workplaces of the Future* (Basingstoke: Macmillan – now Palgrave).

Murray, C. (1984) *Losing Ground: American Social Policy, 1950–80* (New York: Basic Books).

Murray, C. (1990) *The Emerging British Underclass* (London: Institute of Economic Affairs).

Murray, C. (1994) *Underclass; The Crisis Deepens* (London: Institute of Economic Affairs).

Newby, H. (1977) *The Deferential Worker* (London: Allen Lane).

Nichols, T. and Armstrong, P. (1976) *Workers Divided* (London: Fontana).

Nichols, T. and Davidson, J.O. (1993) 'Privatisation and Economism: An Investigation Among Producers in Two Privatised Utilities in Britain', *Sociological Review*, **41**, 705–30.

Noble, T. (2000) 'The Mobility Transition: Social Mobility Trends in the First-Half of the Twenty-First Century', *Sociology*, **34**, 35–51.

Noon, M. and Blyton, P. (1997) *The Realities of Work* (Basingstoke: Macmillan – now Palgrave).

Ophem J. van and Hoog K. de (1998) 'Differences in Leisure Behaviour of the Poor and the Rich in the Netherlands at the Beginning of the 1990s', in J. W. te Kloetze (ed.), *Family and Leisure in Poland and the Netherlands* (Garant: Leuven-Apeldoorn), 115–32.

Pakulski, J. and Waters, M. (1996) *The Death of Class* (London: Sage).

Parkin, F. (1968) *Middle Class Radicalism*, Manchester University Press.

Parkin, F. (1971) *Class Inequality and Political Order* (London: MacGibbon & Kee).

Payne, G. (1999) 'Does Economic Development Modify Social Mobility?', Paper presented to *British Sociological Association Conference*, Glasgow.

Payne, J. (1987) 'Does Unemployment Run in Families?', *Sociology*, **21**, 199–214.

Payne, J. (1989) 'Unemployment and Family Formation Among Young Men', *Sociology*, **23**, 171–91.

Penn, R., Rose, M. and Rubery, J. (1994) *Skill and Occupational Change* (Oxford: Oxford University Press).

Peterson, R.A. and Kern, R.M. (1996) 'Changing Highbrow Taste: From Snob to Omnivore', *American Sociological Review*, **61**, 1996, 900–7.

Pollock, G. (1997) 'Uncertain Futures: Young People In and Out of Employment Since 1940', *Work, Employment and Society*, **11**, 615–38.

Prandy, K. (1965) *Professional Employees* (London: Faber).

Prandy, K. (1990) 'The Revised Cambridge Scale of Occupations', *Sociology*, **24**, 629–55.

Prandy, K. (1998a) 'Deconstructing Classes: Critical Comments on the Revised Social Classification', *Work, Employment and Society*, **12**, 743–53.

Prandy, K. (1998b) 'Class and Continuity in Social Reproduction: An Empirical Investigation', *Sociological Review*, **46**, 340–64.

Prandy, K. and Blackburn, R.M. (1997) 'Putting Men and Women into Classes: But is this Where They Belong?' *Sociology*, **31**, 143–52.

Prandy, K. and Bottero, W. (2000) 'Social Reproduction and Mobility in Britain and Ireland in the Nineteenth and Early Twentieth Centuries', *Sociology*, **34**, 265–81.

Prowse, P. and Turner, R. (1996) 'Flexibility and Coal', *Work, Employment and Society*, **10**, 151–60.

Purcell, K., Hogarth, T. and Simm, C. (1999) *Whose Flexibility?* (York: Joseph Rowntree Foundation).

Rannie, A. (1985) 'Is Small Beautiful?', *Sociology*, **19**, 213–4.

Randle, K. (1996) 'The White Coated Worker: Professional Autonomy in a Period of Change', *Work, Employment and Society*, **10**, 737–53.

Redman, T., Wilkinson, A. and Snape, E. (1997) 'Stuck in the Middle? Managers in Building Societies', *Work, Employment and Society*, **11**, 101–14.

Reid, I. (1998) *Class in Britain* (Cambridge: Polity Press).

Rex, J. and Tomlinson, S. (1979) *Colonial Immigrants in a British City* (London: Routledge).

Ridig, W., Bennie, L.G. and Franklin, M.N. (1991) *Green Party Members: A Profile* (Glasgow: Delta Publications).

Robbins Report (1963) *Higher Education* (London: HMSO).

Roberts, B.C., Loveridge, R. and Gennard, J. (1972) *Reluctant Militants* (London: Heinemann).

Roberts, K., Barton, A., Buchanan, J. and Goldson, B. (1997) *Evaluation of a Home Office Initiative to Help Offenders into Employment* (London: Home Office).

Roberts, K. and Chadwick, C. (1991) *Transitions into the Labour Market: The New Routes of the 1980s*, Youth Cohort Series 16, Research and Development Series 65 (Sheffield: Employment Department).

Roberts, K., Clark, C.S., Cook, F.G. and Semeonoff, E. (1977) *The Fragmentary Class Structure* (London: Heinemann).

Roberts, K. and Parsell, G. (1991) 'Young People's Sources and Levels of Income, and Patterns of Consumption in Britain in the Late-1980s', *Youth and Policy*, **35**, December, 20–5.

Roberts, S. and Marshall, G. (1995) 'Intergenerational Class Processes and the Asymmetry Hypothesis', *Sociology*, **29**, 43–58.

Robertson, D. (1984) *Class and the British Electorate* (Oxford: Blackwell).

Robinson, P. (1999) 'Explaining the Relationship between Flexible Employment and Labour Market Regulation', in A. Felstead and N. Jewson (eds), *Global Trends in Flexible Labour* (Basingstoke: Macmillan – now Palgrave).

Rojek, C. (2000) 'Leisure and the Rich Today: Veblen's Thesis After a Century', *Leisure Studies*, **19**, 1–15.

Rose, D. (1998) 'Once More Unto the Breach: In Defence of Class Analysis Yet Again', *Work, Employment and Society*, **12**, 755–67.

Rose, D. and O'Reilly, K. (eds) (1997) *Constructing Classes* (Swindon: ESRC/ONS).

Rose, R. and McAllister, I. (1990) *The Loyalties of Voters* (London: Sage).

Routh, G. (1965) *Occupations and Pay in Great Britain*, 1906–1960 (London: Cambridge University Press).

Runciman, W.G. (1990) 'How Many Classes are there in Contemporary British society?' *Sociology*, **24**, 377–96.

Rutter, M. and Madge, N. (1976) *Cycles of Disadvantage* (London: Heinemann).

Sanders, D. (1997) 'Voting and the Electorate', in P. Dunleavy, A. Gamble, I. Holliday and A. Peele (eds), *Developments in British Politics* (Basingstoke: Macmillan – now Palgrave).

Sarlvik, B. and Crewe, I. (1983) *Decade of Dealignment* (Cambridge: Cambridge University Press).

Saunders, P. (1978) 'Domestic Property and Social Class', *International Journal of Urban and Regional Research*, **2**, 233–51.

Saunders, P. (1981) 'Beyond Housing Classes: The Sociological Significance of Private Property rights in the means of consumption', *International Journal of Urban and Regional Research*, **5**, 202–27.

Saunders, P. (1990) *A Nation of Home Owners* (London: Unwin Hyman).

Saunders, P. (1995a) 'Might Britain be a Meritocracy?', *Sociology*, **29**, 23–41.

Saunders, P. (1995b) *Capitalism: A Social Audit* (Buckingham: Open University Press).

Saunders, P. (1997) 'Social Mobility in Britain: An Empirical Evaluation of Two Competing Explanations', *Sociology*, **31**, 261–88.

Saunders, P. and Harris, C. (1994) *Privatization and Popular Capitalism* (Milton Keynes: Open University Press).

Savage, M., Barlow, J., Dickens, P. and Fielding, T. (1992) *Property, Bureaucracy and Culture* (London: Routledge).

Savage, M. and Egerton, M. (1997) 'Social Mobility, Individual Ability and the Inheritance of Class Inequality', *Sociology*, **31**, 645–72.

Scase, R. and Goffee, R. (1989) *Reluctant Managers* (London: Unwin Hyman).

Scott, J. (1982) *The Upper Classes* (London: Macmillan – now Palgrave).

Scott, J. (1991) *Who Rules Britain?* (Cambridge: Polity Press).

Scott, J. (1997) *Corporate Business and Capitalist Classes* (Oxford: Oxford University Press).

Scott, J and Griff, C. (1984) *Directors of Industry: The British Corporate Network, 1904–76* (Oxford: Polity Press).

Seabrook, J. (1971) *City Close-Up* (London: Allen lane).

Seabrook, J. (1988) *The Leisure Society* (Oxford: Blackwell).

Searle-Chatterjee, M. (1999) 'Occupations, Biography and New Social Movements', *Sociological Review*, **47**, 258–79.

Skeggs, B. (1997) *Formations of Class and Gender* (London: Sage).

Smith, C. (1987) *Technical Workers: Class, Labour and Trade Unionism* (Basingstoke: Macmillan – now Palgrave).

Stanworth, M. (1984) 'Women at Class Crossroads: a Reply to Goldthorpe', *Sociology*, **18**, 159–70.

Stewart, S., Prandy, K. and Blackburn, R.M. (1980) *Social Stratification and Occupations* (London: Macmillan – now Palgrave).

Sullivan, O. (1989) 'Housing Tenure as a Consumption Sector Divide: A Critical Perspective', *International Journal of Urban and Regional Research*, **13**, 183–200.

Taylor, M.P. (1994) *Earnings, Independence or Unemployment?* Working Paper no. 26, British Household Panel Survey, University of Essex.

Thompson, P. (1983) *The Nature of Work* (London: Macmillan – now Palgrave).

Touraine, A., Hegedus, Z., Dubet, F. and Wievorka, M. (1983) *Anti-Nuclear Protest* (Cambridge: Cambridge University Press).

Travis, A. (1999) 'Sex in the 90s: The Young Take a Moral Stand', *Guardian*, 29 December, 3.

Traxler, F. (1996) 'Collective Bargaining and Industrial Change: A Case of Disorganisation?' *European Sociological Review*, **12**, 271–87.

Truss, C.J.G. (1993) 'The Secretarial Ghetto: Myth or Reality. A Study of Secretarial Work in England, France and Germany', *Work, Employment and Society*, **7**, 561–84.

Turnbull, P. and Wass, V. (1994) 'The Greatest Game No More – Redundant Dockers and the Demise of Dock Work', *Work, Employment and Society*, **8**, 487–506.

Turner, G. (1963) *The Car-Makers* (London: Eyre & Spottiswoode).

Turok, I. and Edge N. (1999) *The Jobs Gap in Britain's Cities: Employment Loss and Labour Market Consequences* (York: Policy Press).

Tyler, M. and Abbott, P. (1998) 'Chocs Away: Weight Watching in the Contemporary Airline Industry', *Sociology*, **32**, 433–50.

Wait, P. (1996) 'Social Stratification and Housing Mobility', *Sociology*, **30**, 533–50.

Walby, S. (1999) 'The New Regulatory State: The Social Powers of the European Union', *British Journal of Sociology*, **50**, 118–40.

Walkerdine, V., Lucey, H. and Melody, J. (2001) *Growing Up Girl: Psychosocial Explorations of Gender and Class* (Basingstoke: Palgrave).

Walsh, T.J. (1990) 'Flexible Labour Utilisation in the Private Service Sector', *Work, Employment and Society*, **4**, 517–30.

Warde, A. (1995) 'Cultural Change and Class Differentiation: Distinction and Taste in the British Middle Classes, 1968–88', in K. Roberts (ed.), *Leisure and Social Stratification*, Leisure Studies Association, Publication no. 53, Eastbourne.

Warhurst, C. and Thompson, P. (1998) 'Hands, Hearts and Minds: Changing Work and Workers at the End of the Century', in P. Thompson and C. Warhurst (eds), *Workplaces of the Future* (Basingstoke: Macmillan – now Palgrave).

Watson, T. and Harris, P. (1999) *The Emergent Manager* (London: Sage).

Weakliem, D. (1989) 'Class and Party in Britain, 1964–1983', *Sociology*, **23**, 285–97.

Webb, J. (1999) 'Work and the New Public Service Class?' *Sociology*, **33**, 747–66.

Weiner, M.J. (1981) *English Culture and the Decline of the Industrial Spirit* (Cambridge: Cambridge University Press).

Westergaard, J. (1992) 'About and Beyond the Underclass: Some Notes on the Influence of Social Climate on British Sociology', *Sociology*, **26**, 575–87.

Westergaard, J. (1994) *Who Gets What?* (Cambridge: Polity Press).

Westergaard, J. and Resler, H. (1975) *Class in a Capitalist Society* (London: Heinemann).

Whitburn, J. *et al.* (1976) *People in Polytechnics*, Society for Research into Higher Education, Guildford).

Whitley, R. (1973) 'Commonalities and Connections Among Directors of Large Financial Institutions', *Sociological Review*, **21**, 613–32.

Whyte, W.H. (1957) *The Organization Man* (New York: Anchor Books).

Wilson, W.J. (1987) *The Truly Disadvantaged* (Chicago: University of Chicago Press).

Windolf, P. (1998) 'Elite Networks in Germany and Britain', *Sociology*, **32**, 321–51.

Witz, A. (1992) *Professions and Patriarchy* (London: Routledge).

Wright, D. (1994) *Workers Not Wasters* (Edinburgh: Edinburgh University Press).

Wright, E.O. (1979) *Class, Crisis and the State* (London: Verso).

Wright, E.O. (1985) *Classes* (London: Verso).

Wright, E.O. (1994) *Interrogating Inequality* (New York: Verso).

Wright, E.O. (1996) *Class Counts* (Cambridge: Cambridge University Press).

Wright-Mills, C. (1956) *White-Collar* (New York: Galaxy).

Wynne, D. (1998) *Leisure, Lifestyle and the New Middle Class* (London: Routledge).

Young, M. and Willmott, P. (1957) *Family and Kinship in East London* (London: Routledge).

Zipp, J.F. and Plutzer, E. (1996) 'Wives and Husbands: Social Class, Gender and Identification in the US', *Sociology*, **30**, 235–52.

Zweig, F. (1961) *The Worker in an Affluent Society* (London: Heinemann).

Zweig, F. (1976) *The New Acquisitive Society* (London: Brian Rose).

Index

261

Index